Cognitive Behaviour Therapy

CBT: A Guide for the Practising Clinician, Volume 2 brings the practising clinician up to date with recent developments in the continuously expanding field of cognitive behaviour therapy (CBT). As with the first volume, this book is a clinically orientated and techniques-focused CBT manual, dealing with specific clinical conditions, skilfully blending guiding theories, focused techniques and clinical flexibility.

With contributions from distinguished clinicians and researchers, a variety of specific disorders are examined, including:

- Social anxiety disorder, CBT for psychoses, preventing relapse in depression;
- Post-traumatic stress disorder, health anxiety;
- Body dysmorphic disorder, pathological gambling, medical illness.

These disorders are also discussed in the context of up-to-date processes and approaches, such as homework assignments, compassion-focused therapy and metacognitive-focused therapy. As such this book, along with the first volume, will be essential reading for all CBT practitioners, mental health professionals and students alike.

Gregoris Simos is a Founding Fellow of the Academy of Cognitive Therapy and also a cognitive behavioural clinician at the Aristotelian University of Thessaloniki, Greece.

Cognitive Behaviour Therapy

A Guide for the Practising Clinician
Volume 2

Edited by Gregoris Simos

Routledge
Taylor & Francis Group

LONDON AND NEW YORK

First published 2009
by Routledge
27 Church Road, Hove, East Sussex BN3 2FA

Simultaneously published in the USA and Canada
by Routledge
270 Madison Avenue, New York, NY10016

Routledge is an imprint of the Taylor & Francis Group, an informa business

Copyright © 2009 Selection and editorial matter, Gregoris Simos; individual
chapters, the contributors

Typeset in Times by Garfield Morgan, Swansea, West Glamorgan
Printed and bound in Great Britain by T J International Ltd, Padstow,
Cornwall
Paperback cover design by Anú Design

This publication has been produced with paper manufactured to strict
environmental standards and with pulp derived from sustainable forests.

British Library Cataloguing in Publication Data
A catalogue record for this book is available from the British Library

Library of Congress Cataloging in Publication Data
A catalog record for this book is available from the Library of Congress

ISBN: 978-0-415-44963-2 (hbk)
ISBN: 978-0-415-44964-9 (pbk)

Contents

Contributors

Gordon J. G. Asmundson, PhD University of Regina, Regina, Saskatchewan, Canada S4S 0A2. Gordon.Asmundson@Uregina.ca

Thorsten Barnhofer, PhD Oxford University, Department of Psychiatry, Warneford Hospital, Oxford OX3 7JX, UK. thorsten.barnhofer@psych.ox.ac.uk

Michelle A. Blackmore, MA Department of Psychology, Temple University, Weiss Hall, 1701 North 13th Street, Philadelphia, PA 19122-6085, USA. mblackmo@temple.edu

Kelsey C. Collimore, BHSc Department of Psychology, University of Regina, Regina, Saskatchewan, Canada S4S 0A2. collimok@uregina.ca

Jeanne Daniel, PhD School of Psychology, Massey University, Private Bag 102904, NSMC, Albany, Auckland, New Zealand. jdaniel@kiwidreaming.co.nz

Melanie J. V. Fennell, PhD Oxford University, Department of Psychiatry, Warneford Hospital, Oxford OX3 7JX, UK. melanie.fennell@psych.ox.ac.uk

Edna B. Foa, PhD Center for the Treatment and Study of Anxiety, University of Pennsylvania School of Medicine, 3535 Market Street, Philadelphia, PA 19104, USA. foa@mail.med.upenn.edu

Paul Gilbert, PhD, FBPsS Mental Health Research Unit, Kingsway Hospital, Derby DE22 3LZ, UK. p.gilbert@derby.ac.uk

Panagiota Goga, PsyD 89 Tsimiski Street, 546 22 Thessaloniki, Greece.

Richard G. Heimberg, PhD Adult Anxiety Clinic of Temple University, Department of Psychology, Temple University, Weiss Hall, 1701 North 13th Street, Philadelphia, PA 19122-6085, USA. heimberg@temple.edu

Matthew Jacofsky, PsyD Bio-Behavioral Institute, 935 Northern Blvd., Great Neck, NY 11021, USA.

Nikolaos Kazantzis, PhD School of Psychology, Massey University at Albany, Private Bag 102904, NSMC, Auckland, New Zealand. N.Kazantzis@massey.ac.nz

Sony Khemlani-Patel, PhD Bio-Behavioral Institute, 935 Northern Blvd., Great Neck, NY 11021, USA.

David Kingdon, MD, MRCPsych University of Southampton, Department of Psychiatry, Royal South Hants Hospital, Southampton SO14 0YG, UK. dgk@soton.ac.uk

Lefteris Konstadinidis, PsyD 89 Tsimiski Street, 546 22 Thessaloniki, Greece. leftkon@otenet.gr

Michael Kyrios, PhD PsyCHE Research Centre and Brain Sciences Institute, Faculty of Life and Social Sciences, Swinburne University of Technology, PO Box 218, Hawthorn, VIC 3122, Australia. mkyrios@swin.edu.au

Robert L. Leahy, PhD American Institute for Cognitive Therapy, 136 East 57th Street, Suite 1101, New York, NY 10022, USA. AICT@aol.com

David M. Ledgerwood, PhD Department of Psychiatry and Behavioral Neurosciences, Wayne State School of Medicine, Substance Abuse Research Division, 2761 E. Jefferson Ave., Detroit, MI 48207, USA.

Benjamin J. Morasco, PhD Behavioral Health and Clinical Neurosciences Division, Portland VA Medical Center (P3MHDC) and Department of Psychiatry, Oregon Health and Science University, 3710 SW US Veterans Hospital Road, Portland, OR 97239, USA.

Fugen Neziroglu, PhD, ABBP Bio-Behavioral Institute, 935 Northern Blvd., Great Neck, NY 11021, USA. Neziroglu@aol.com

Costas Papageorgiou, PhD University of Lancaster, Institute for Health Research, The Priory Hospital Altrincham, Rappax Road, Hale, Cheshire WA15 0NX, UK. c.papageorgiou@lancaster.ac.uk

Nancy M. Petry, PhD Department of Psychiatry, MC-3944, University of Connecticut Health Center, 263 Farmington Avenue, Farmington, CT 06030-3944, USA. NPetry@uchc.edu

Antonio Pinto, MD Piazza Ettore Vitale n 28, 80126, Napoli, Italy. dott.antonio.pinto@virgilio.it

Sheila A. M. Rauch, PhD PTSD Clinical Team, University of Michigan Medical School, VA Ann Arbor Healthcare System, 2215 Fuller Road (116c), Ann Arbor, MI 48105, USA. sherauch@med.umich.edu

Gregoris Simos, MD, PhD CMHC/2nd Department of Psychiatry, Aristotelian University of Thessaloniki, 1 Karaoli and Dimitriou Street, 54630 Thessaloniki, Greece. simos@med.auth.gr

Steven Taylor, PhD Department of Psychiatry, University of British Columbia, 2255 Wesbrook Mall, Vancouver, BC, Canada, V6T 2A1. taylor@unixg.ubc.ca

Douglas Turkington, MD, PhD Professor of Psychosocial Psychiatry, Newcastle University, Department of Psychiatry, Royal Victoria Infirmary, Newcastle-upon-Tyne, Tyne and Wear NE4 4LP, UK. douglas.turkington@ncl.ac.uk

Jeremiah Weinstock, PhD Department of Psychiatry, MC-3944, University of Connecticut Health Center, 263 Farmington Avenue, Farmington, CT 06030-3944, USA.

Preface

It is well known that cognitive behaviour therapy (CBT) is the most extensively researched form of psychotherapy and that CBT is becoming the treatment of choice for an increasing number of mental disorders and problems. Like any other living organism, CBT has not stopped evolving and it continually accommodates new theoretical speculations and incorporates new treatment techniques. At the same time, contemporary CBT extends its focus not only to the management of new disorders, but also to understanding and handling various variables of a given disorder, as well as the therapeutic relationship itself. As a consequence, we witness a considerably growing number of CBT books, which, I guess, is difficult for the practising clinician to monitor, select, and read.

As the fields of effective application of CBT are expanding, a clinically oriented and updated manual is always necessary. Concentrated and concisely presented new knowledge on a variety of topics – therapeutic, as well as procedural – by leading clinicians and researchers is what clinicians can afford in their everyday practice. This book is written for both the novice and the more experienced cognitive behaviour therapist, for whom more extended and specific problem- and processes-oriented texts are always available. It is true that there is a growing number of such excellent books, but the careful selection of topics and authors of the present textbook makes this book unique.

CBT: A Guide for the Practising Clinician, Volume 2 comes as an inevitable consequence of its predecessor, published in 2002. This first book focused on the most prevalent areas of CBT application (depression, anxiety disorders, eating disorders, personality disorders, couples and family problems, and disorders of childhood and adolescence), but even from its publication it was evident that new topics could and should be included in such a book. It seems that the time has come for this.

Like its predecessor, this book is a clinically oriented and techniques-focused CBT manual. This volume covers two broad areas: (a) CBT for specific disorders and problems, and (b) specific processes and techniques in CBT.

The first part of the book focuses on those disorders that were not covered in Volume 1, either because the inclusion of such disorders (e.g. psychoses, social anxiety disorder, post-traumatic stress disorder) would have made it too long a book, or because CBT with specific disorders (pathological gambling, health anxiety, body dysmorphic disorder, and CBT in medical illness) was not so popular, as at that time it seemed that CBT was not definitely an evidence-based therapeutic process. This part of the book also focuses on newer solutions to old problems (e.g. meta-cognitive therapy for depressive rumination; mindfulness-based CBT for relapse prevention of depression).

The second part of the book focuses on CBT-relevant general processes and techniques. Early-phase socialization of a patient in CBT, effective application of homework assignments, resolution of resistance, and reduction of self-criticism and shame via developing emotional experiences of reassurance and self-compassion are increasingly becoming necessary and integral parts of contemporary CBT.

CBT: A Guide for the Practising Clinician was especially welcome for several reasons. It focused on specific clinical conditions; it skilfully blended guiding theories, focused techniques and clinical flexibility; and it was written by distinguished researchers and clinicians. Its clarity and up-to-date quality resulted in its inclusion as standard reading in several psychology courses around the world. *CBT: A Guide for the Practising Clinician, Volume 2* could not be inferior to its predecessor, and, allow me to say, it is not. It shares all the good qualities of the first volume, since well-known clinicians and researchers have contributed their expertise to the present book, and it also aims to provide both the novice and the experienced clinician with the necessary resources for a more efficient application of contemporary CBT.

Volume 2 also introduces some chapters written by Greeks or those of Greek origin. I hope that readers will understand the challenge I had to face. These clinicians and researchers were invited to contribute their chapters not just because they are Greek, but – believe me – because they are great at what they do.

Gregoris Simos, MD, PhD

Cognitive behaviour therapy for psychosis: enhancing the therapeutic relationship to improve the quality of life

Antonio Pinto, Douglas Turkington and David Kingdon

Overview

Therapeutic and rehabilitative programmes have spread remarkably in recent years, aimed at alleviating the severe personal, familial and social consequences that can occur with psychoses, especially schizophrenia. Substantial progress has been made in understanding the biological, psychological and social determinants of psychosis at different levels of complexity:

1   The view of schizophrenia as a syndrome has been based on two main streams: Kraepelin (1919) identified a single-disease model mainly on the basis of course and outcome features; Bleuler (1911) was more focused on 'primary' or 'essential' symptomatologic features. Modern nosographies, DSM-IV-TR and ICD-10, utilize both streams. Categorical approaches could not, however, identify a paradigmatic nucleus as concerns the psychopathologic manifestation of what Schneider (1980) describes as schizophrenia. Modern genetic findings and clinical experience are now moving strongly towards the concept of a psychosis spectrum, and it is looking increasingly possible that this will form the basis of the relevant section of DSM-V (Kingdon et al., 2007).

2   Directly linked to the variability of definition and diagnostic ascertainment of schizophrenia has been the difficulty in accurately assessing long-term course and outcome. But there is now very good evidence that a substantial proportion of patients can recover to independent levels of social functioning. Warner (1994), reviewing around 40 long-term follow-up studies published since 1956, has shown that with time 22 per cent of the patients fully recover from their symptoms, regaining their premorbid level of functioning, while another 44 per cent achieve social recovery, meaning they become economically independent and maintain a low level of social dysfunction.

3   Biological, psychological and social determinants have emerged as relevant to the aetiopathogenesis of psychosis. The relevance of psychosocial factors, in particular, to treatment and outcome is becoming

increasingly pertinent. Pharmacological and psychological interventions can preserve the individual's cognitive skills and allow his/her full functional recovery.

Through the years, different types and models of therapeutic intervention with schizophrenic subjects have been developed, aiming mainly at remission of the symptoms and better management of the patient's dysfunctional behaviours (Hogarty et al., 2004). Such interventions are part of a bio-psycho-social approach (Penn & Mueser, 1996) and range from a hospital treatment model for crisis management to psychosocial rehabilitation, mainly implemented within community-based structures.

Common criteria for evaluating the psychic well-being of an individual include:

- adherence to 'reality'
- adaptation to 'reality'
- self-preservation
- interests and social activities
- psychological independence
- tolerance of frustration
- mental flexibility
- objective and logical thinking
- self-acceptance
- long-term hedonism
- realism in opposition to an excessive utopianism
- risk acceptance
- acceptance of one's responsibility for one's emotional reactions
- acceptance of uncertainty
- pursuit of creative interests.

Such goals are hard to achieve if the resources of the patient are absorbed by delusions and hallucinations and/or he/she cannot find a proper way to manage them; at the same time, the complex nature of the pathology does not always allow one to assess, at the beginning of a treatment, to what extent symptoms will reduce. It is therefore appropriate to structure a setting in which the remission of the patients' most florid symptoms is not the main and only purpose, nor the focus of their adherence to treatment. The main goal of an intervention within this complex model is the improvement of the subject's functioning and his/her own increased feeling of well-being regardless of the reduction of the symptoms.

Individuals and their families may find it much more appropriate to shift from treating symptoms to solving problems (Perris, 1989) and work with the aim of increasing their control over the environment and maximize their ability to predict possible events and cope with their own reactions to stressful events (Kelly, 1955). Explaining the problem merely from a bio-medical point of view, regarding symptoms as expressions of dysfunction in the central nervous system, may lead the patient to a passive and quieter attitude towards the matters to be addressed on the psychotherapeutic path. Moreover, seeing delusions and hallucinations as expressions of a disabling pathology with a strong tendency towards chronicity reinforces the stigma perceived by patients and families, as well as their sense of not belonging to people's ordinary problems. Problem-solving training is therefore designed with an eye on the patients' perspective and personal point of view. What patients consider as problems will become the object of their therapy; their delusional themes, their worries and anxiety about the origin of the voices and content of their messages, their apparently illogical behaviours deter-mined by bizarre beliefs, their unmotivated social isolation, and any other factors lowering the quality of their lives will be accepted by the therapist as they are. This setting will allow cognitive behaviour therapy (CBT) not to cause any break in the therapeutic relationship, but consolidate it instead. It is in fact important for the patients to perceive the therapist's will to help them solve what they perceive as problems, besides curing what is explained to be part of a pathology. The schizophrenic experience, perhaps for the first time in the patients' life, may therefore shift from being an example of isolation, stigma and alienation to being a relational experience, allowing them to confront this experience with another individual who will not judge or marginalize them, but welcome and share their requests, offering them as the first thing the chance to feel validated as persons and bring their experience back to common and meaningful phenomenal categories (nor-malization) (Lorenzini & Sassaroli, 1992). Subsequently, through more complex dialogue techniques (Socratic dialogue, peripheral questioning, inference chaining, etc.), patients will be able to test the hold and reliability of their beliefs, with the possibility to change them at least partially.

This way, the dual nature of the therapeutic goals should be pursued: the goal of the therapist, who reasonably sees the reduction/remission of the symptoms as a tangible and verifiable sign of change and the goal of the patient, whose main aspiration is being plausibly understood and finding someone to trust. The perception of a global improvement in the quality of the patient's life will thus derive from a sum of these two elements, which will be the basis for structured interventions through medication and CBT.

Evidence

The evidence-base relevant to the use of cognitive therapy in schizophrenia is now well developed. Beck published the first case of therapy utilizing cognitive behavioural principles (Beck, 1952). There was little further work for another 40 years. In the late 1990s, randomized, controlled studies began to emerge (Kingdon & Turkington, 2005). Meta-analyses (Zimmermann et al., 2005) and more than 20 randomized, controlled studies have now established the efficacy of CBT in schizophrenia in reduction of persistent positive symptoms in patients (Turkington et al., 2006b).

The evidence in early schizophrenia is less strong, although small durable benefits were found in the one large study in this area (Lewis et al., 2002; Tarrier et al., 2004). Preliminary studies of the use of CBT in the prodromal phase (prior to diagnosis of schizophrenia) show effects on delaying transition to psychosis (McGorry et al., 2002; Morrison et al., 2004). Motivational interviewing with CBT and family work for people with psychosis and substance misuse are promising (Barrowclough et al., 2001; Haddock et al., 2003).

Benefits can accrue when delivered in community settings (Turkington et al., 2002, 2006a). Acceptability in clinical practice has also been demonstrated (Kingdon & Kirschen, 2006). In the UK, guidelines on schizophrenia (National Institute for Clinical Excellence, 2002) recommend CBT on an individual basis (at least 10 sessions over at least 6 months) for all people with schizophrenia.

Despite these data clearly showing the effectiveness of CBT in addition to pharmacological treatment, there are several difficulties to be taken into account in order to maximize the results and reduce the dropout rate among non-responders or partial responders. Certainly, one is gaining the patients' collaboration, which, with other elements, led to this population being considered unsuitable for a structured therapeutic treatment in the past. However, we believe that such collaboration is achievable through developing the therapeutic alliance.

Developing a therapeutic relationship

Engagement with the individual who is experiencing psychotic symptoms can be straightforward and immediate. Many people in this situation are very prepared to discuss the concerns they have as long as there is somebody who is prepared to listen and take their beliefs seriously. That does not mean providing unconditional agreement but does mean providing time for them to explain what they are experiencing and what they believe about these experiences. However, it is so common that they have not been provided with an accepting listening approach by those with whom they have tried to speak that they anticipate the worst. This means they are either reluctant to disclose their concerns or very distrustful of those in health services who are trying to work with them. There are also many other influences on engagement, such as

- previous experience of services
- current situation (e.g. detained in hospital)
- family and cultural issues

- symptoms, such as paranoia, command hallucinations (such as a voice saying, 'don't talk to him'), depression, and poor motivation.

A therapeutic collaboration is possible if:

- the therapist is able to establish with the patient the necessary trust and agreement on specific goals
- the therapist is able to let the patient's families, if actively involved in the treatment, feel that the patient can learn to cope with the difficulties of life
- the therapist is able to show, with a honest, genuine and empathic attitude, that he/she believes in recovery from psychosis depending on the patient's approach, his/her relatives' reactions, and an optimistic therapeutic attitude.

Assessment and formulation

Assessment of an individual with psychosis is very similar to that of any person referred for cognitive therapy. It builds on a good general assessment of their background, current circumstances, and mental state. The links between feelings, thoughts and behaviour are teased out as the assessment and subsequent therapy progress. Psychotic symptoms, such as delusions and hallucinations, will be explored and a dimensional approach used to these, examining such aspects as degree and nature of distress (if any), frequency, amount of preoccupation and effect on the individual's functioning. Understanding the content of the delusional beliefs and hallucinations and beliefs about them is necessary to discuss and debate them (see later).

Formulation can follow using standard CBT formats, although the amount of information gathered with complex patients can seem overwhelming, and we have developed a format (see Figure 1.1) that allows information of significance to be assembled as a case summary. It is then possible to extract particular issues to focus upon, such as using an ABC formulation to understand activating events (e.g., a voice), beliefs (e.g., that the voice is speaking the truth), and consequences (e.g., fear and guilt with behavioural avoidance), and subsequently challenge them.

Working with delusions

Delusions are formulated as understandable responses to or ways to make sense of specific experiences, and a personal, meaningful alternative is constructed. Everyone, including patients, is subject to many biases in judgement and reasoning that can lead to maintaining strong beliefs with little rational support. Delusional content represents the attempt of the

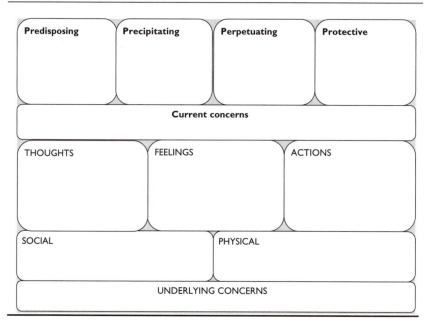

Figure 1.1 Diagram: 'making sense'

patient to make sense of a previous experience, and therefore the therapy should be addressed to both the form and content of delusional beliefs (Sassaroli & Lorenzini, 1998).

Within this theoretical framework the goal of the intervention is focused on:

- helping patients replace maladaptive beliefs with more functional beliefs that could contribute to give a more adaptive sense to their experiences
- helping patients develop better competence in analysing and evaluating their self-beliefs on the basis of the available evidence.

The phases of the intervention protocol must be approached in an extremely flexible way. Duration and frequency of sessions will be adapted to the patient's needs and wishes. Furthermore, especially in the initial phases, if patients are unwilling to go to the therapist's office, home sessions are often needed.

Initial phase

The main goal is building and establishing a collaborative therapeutic relationship in an empathic atmosphere that will be the basis for developing the patient's motivation to treatment. Ample room is hence given to allow patients to feel free to tell their story and express their private truths (Lorenzini & Sassaroli, 1992). Patients talk about their problems from their own perspective, and the therapist respects their subjective view of events, and that should make them feel that their concerns are taken seriously. The therapist will show good listening skills, such as empathic listening and comment summaries to close in on what the patient has been saying; furthermore he/she will collect information to develop a personalized cognitive formulation of the patient's problem.

The therapist should clarify their total non-involvement with what happened to the patient until that moment and that their task is to help him/her cope with the difficult time he/she is going through. Accepting the patients' requests and their perspective on events does not imply colluding with delusional thinking: therapists, particularly at this early stage of the therapy, will suspend judgement with regard to the patient's delusions.

In this phase, a clear picture of the development of the relevant beliefs is built up. This involves exploration of the period before they emerged, to identify life stresses and circumstances. The process by which the beliefs arose from these events is uncovered, and the reasons for the conclusions the person came to are examined with them. This re-examination is very important in establishing how patients acquired their current beliefs and allows both therapists and patients to collaborate and understand the reasoning process. It may identify where there has been 'jumping to conclusions' or personalizing, although it may not be agreed at this stage that this has happened.

'Reality testing'

The goal of CBT is not to try to persuade or force the patient to agree that he/she has symptoms of mental illness. Rather the goal is to reduce the severity of, or distress from, the symptoms regardless of whether the patient accepts a diagnostic label (Turkington et al., 2006b). The therapist will try to understand through Socratic dialogue which problems and subjective meanings within the story of their lives and development underlie their delusions. This can be considered as a means for patients to express their fears, sensations, anguish, and states of mind due to particular beliefs (automatic thoughts, dysfunctional assumptions), which are important to identify, as they allow a better knowledge of the patients and can be of help in their recovery. Patients may of course be defensive towards collaborative attitudes, which can be seen as invasive and intrusive, especially if the object of the discussion is one of the core themes at the base of their personality structure, or can determine a significant emotional resonance in them. Therapists aim to involve patients in a maximally collaborative search for possible alternative explanations.

The use of peripheral questioning (Kingdon & Turkington, 2005) may allow the therapist safer access to the core themes of delusional ideation. The discussion will initially deal with those matters that are considered to be less relevant in relation to the structure of a delusion, in order to allow the patient to get used to the possibility of a dialogue in which some of his/her impressions can eventually be called into question, without causing him/her to feel invalidated or affecting the therapeutic relationship. Inference chaining is particularly suitable to address the most complex delusions (Kingdon & Turkington, 2005). This involves discussing with the person the inference of their beliefs; e.g., 'If it was accepted that you were being persecuted by your employer, what is it about that persecution which causes you most distress? And what could we do about it?' As we go through the therapy, the content of a delusional idea may gradually be called directly into question – ideally, by the person themselves beginning to express ambivalence. Adopting the typical strategies of the disputing of irrational beliefs (verbal challenge or planned reality testing) can then become relevant to use. Yet it is important that we try to work directly on delusional beliefs only after having understood what they arise from, and after the patient has been placed in a condition in which he/she feels free to make mistakes. Otherwise, trying to modify patients' ideas earlier in the process, with evidence or with disputing of irrational beliefs, could be dangerous and ineffective. A direct attack to the core structure of a delusion, not having taken the precautions mentioned above, may cause the patient to consider the therapist also to be part of his/her delusion, or start to disengage from therapy. This could make the therapeutic relationship collapse, preventing further work and meaning a new relational failure for the patient.

Working with hallucinations

Establishing with the individual exactly what their perceptual experience is like can be helpful: 'Is it like me talking to you now?/Can you see it now?' Individuals will usually respond affirmatively and be relieved that the therapist recognizes that the experience feels very 'real'. Further discussion about their beliefs about the experiences can help clarify them: 'Do you think others can hear these voices or see what you see?' Usually, they will have worked out that others do not share their experiences, and this allows exploration of the reasons why they believe this should be the case. They may give a religious or apparently delusional reason, but quite frequently they are unsure themselves. Such uncertainty can allow the therapist to discuss the nature of hallucinations and 'normalize' them.

These symptoms will be explained as reactions that can occur to stressful events or conditions of physical or psychic discomfort (e.g., metabolic alterations, sleep deprivation or prolonged social isolation). In such situations, the brain may form the impression of hearing voices or sounds that others cannot hear or, if we are particularly sensitive to or worried about other people's comments or judgements, the patient has the impression of being continually observed and commented upon. In other words, symptoms of schizophrenia vary only quantitatively from 'normal' processes and occur at the end of a continuum or spectrum that spans from 'normal' to 'pathological'. Hallucinations are located at the extreme end of a continuum that ranges from dreams and normal imagination to illusions and hallucinations, with even 'normal' individuals experiencing hallucinations during periods of sensory or sleep deprivation (Kingdon & Turkington, 1994).

In this way, patients develop a better sense of themselves and of control over the events happening in their lives, including their own psychotic symptoms, which often cause them extreme anxiety and anguish. Learning to predict and understand their own emotional and behavioural reactions, patients can feel that they are not at the mercy of events or 'mysterious forces'. This increases their self-esteem and personal sense of worth.

This can also be the subject of a collaborative yet structured work. The therapist identifies the elements involved in the hearing voices phenomenon: whose voices patients hear, where they come from, what power patients assign to them, and to what extent they are able to resist their eventual command. What do patients themselves think of the voices: are they a positive element or a source for stress? What level of social impairment do they determine? Which specific coping strategies do patients spontaneously adopt and to what extent can they be considered dysfunctional? In what circumstances do patients hear the voices and what beliefs are associated? Using the ABC technique, it may be possible to highlight how hearing voices may be the consequence of a stressful event (Chadwick et al., 1996), and patients can be taught ways to cope with a phenomenon they should by now understand better (Tarrier et al., 1990). Such tools can include:

- *distraction techniques*: allowing patients to distract their attention from the voices and direct it to audio sources (listening to the radio, using headphones, turning on the television, reading aloud) or focus on activities (e.g., exercise or computer games)
- *relaxation techniques*: using self-instruction or autogenic training while doing physical activity, or taking a bath
- *sharing*: patients actively find someone they can talk with and discuss what is happening to them at that particular moment
- *'mindfulness'*: helping patients to non-judgementally observe the phenomenon they are experiencing, learning how to accept it without being overly troubled by it (Chadwick, 2006).

Once the therapist and patient identify the most troublesome areas, they can explore the coping strategies that are spontaneously adopted by the patient to deal with the stress and discomfort caused by specific events. Then the subjective advantages and disadvantages of those strategies will be evaluated. Do they, for example, help eliminate or solve underlying problems? What is the cost-benefit balance of such behaviours? What will be their impact on the patient's relationships and on those who live with him/her? etc. Alternative strategies are then explored together, eventually finding more functional and convenient ones that can be used along with or instead of the others.

The aim of this intervention is to help patients start to see that what they do is understandable. We can try together to find the reasons and events that lead them to act in certain ways. Such reasons can easily be found through an accurate analysis of the antecedents and consequences of specific behaviour (Garety, 1992).

An analysis of the triggering events is performed. Patients can learn to predict which situations they perceive as particularly dangerous and stressful and reinforce their coping strategies in order to be able to face them in a better way. This will allow the patient's initiative to respond to stressful life events to be validated and lead the patient towards cognitive distancing, which will be a basis for a further intervention through different tools such as stress-solving strategies and other techniques fostering a better comprehension and ability to cope with the situations that generate misinterpretation of reality.

Work with negative symptoms

Negative symptoms are the most disabling aspect of psychosis and, once the acute episode has settled, the area of most concern to families and other carers. They involve diminished drive (amotivation) with social withdrawal, reduced conversation and content of conversation (alogia), flattening of emotional expression (affective blunting), and poor attention and concentration. These interfere seriously with the person's ability to relate to others, find employment and even look after themselves. As it has become possible to understand the development of these symptoms, so it has become possible to develop treatment strategies (see, for more detail, Kingdon & Turkington, 2005). Essentially, these seek to understand how the negative symptoms have emerged – frequently they have followed a period of increasing anxiety, reduced attention and concentration, and subsequently frustrated attempts to meet unachievable goals. These inevitably lead to demoralization and 'giving up'. When this occurs, guilt and depression can supervene, complicated by psychotic symptoms such as ideas of reference, thought broadcasting and paranoia.

Treatment programmes for negative symptoms focus on taking the pressure off the individual and carers. Long-term goals are needed to maintain hope and, in the longer-term, establish direction. Short-term goals, however, need to be readily achievable, such as coming downstairs to have a mid-afternoon cup of tea, and timed collaboratively: 'when you feel ready to start this'. Carers are enlisted in this process to ensure that their expectations are adjusted to what is achievable in the short term. As small steps are taken, so progress takes place and demoralization can begin to lift. It is also during this early period that work on understanding delusions and hallucinations can take place in preparation for re-engaging in relationships or even just being able to leave the house. Social anxiety and depressive symptoms may also contribute and require work in their own right.

As progress commences, at the individual's pace, specific social skills and neurocognitive deficits may emerge, and these can become a focus in their own right.

Social skills training

Patients can have primary or secondary negative symptoms due to medication side effects or to dysfunctional coping strategies, such as avoidance. They may have a limited repertoire of social skills and/or impairment of social functioning, with social withdrawal, poor self-care and loss of interest. These can feed the patient's sense of not belonging to his/her community and family, who may in their turn adopt a 'critical' attitude – often with the best of intentions, as it is aimed at motivating the patient. However, in practice, this can lead to patients feeling guilty for their behaviours and impair still further their functioning.

Furthermore, social isolation and loss of interest in any goal-oriented activity will increase the gap between patients and the surrounding world, along with the effect of their psychotic symptoms, pushing them more and more out of those dimensions in which encountering 'the other' is possible (Buber, 1954). Individuals with schizophrenia may have difficulty sustaining social relationships and have deficits in language, motion, expression, and the ability to decode and evaluate messages coming from the environment and respond to them. For this reason, social skills training and homework assignments, opportunely integrated in the structure of the above setting, can be very helpful for patients to:

• maintain contact with reality through better organized time management
• practise programming and implementing goal-oriented activities requiring cognitive functions (attention, memory, executive skills, etc.)
• increase self-esteem, self-confidence and sense of autonomy through social skills learning
• improve interpersonal communication skills and therefore the ability to express their needs.

As patients get used to spending more time with others again and start sharing a common goal with them, they should be helped to shift from a hypertrophic agonistic internal working model, which is likely to have determined part of their interpersonal relations until that moment, to an empowering of the more functional internal working model of peripatetic cooperation (Liotti, 1995). In other words, they will be able to learn alternative ways of being in the world, in which their defensive mode might not be essential for survival. Using individualized case formulations, clinicians implemented elements of CBT or social skills training (SST) such as role play, modelling, *in vivo* exercises, positive reinforcement and homework assignments.

Skills training methods integrated with CBT have been used to improve social behaviours, including self-care, self-managed medication, social conversation, interpersonal problem-solving, self-directed recreation, family communication and management of personal resources (Pinto et al., 1999). This approach (Kopelowicz et al., 2006) has been endorsed by several studies, proving that the ability and possibility to lead a more self-sufficient life, in all of its aspects, is prognostic of better intermediate and long-term outcomes (De Girolamo, 1993).

SST uses three modules:

- basic skills training
- problem-solving training
- attention-focusing skills training.

Patients' specific needs will determine the choice of which module to start from. Active participation is required in the sessions, which may last from 10–15 minutes to 2 hours, according to the patient's attention and concentration skills. As previously mentioned, integrating the programme with homework assignments or *in vivo* exercises allows transfer of learning to everyday life.

Each module includes seven sequential activities:

- introduction
- video demonstration
- role playing
- generation and evaluation of scenarios for resource management
- generation and evaluation of scenarios for outcome prediction
- *in vivo* performance of assigned tasks
- performance of assigned homework.

For further detailed information on this approach and its application methods, see the available literature (Kopelowicz et al., 2006).

Neuropsychological deficits

Consistent evidence suggests the presence of abnormalities on neurocognitive testing of people with schizophrenia: executive function disorders; memory, attention and vigilance disorders; and perception disorders. Such abnormalities may determine more complex dysfunctions of information processing such as difficulty in filtering or gating stimuli (gating failure), inability to select significant sensory perceptions from background noise (over-inclusion), and deficit in the automatic association of neurosensory inputs and planned responses. Present research is now clarifying the role of nuclear cognitive alterations in the delusional and hallucinatory themes of patients and in their dysfunctional behaviour schemes (Wykes & Reeder, 2005). Basic information-processing disorders (such as attention deficit) do in fact affect more complex cognitive abilities, such as abstraction and conceptualization, determining within vicious circles, pervasive alterations in the subject's social skills such as 'bottom-up' (from primary cognitive disorders to social dysfunctions) and 'top-down' (social skills deterioration worsens the cognitive deficit).

In the past few years, intervention programmes have proliferated (process-based approaches) and are sometimes described as cognitive therapy. However, these approaches need to be distinguished from formulation-based Beckian cognitive therapy described elsewhere in this chapter. More commonly, they are described as cognitive rehabilitation or remediation, with the main purpose of recognizing and correcting nuclear cognitive deficits in order to foster the correction of dysfunctional behaviour schemes. This approach focuses on cognitive abilities from a neuropsychological perspective (that is, attention, concentration and memory). The interventions typically involve repetitive microskills training, conceptualized as deficient in the cognitive abilities of schizophrenics. They can be aimed at improving social perception, and there is now some evidence that this may generalize to improvement in social and vocational outcome (Wykes et al., 2007).

Medication issues

Antipsychotics reduce psychotic symptoms and potential for relapse in most people who develop psychosis. However, many discontinue medication against medical advice. There are a number of reasons for this. Some patients do not agree that they are ill and so stop medication. Side effects of the drugs used in the past have been unpleasant for many patients and so may also be a reason. The introduction of atypical antipsychotics has been seen as a major step forward in regard to this. The more favourable profile in terms of extrapyramidal side effects of medications such as risperidone, olanzapine, quietapine, aripiprazole and clozapine has been clearly demonstrated, but, unfortunately, other side effects, such as weight gain, sedation and development of diabetes, have proved problematic. Clozapine has been shown to be more effective in those patients resistant to other medications who can and will take it, but this is not the case for the group as a whole (Lieberman et al., 2005). Some patients will prefer to take the risk of relapse to experiencing side effects or simply for reasons of autonomy – they do not wish to take medication, especially if they are not convinced that it works. Collaboration over treatment needs is a key issue and an approach which incorporates the patient's wishes and needs as fully as possible is most likely to be effective. Cognitive therapy involves discussion of the context and current concerns of the person for whom medication may have a role in helping them cope and prevent relapse. Direct focus on 'compliance' has not been shown to be effective (Byerly et al., 2005; O'Donnell et al., 2003).

Strategies to prevent relapse

Relapse causes distress to individuals and their carers, and it is a major cause of increasing disability. Gains made previously may be lost and demoralization increase. Work with both patients and their relatives can minimize this by developing an understanding of the signs of relapse so that it can be avoided or minimized. A psychoeducational model has been described which can be developed to incorporate cognitive behavioural principles (Gumley et al., 2003). This can increase understanding of:

- the nature of psychosis and associated problems, such as substance misuse, anxiety and depression
- specific symptoms, with particular emphasis on understanding patient behaviour and discourse, especially where it seems strange and unusual
- how to help patients better cope with psychotic symptoms
- how to recognize early signs of relapse of psychotic symptoms and propose adequate behavioural strategies to manage the situation
- the stress-vulnerability model: explaining which specific stress factors may trigger the patient (whether subjective or related to the family environment).

Issues related to the family atmosphere and coping abilities have been demonstrated to be important. The expressed emotion (EE) within a family has been analysed, and three main components have been highlighted in one or more family members classified as high in EE: criticism, hostility and over-involvement. Each of these components was substantially linked to schizophrenic relapse, which, in a family with high EE levels, would determine the prevalent emotional tone as well as the quality of interpersonal relations and therefore the patient's ability to cope functionally with the problems related to his/her pathology. Work with families focuses on the following (Barrowclough & Tarrier, 1992):

- providing information about schizophrenia
- teaching problem-solving skills
- improving communication skills
- covering emotional issues
- reducing physical contact between relatives and patients
- lowering expectations
- using the therapist as a reference person.

Summary

Cognitive therapy is now established as an evidence-based intervention for people with psychosis through a series of randomized, controlled studies and the conclusions of meta-analyses. In some countries, it is now forming part of government and professional guidelines for the management of schizophrenia. It builds on good clinical practice and cognitive therapy as developed in the treatment of depression. Engagement is a particular focus, as patients have often become alienated from services, or their concerns – whether psychotic or not – have not been given due attention and understanding, and, where appropriate, are normalized. Assessment and formulation form a basis for interventions with hallucinations, delusions and negative symptoms. Work on relapse prevention and with families also has an important place in assisting recovery.

References

Barrowclough, C., Haddock, G., Tarrier, N., Lewis, S. W., Moring, J., O'Brien, R., et al. (2001). Randomized controlled trial of motivational interviewing, cognitive behavior therapy, and family intervention for patients with comorbid schizophrenia and substance use disorders. *American Journal of Psychiatry, 158*, 1706–1713.

Barrowclough, C., & Tarrier, N. (1992). *Families of Schizophrenic Patients: A Cognitive Behavioural Intervention*. London: Chapman & Hall.

Beck, A. T. (1952). Successful outpatient psychotherapy of a chronic schizophrenic with a delusion based on borrowed guilt. *Psychiatry: Journal for the Study of Interpersonal Processes, 15*, 305–312.

Bleuler, E. (1911). *Dementia Praecox oder Gruppe der Schizophrenien*. Leipzig: Deutick.

Buber, M. (1954). *Das Problem des Menschen*. Heidelberg: Lambert Schneider.

Byerly, M. J., Fisher, R., Carmody, T., & Rush, A. J. (2005). A trial of compliance therapy in outpatients with schizophrenia or schizoaffective disorder. *Journal of Clinical Psychiatry, 66*, 997–1001.

Chadwick, P. (2006). *Person-Based Cognitive Therapy for Distressing Psychosis.* Chichester: John Wiley & Sons.

Chadwick, P. D., Birchwood, M. J., & Trower, P. (1996). *Cognitive Therapy for Delusions, Voices and Paranoia.* Chichester: Wiley.

De Girolamo, G. (1993). La valutazione in psichiatria tra qualità ed efficacia. In F. Asioli, A. Ballerini, & G. Ceroni (eds), *Psichiatria nella comunità* (pp. 339–354). Torino: Bollati Boringhieri.

Garety, P. (1992). Making sense of delusions. *Psychiatry, 55,* 282–291.

Gumley, A., O'Grady, M., McNay, L., Reilly, J., Power, K., & Norrie, J. (2003). Early intervention for relapse in schizophrenia: results of a 12-month randomized controlled trial of cognitive behavioural therapy. *Psychological Medicine, 33,* 419–431.

Haddock, G., Barrowclough, C., Tarrier, N., Moring, J., O'Brien, R., Schofield, N., et al. (2003). Cognitive-behavioural therapy and motivational intervention for schizophrenia and substance misuse: 18-month outcomes of a randomised controlled trial. *British Journal of Psychiatry, 183,* 418–426.

Hogarty, G. E., Flesher, S., Ulrich, R., Carter, M., Greenwald, D., Pogue-Geile, M., et al. (2004). Cognitive enhancement therapy for schizophrenia: effects of a 2-year randomized trial on cognition and behavior. *Archives of General Psychiatry, 61,* 866–876.

Kelly, G. (1955). *The Psychology of Personal Construct.* New York: Norton.

Kingdon, D. G., Kinoshita, Y., Naeem, F., et al. (2007). Schizophrenia can and should be renamed. *British Medical Journal, 334,* 221–222.

Kingdon, D. G., & Kirschen, H. (2006). Who does not get cognitive-behavioral therapy for schizophrenia when therapy is readily available? *Psychiatric Services, 57,* 1792–1794.

Kingdon, D. G., & Turkington, D. (1994). *Cognitive Behavioral Therapy of Schizophrenia.* New York: Guilford.

Kingdon, D. G., & Turkington, D. (2005). *Cognitive Therapy of Schizophrenia.* New York: Guilford.

Kopelowicz, A., Liberman, R. P., & Zarate, R. (2006). Recent advances in social skills training for schizophrenia. *Schizophrenia Bulletin, 32,* S12–S23.

Kraepelin, E. (1919). *Dementia Praecox and Paraphrenia.* Edinburgh: Livingstone.

Lewis, S., Tarrier, N., Haddock, G., Bentall, R., Kinderman, P., Kingdon, D., et al. (2002). Randomised controlled trial of cognitive-behavioural therapy in early schizophrenia: acute-phase outcomes. *British Journal of Psychiatry, 181* (Suppl 43), S91–S97.

Lieberman, J. A., Stroup, T. S., McEvoy, J. P., Swartz, M. S., Rosenheck, R. A., Perkins, D. O., et al. (2005). Effectiveness of antipsychotic drugs in patients with chronic schizophrenia. *New England Journal of Medicine, 353,* 1209–1223.

Liotti, G. (1995). *La dimensione interpersonale della coscienza.* Roma: NIS.

Lorenzini, R., & Sassaroli, S. (1992). Perchè si delira. In R. Lorenzini & S. Sassaroli (eds), *La verità privata. Il delirio e i deliranti* (pp. 39–49). Rome: La Nuova Italia Scientifica.

McGorry, P. D., Yung, A. R., Phillips, L. J., Yuen, H. P., Francey, S., Cosgrave, E. M., et al. (2002). Randomized controlled trial of interventions designed to reduce the risk of progression to first-episode psychosis in a clinical sample with subthreshold symptoms. *Archives of General Psychiatry, 59*(10), 921–928.

Morrison, A. P., French, P., Walford, L., Lewis, S. W., Kilcommons, A., Green, J., et al. (2004). Cognitive therapy for the prevention of psychosis in people at ultra-high risk: randomised controlled trial. *British Journal of Psychiatry*, *185*, 291–297.

National Institute for Clinical Excellence (2002). *Clinical Guideline: Schizophrenia* (CG1). London: Department of Health.

O'Donnell, C., Donohoe, G., Sharkey, L., Owens, N., Migone, M., Harries, R., et al. (2003). Compliance therapy: a randomised controlled trial in schizophrenia. *British Medical Journal*, *327*, 1–4.

Penn, D. L., & Mueser, K. T. (1996). Research update on the psychosocial treatment of schizophrenia. *American Journal of Psychiatry*, *153*, 607–617.

Perris, C. (1989). *Cognitive Therapy with Schizophrenic Patients*. New York: Guilford.

Pinto, A., La, P. S., Mennella, R., Giorgio, D., & DeSimone, L. (1999). Rehab rounds. Cognitive-behavioral therapy and clozapine for clients with treatment-refractory schizophrenia. *Psychiatric Services*, *50*, 901–904.

Sassaroli, S., & Lorenzini, R. (1998). Pathogeny and therapy. In C. Perris & P. McGorry (eds), *Cognitive Psychotherapy of Psychotic and Personality Disorders* (pp. 282–312). Chichester, UK: Wiley.

Schneider, K. (1980). *Klinische Psychopatologie*. Stuttgart: Georg Thieme.

Tarrier, N., Harwood, S., Yusupoff, L., Beckett, R., & Baker, A. (1990). Coping strategy enhancement (CSE): a method of treating residual schizophrenic symptoms. *Behavioural Psychotherapy*, *18*, 283–293.

Tarrier, N., Lewis, S., Haddock, G., Bentall, R., Drake, R., Kinderman, P., et al. (2004). Cognitive-behavioural therapy in first-episode and early schizophrenia. 18-month follow-up of a randomised controlled trial. *British Journal of Psychiatry*, *184*, 231–239.

Turkington, D., Kingdon, D., Rathod, S., Hammond, K., Pelton, J., & Mehta, R. (2006a). Outcomes of an effectiveness trial of cognitive-behavioural intervention by mental health nurses in schizophrenia. *British Journal of Psychiatry*, *189*, 36–40.

Turkington, D., Kingdon, D., & Turner, T. (2002). Effectiveness of a brief cognitive-behavioural therapy intervention in the treatment of schizophrenia. *British Journal of Psychiatry*, *180*, 523–527.

Turkington, D., Kingdon, D., & Weiden, P. J. (2006b). Cognitive behavior therapy for schizophrenia. *American Journal of Psychiatry*, *163*, 365–373.

Warner, R. (1994). *Recovery from Schizophrenia* (2nd edn). London: Routledge.

Wykes, T., & Reeder, C. (2005). *Cognitive Remediation Therapy for Schizophrenia. Theory and Practice*. London: Routledge.

Wykes, T., Reeder, C., Landau, S., Everitt, B., Knapp, M., Patel, A., et al. (2007). Cognitive remediation therapy in schizophrenia: randomised controlled trial. *British Journal of Psychiatry*, *190*, 421–427.

Zimmermann, G., Favrod, J., Trieu, V. H., & Pomini, V. (2005). The effect of cognitive behavioral treatment on the positive symptoms of schizophrenia spectrum disorders: a meta-analysis. *Schizophrenia Research*, *77*, 1–9.

Chapter 2

Cognitive behaviour therapy, depressive rumination and metacognition

Costas Papageorgiou

Cognitive-behaviour therapy (CBT) for depression (Beck, Rush, Shaw, & Emery, 1979) has been highly influential in the psychological conceptualization and treatment of this common and disabling problem. CBT for depression is a structured, time-limited, and problem-focused approach that aims to modify negative thoughts and beliefs or schemas, and reverse behaviours associated with problem maintenance. CBT for depression is perhaps the most extensively evaluated psychological treatment for emotional disorders. CBT has been shown to be an effective treatment for mild to moderate depression (e.g., Clark, Beck, & Alford, 1999; DeRubeis & Crits-Christoph, 1998) and more effective than antidepressant medication when they are both withdrawn shortly after recovery (e.g., Blackburn, Eunson, & Bishop, 1986; Shea et al., 1992). However, a significant proportion of individuals treated with CBT do not fully remit or they relapse and experience recurrences of depression. Estimates of relapse following CBT for depression vary between 25 per cent (DeRubeis & Crits-Christoph, 1998) and 50 per cent (Nezu, Nezu, Trunzo, & McClure, 1998). Therefore, treatment outcome data show that a significant number of individuals with depression who receive CBT do not fully benefit from this intervention, and given the nature, impact and prevalence of depression, there is an urgent need to maximize treatment effectiveness. For this to be achieved, clinical researchers have argued that interventions should aim to target core psychological processes implicated in the development, maintenance, and recurrence of depression (e.g., Papageorgiou & Wells, 2000, 2004; Wells, 2000; Wells & Matthews, 1994). A number of core psychological or cognitive processes have been implicated in the onset, perpetuation, and recurrence of depression. Persistent, recyclic, negative thinking, in the form of rumination, has attracted increasing theoretical, empirical, and clinical interest in the past few years (Papageorgiou & Wells, 2004). This chapter begins by reviewing the phenomenology of depressive rumination. It then describes a clinical metacognitive model of rumination and depression. In the final section, a brief overview is provided of metacognitive therapy for depressive rumination.

Phenomenology of depressive rumination

The concept of depressive rumination

Rumination is considered to be a relatively common response to negative moods (Rippere, 1977) as well as a salient cognitive feature of dysphoria and DSM-IV (American Psychiatric Association, 1994) major depressive disorder. Rumination may be symptomatic of dysphoria or depression, but it may also be perceived as serving a function. The content of rumination is experienced in both verbal and imaginal form and has been found to be similar in depressed and non-depressed individuals (Papageorgiou & Wells, 1999a, 1999b, 2004). Consistent with the content-specificity hypothesis (Beck, 1967, 1976), rumination involves themes of past personal loss and failure. Ruminative thinking is characterized by 'Why'-type questions. For example, 'Why did it happen to me?', 'Why do I feel so depressed?', and 'Why don't I feel like doing anything?'

The definition of depressive rumination

A specific and commonly used definition of depressive rumination was proposed by Susan Nolen-Hoeksema. According to the response styles theory of depression (Nolen-Hoeksema, 1991), rumination is a form of repetitive and passive thinking about symptoms of depression and the possible causes and consequences of these symptoms. In this theory, rumination consists of 'repetitively focusing on the fact that one is depressed; on one's symptoms of depression; and on the causes, meanings and consequences of depressive symptoms' (Nolen-Hoeksema, 1991, p. 569). Other more recent definitions of rumination have focused on current feelings of sadness or 'rumination on sadness' (Conway, Csank, Holm, & Blake, 2000) where rumination 'consists of repetitive thoughts concerning one's present distress and the circumstances surrounding the sadness' (p. 404). Alloy and colleagues (Alloy et al., 2000; Robinson & Alloy, 2003) proposed the concept of stress-reactive rumination to refer specifically to the tendency to ruminate on negative inferences following stressful life events. Stress-reactive rumination has been shown to play a key role in depression (Alloy et al., 2000; Robinson & Alloy, 2003). Treynor, Gonzalez and Nolen-Hoeksema (2003) revised the Ruminative Responses Scale (RRS) (Nolen-Hoeksema & Morrow, 1991) and produced a new measure of rumination, which was unconfounded with depression content. Factor analysis yielded a two-factor solution with one factor labelled 'reflection' and the other 'brooding'. Reflection was concerned with efforts to overcome problems and difficulties, whereas brooding was related to thinking anxiously and/or gloomily about events. Although both factors were significantly correlated with indices of depression, reflection was linked to less depression over time while brooding was associated with more depression, suggesting that only the brooding factor may be related to the style of persistent negative thinking characterized by rumination.

The maladaptive nature of depressive rumination

Rumination can be a normal as well as a pathological cognitive process. A number of factors determine when rumination becomes a maladaptive activity. Although the content of rumination is not likely to influence whether this process is normal or abnormal, its frequency and duration is certainly likely to contribute to psychopathology. In the self-regulatory executive function (S-REF) model of emotional disorders, Wells and Matthews (1994, 1996) suggest that there are at least three factors that contribute to rumination and other forms of perseverative negative thinking becoming pathological. For purposes of assessment, it may be useful to view these factors as the 3-Ws: (1) When rumination is used (e.g., in response to negative mood); (2) What rumination may be used for (e.g., a predominant problem-solving and coping strategy); and (3) Whether rumination is negatively appraised (e.g., 'I have no control over my rumination'). The contribution of these factors to pathological varieties of rumination is clearly supported by empirical evidence (for reviews, see Papageorgiou & Wells, 2004; Wells, 2000).

Comparisons between depressive rumination and worry, negative automatic thoughts, and self-focused attention

Similarities and differences exist between depressive rumination and other related cognitive processes and products, namely worry, negative automatic thoughts, and self-focused attention. We (Papageorgiou, 2006; Papageorgiou & Wells, 1999a, 2004) have suggested that the study of similarities and differences between rumination and other related cognitive processes or products offers a number of opportunities for the conceptualization and treatment of depressive rumination. For instance, the overlap between rumination and worry may help to explain the high levels of comorbidity often detected between depressive and anxiety disorders.

Previous research examining the nature of depressive (ruminative) and anxious (worrisome) thinking showed that these types of cognitions are clearly distinct phenomena (Clark & de Silva, 1985; Clark & Hemsley, 1985). Chains of ruminative and worrisome thinking differ not only at the content level (Beck, 1967, 1976; Borkovec, Robinson, Pruzinski, & DePree, 1983), but also at the process (e.g., attentional involvement, dismissability, distraction, etc.) and metacognitive (e.g., beliefs or appraisals about thinking and ability to monitor, objectify and regulate thinking) levels (Wells

& Matthews, 1994, 1996). Papageorgiou and Wells (1999a) found that although ruminative and worrisome thinking shared a number of similarities, they also differed on several process and metacognitive dimensions in a non-clinical sample. In comparison with rumination, worry was found to be significantly greater in verbal content, and associated with more compulsion to act, and with more effort and confidence in problem solving. Rumination was significantly more past oriented than worry. In a subsequent study, Papageorgiou and Wells (1999b, 2004) found that in comparison with the worry of a panic disorder group, the rumination of a depressed group was rated as significantly longer in duration, less controllable, and less dismissable, and was associated with lower effort to problem-solve, lower confidence in problem solving, and greater past orientation. Other relevant studies investigating the relationships between rumination, worry, depression, and anxiety have relied on self-report measures of these constructs and found that they can also be distinguished (e.g., Fresco, Frankel, Mennin, Turk, & Heimberg, 2002; Goring & Papageorgiou, 2008; Hong, 2007; Muris, Roelofs, Meesters, & Boomsma, 2004). For instance, in a factor analytic study of measures of rumination and worry, Goring and Papageorgiou (2008) found that rumination and worry can be distinguished in individuals with depression, as items from the two measures loaded on separate factors. These data are consistent with the notion that different components of thinking style are associated with emotional experience (Wells & Matthews, 1994, 1996).

Rumination can also be distinguished from the negative automatic thoughts that are characteristic of depression. Papageorgiou and Wells (2001a) argued that although negative automatic thoughts are relatively brief shorthand appraisals of loss and failure in depression, rumination consists of longer chains of repetitive, recyclic, negative and self-focused thinking that may be activated as a response to initial negative automatic thoughts. Empirical evidence has also demonstrated that rumination predicts depression over and above its shared variance with several types of negative cognitions (e.g., Nolen-Hoeksema, Parker, & Larson, 1994; Spasojevic & Alloy, 2001).

Finally, a distinction can be made between rumination and the depressive self-focusing style (Pyszczynski & Greenberg, 1987). The focus of the depressive style is on reducing discrepancies between ideal and real states following failure (Pyszczynski, Greenberg, Hamilton, & Nix, 1991). However, the focus of rumination is more specific and is thought to involve coping in the form of problem-solving, which does not necessarily occur following failure (Wells & Matthews, 1994). Ruminative thinking can also be differentiated from private self-consciousness (Fenigstein, Scheier, & Buss, 1975), a disposition chronically to self-focus and self-analyse regardless of mood. Nolen-Hoeksema and Morrow (1993) showed that although rumination remained a significant predictor of depressed mood after statistically controlling for private self-consciousness, private self-consciousness was not a significant predictor of depression after controlling for rumination. Moreover, Papageorgiou and Wells (2001a) pointed out that while rumination in depression is likely to involve self-relevant chains of negative thoughts, not all forms of ruminative thinking are necessarily self-relevant. Papageorgiou and Wells (2004) suggested that depressive rumination specifically consists of self-focused thinking and negative appraisals of the self, emotions, behaviours, situations, life-stressors, and coping. Therefore, self-focus can be viewed as a component of rumination that links to some, but not all, aspects of the content or form that ruminative thinking takes.

The consequences of depressive rumination

The negative consequences of dysphoric or depressive rumination have been extensively researched and documented in the literature (for comprehensive review, see Lyubomirsky & Tkach, 2004). Empirical evidence attesting to the numerous negative consequences associated with depressive rumination derives from both experimental and questionnaire-based studies. In their review, Lyubomirsky and Tkach (2004) list the following key consequences associated with rumination: (1) negative affect and depressive symptoms, (2) negatively biased thinking, (3) poor problem-solving, (4) impaired motivation and inhibition of instrumental behaviour, (5) impaired concentration and cognition, and (6) increased stress and specific problems (e.g., threats to physical health, impaired social relationships, stress and emotional adjustment). From an applied perspective, rumination has also been found to delay recovery from depression during CBT (Siegle, Sagrati, & Crawford, 1999). Therefore, the literature documents the extensive deleterious consequences associated with rumination, hence reinforcing the need to advance our knowledge of this process and, in particular, develop effective interventions that directly target depressive rumination in treatment.

A clinical metacognitive model of rumination and depression

Despite the numerous negative consequences associated with depressive rumination, it may seem unclear why certain individuals choose to engage in rumination when they encounter specific stressors. However, knowledge of the factors implicated in proneness to rumination may contribute to our understanding of the mechanisms underlying the frequency and severity of rumination and depressive symptoms. In addition, the modification of these factors may assist in reducing vulnerability to rumination and maximizing the efficacy of CBT and other psychological interventions for depression. Several hypotheses have been advanced to account for the role of rumination in depression. Rumination has been conceptualized as resulting from a failure to achieve higher-order goals (Martin & Tesser, 1989, 1996), as a way of helping individuals to focus inwardly and evaluate the feelings and the problematic situation in order to gain insight (Nolen-Hoeksema, 1991), and as a primary coping activity (Papageorgiou & Wells, 2003, 2004). In particular, rumination can be viewed as a strategy used to understand one's problems, emotions and circumstances, and as a means of finding solutions to the problems precipitating depression (Papageorgiou & Wells, 2001a; Wells & Matthews, 1994, 1996).

A systematic account of rumination should specify the mechanisms responsible for initiating and maintaining this activity and the factors contributing to the development of its pathological form. Wells and Matthews' (1994, 1996) S-REF model of emotional disorders accounts for the information-processing mechanisms that initiate and maintain styles of perseverative negative thinking, such as depressive rumination, and the pathological consequences of these styles of thinking. In the S-REF model, a particular cognitive attentional 'syndrome', consisting of heightened self-focus, repetitive negative thinking, maladaptive coping behaviours and threat monitoring, contributes to emotional disturbance. An important component of this syndrome is perseverative negative thinking in the form of rumination or worry. The S-REF model views these processes as coping strategies that have counterproductive effects of perpetuating emotional disorders. Selection and execution of rumination are linked to particular metacognitive beliefs and processes. Metacognition refers to the aspects of the information-processing system that monitors, interprets, evaluates and regulates the contents and processes of its organization (Flavell, 1979; Wells, 2000). Building on the S-REF model, a specific clinical metacognitive model of rumination and depression (Papageorgiou & Wells, 2003, 2004) has been developed and evaluated, and it suggests specific ways in which rumination is initiated, maintained and becomes pathological. According to this model, following a specific trigger (e.g., a negative thought or image, a memory of loss or failure, or an external non-cognitive event), positive metacognitive beliefs about the benefits and advantages of rumination motivate individuals with depression to engage in sustained ruminative thinking. Depressed individuals may believe that 'ruminating about my depression helps me to understand past mistakes and failures'. Once rumination is activated, and because of the numerous negative consequences associated with this process, individuals then appraise rumination as both uncontrollable and harmful (i.e., negative beliefs 1, as in 'It is impossible not to ruminate about the bad things that have happened in the past') and likely to produce detrimental interpersonal and social consequences (i.e., negative beliefs 2, as in 'Everyone would desert me if they knew how much I ruminate about myself'). This model asserts that the activation of negative beliefs about rumination contributes to depression. Thus, vicious cycles of rumination and metacognition are responsible for the experience of depression.

Empirical evidence supporting the clinical metacognitive model of rumination and depression comes from several studies. In an initial investigation, Papageorgiou and Wells (2001a) found that all individuals with depression in their study reported both positive and negative metacognitive beliefs about rumination. On the basis of this, the Positive Beliefs about Rumination Scale (PBRS) (Papageorgiou & Wells, 2001b) and the Negative Beliefs about Rumination Scale (NBRS) (Papageorgiou, Wells, & Meina, in preparation) were developed. Both the PBRS and NBRS have been shown to have good psychometric properties of reliability and validity (e.g., Luminet, 2004; Papageorgiou & Wells, 2001b). Studies have shown that the PBRS is significantly and positively associated with rumination and depression in non-clinical samples (Papageorgiou & Wells, 2001b, Study 4; 2001c; 2003, Study 2) and patients with depression (Papageorgiou & Wells, 2003, Study 1; Papageorgiou et al., in preparation). In addition, both subtypes of negative metacognitive beliefs about rumination (i.e., beliefs concerning uncontrollability and harm, and the interpersonal and social consequences of rumination) have been shown to be significantly and positively correlated with rumination and depression in non-clinical samples (Papageorgiou & Wells, 2001c, 2003, Study 2) and patients with depression (Papageorgiou & Wells, 2003, Study 1; Papageorgiou et al., in preparation). Studies have also shown that both positive and negative metacognitive beliefs about rumination significantly distinguish patients with recurrent depression from patients with panic disorder and agoraphobia, and patients with social phobia (Papageorgiou & Wells, 2001b, Study 5; Papageorgiou et al., in preparation), suggesting specificity associated with such metacognitive beliefs. In another study, Sanderson and Papageorgiou (in preparation) found that positive and negative beliefs about rumination did not significantly discriminate between currently and previously depressed individuals, suggesting that these beliefs may act or persist as a vulnerability factor. In a further study, Papageorgiou and Wells (2001c) conducted a prospective study to examine the causal status of the relationships between rumination, negative metacognitive beliefs about rumination, and depression in a non-clinical sample. Negative metacognitive beliefs about the uncontrollability and harm associated with rumination predicted depression prospectively even after controlling statistically for initial levels of depression and rumination. Finally, using structural equation modelling, a good statistical model fit has been found for the clinical metacognitive model of rumination and depression in a depressed sample (Papageorgiou & Wells, 2003, Study 1) and a similar model in a non-depressed sample (Papageorgiou & Wells, 2003, Study 2; Roelofs, Papageorgiou, Gerber, Huibers, Peeters, & Arntz, 2007).

A brief overview of metacognitive therapy for depressive rumination

CBT for depression focuses specifically on modifying the content of negative thoughts and beliefs and reversing associated behaviours. CBT places little or no emphasis on targeting the process of ruminative thinking and the metacognitive factors responsible for initiating and maintaining this activity. Therefore, the development and implementation of a metacognitive therapy for depressive rumination has been advocated (Wells, 2000; Wells & Papageorgiou, 2004). Why develop a specific metacognitive treatment for depressive rumination? There are at least two primary lines of work that support the need for developing specific therapeutic interventions targeting the process, rather than the content, of rumination in depression. First, as we have seen so far in this chapter, rumination and metacognition play a key role in depression. And second, this role is clearly supported by theoretical developments (e.g., Wells & Matthews, 1994, 1996) and empirical evidence (e.g., Papageorgiou & Wells, 2003, 2004). In view of this, Wells and Papageorgiou (2004) proposed a specific metacognitive therapy for depressive rumination, which also draws on the metacognitive therapy of generalized anxiety disorder (Wells, 1997, 2000). According to Wells and Papageorgiou (2004), metacognitive therapy for depressive rumination should consist of the following basic goals and stages: (1) assessment of rumination and metacognition, (2) case conceptualization, (3) socialization, (4) facilitating abandonment of rumination, (5) enhancing flexible control over cognition, (6) modifying negative and positive metacognitive beliefs, and (7) de-catastrophizing emotion. In the remainder of this chapter, brief descriptions of the features of each one of these stages will be presented.

Assessment of rumination and metacognition

Following psychological assessment and diagnostic screening, the aim is to assess the nature of rumination and the metacognitive beliefs supporting this activity. The frequency, content, duration of rumination and depression associated with it can be monitored by diaries. The use of standardized psychometric tools can facilitate assessment of rumination and other important variables associated with it. The RRS (Nolen-Hoeksema & Morrow, 1991) can be used to assess rumination itself. Other self-report measures can be used to assess metacognitive beliefs about rumination. These include the PBRS (Papageorgiou & Wells, 2001b) and the NBRS (Papageorgiou, Wells, & Meina, in preparation). In addition to these psychometric instruments, cost-benefit analyses can be conducted to elicit the advantages and disadvantages of rumination, which may reveal idiosyncratic positive and negative metacognitive beliefs about rumination that can be used for subsequent treatment sessions.

Case conceptualization

The first treatment session focuses on reviewing most recent occasions when the patient felt *particularly* depressed and was engaged in rumination, and to gather specific information to construct individual metacognitive formulations of the patient's depression. The key elements of this conceptualization are the trigger(s), positive and negative metacognitive beliefs, and the content of rumination. Papageorgiou and Wells' (2003, 2004) clinical metacognitive model of rumination and depression is used to complete individual case conceptualizations. The primary aim of this stage is to illustrate how metacognitive beliefs are responsible for activating and maintaining rumination in depression. It is useful to review several occasions of depressed mood to demonstrate the goodness of fit of the model.

Socialization

The first treatment session also focuses on reviewing both thinking and behavioural styles associated with triggering depression and its consequences. Again, the aim here is to illustrate fully and clearly to patients how their rumination can be metacognitively activated and perpetuated during episodes of depression. The intermeshed role of behaviour and rumination in maintaining depression is also illustrated. Examples are used to show how rumination leads to the persistence of depressed mood. Brief activity scheduling tasks can be used as behavioural experiments to demonstrate how mood improves by engaging in activity that either blocks or reduces ruminative thinking.

Facilitating abandonment of rumination

During this stage, the problems and negative consequences associated with rumination are identified and listed. Thorough advantages versus disadvantages analyses of rumination are carried out to help the patient identify the beliefs about rumination that can make it difficult to abandon this activity. This analysis provides a means of: (1) showing how rumination is problematic in terms of affect, behaviour, cognition and physical sensations/symptoms, (2) eliciting positive and negative metacognitive beliefs about rumination, and (3) strengthening the perceived disadvantages so that the patient is more motivated to interrupt the activity. The PBRS and NBRS can be used to provide a basis for exploring specific metacognitive beliefs about rumination.

Enhancing flexible control over cognition

In metacognitive treatment for depressive rumination, Wells and Papageorgiou (2004) advocated the use of three primary strategies for enhancing flexible control over cognition: attention training (ATT), prescribed rumination ban, and detached mindfulness. Wells (1990) developed ATT as a means of helping patients train in executive control skills that directly disrupt the cognitive attentional syndrome in the S-REF model. ATT serves as a means of counteracting adhesive self-focus and preoccupation and enhancing flexible control over one's thinking. ATT as a sole treatment strategy seems to be effective across a range of disorders (Cavanagh & Franklin, 2001; Papageorgiou & Wells, 1998, 2000; Wells, 1990; Wells, White, & Carter, 1997). ATT consists of attending flexibly to a range of different external auditory stimuli, and it comprises three phases: selective attention, rapid attention switching, and divided attention. The therapist introduces ATT in the treatment of depression using a rationale that emphasizes the need to interrupt unhelpful thinking styles as follows:

> We have seen how when you become depressed your thinking pattern changes and you begin to focus your attention on your feelings and brood on negative thoughts concerning past, present, or future. This form of preoccupation or rumination is a problem because it keeps depression going. You might be able to see this effect when you think about your own experiences. When you dwell on your negative thoughts and feelings this does not help you to feel better, and when something happens to interrupt this activity you can feel better even if only for a short time. Unfortunately, it probably isn't long before your rumination starts again. In order to make more stable improvements in your mood it is helpful to practise a technique called attention training, which will allow you to reduce your unhelpful patterns of rumination and attention that keep your problem going.
>
> (Wells & Papageorgiou, 2004, p. 265)

Other specific ATT rationales have been developed for panic disorder, social phobia and health anxiety and these rationales, together with the full ATT instructions, can be found in Wells (2000). Following the introduction of ATT, patients are then asked to practise ATT twice a day for homework. Each practice session should be for a period of 10–15 minutes. In order to facilitate ATT compliance, the types of auditory stimuli that patients will use in their home practice environment are carefully reviewed.

In conjunction with ATT, patients are encouraged to notice early signs of rumination and ban it. Motivation to carry out an effective rumination ban is usually increased by the advantages versus disadvantages analysis. Common obstacles to the effective implementation of the rumination ban include: (1) failure by patients to be aware of the pervasiveness of rumination, (2) erroneous metacognitive beliefs that the activity is uncontrollable, and (3) metacognitive beliefs about the need to continue ruminating because it is perceived as helpful. Several strategies (e.g., self-monitoring) can be implemented to overcome these obstacles.

Detached mindfulness is a strategy or metacognitive state which aims to facilitate the interruption of ruminative thinking by learning not to engage actively with thoughts, but to maintain awareness of them as a passive observer (Wells & Matthews, 1994, 1996; Wells, 2000). Instead of challenging the content or validity of individual negative thoughts, patients are encouraged to develop detachment from thoughts that trigger ruminative thinking while maintaining objective awareness of them. A number of strategies can be used to illustrate the basic principle of detached mindfulness and provide the setting conditions for developing this ability. Wells (2006) advocated the use of 10 techniques to facilitate detached mindfulness in metacognitive therapy. These techniques include the following: metacognitive guidance, free association task, prescriptive mind-wandering, suppression counter-suppression experiment, tiger task, clouds image, passenger train analogy, recalcitrant child analogy, verbal loop, and ATT. Once the concept of not engaging with thoughts is grasped, the patient is encouraged to disengage from negative thoughts that trigger rumination each time they occur.

Modifying negative and positive metacognitive beliefs

The negative metacognitive beliefs about the uncontrollability and harm of rumination are tested with the implementation of the prescribed rumination ban and through controlled rumination experiments. In controlled rumination experiments, patients are asked to notice rumination and interrupt it, and to postpone the process until a specified time later in the day. The positive metacognitive beliefs about rumination are challenged by verbal reattribution strategies of questioning how long patients have been ruminating to determine whether they have achieved solutions to their problem of depression. This can be followed by reviewing evidence for and against the belief that rumination is an effective strategy. A rumination modulation experiment can also be used to modify positive beliefs about rumination. Here, the patient is asked to ruminate deliberately for a specified period of time at the beginning of a day and the following day to ban such activity.

De-catastrophizing emotion

Individuals with histories of depression tend to endorse negative beliefs about the consequences of rumination and depression that pertain to themes of danger and fears of depression, relapse or recurrence. The primary focus during this stage of metacognitive treatment of depressive rumination is to assess the presence of these meta-emotional appraisals and responses and modify them by normalization and verbal reattribution strategies with relevant behavioural experiments. This is particularly important since individuals' tendency to engage in meta-emotional appraisals and responses is likely to reactivate positive beliefs about rumination, hence resulting in actual patterns of rumination and contributing to the experience of depression.

Summary and conclusion

Although CBT is an effective treatment for depression, a significant proportion of individuals do not fully benefit from this intervention. In order to maximize treatment effectiveness, core cognitive processes in depression should be targeted. In this chapter, the phenomenology of rumination, which has been shown to play a central role in depression, was reviewed in detail. The development and empirical evidence of a clinical metacognitive model of rumination and depression was described. This model accounts for the mechanisms involved in the initiation and maintenance of rumination in depression. More specifically, metacognitive factors are at centre stage in this model, and they are directly targeted through the implementation of a new, specific, metacognitive therapy for depressive rumination. Growing evidence supports not only a number of individual components of this intervention but also the combined set of strategies and techniques that constitute metacognitive treatment for depressive rumination.

Acknowledgement

I am grateful to Sue Thorgaard for her assistance in the preparation of the manuscript.

References

Alloy, L. B., Abramson, L. Y., Hogan, M. E., Whitehouse, W. G., Rose, D. T., Robinson, M. S., et al. (2000). The Temple–Wisconsin Cognitive Vulnerability to Depression (CVD) Project: lifetime history of Axis I psychopathology in individuals at high and low cognitive vulnerability to depression. *Journal of Abnormal Psychology*, *109*, 403–418.

American Psychiatric Association (1994). *Diagnostic and Statistical Manual of Mental Disorders* (4th edn). Washington, DC: Author.

Beck, A. T. (1967). *Depression: Clinical, Experimental, and Theoretical Aspects*. New York: Harper & Row.

Beck, A. T. (1976). *Cognitive Therapy and the Emotional Disorders*. New York: International Universities Press.

Beck, A. T., Rush, A. J., Shaw, B. F., & Emery, G. (1979). *Cognitive Therapy of Depression*. New York: Guilford Press.

Blackburn, I. M., Eunson, K. M., & Bishop, S. (1986). A two year naturalistic follow-up of depressed patients treated with cognitive therapy, pharmacotherapy and a combination of both. *Journal of Affective Disorders, 10*, 65–75.

Borkovec, T. D., Robinson, E., Pruzinsky, T., & DePree, J. A. (1983). Preliminary exploration of worry: some characteristics and processes. *Behaviour Research and Therapy, 21*, 9–16.

Cavanagh, M. J., & Franklin, J. (2001, July). Attention training and hypochondriasis: preliminary results of a controlled treatment trial. Paper presented at the World Congress of Behavioral and Cognitive Therapies, Vancouver, Canada.

Clark, D. A., Beck, A. T., & Alford, B. A. (1999). *Cognitive Theory and Therapy of Depression*. New York: Wiley.

Clark, D. A., & de Silva, P. (1985). The nature of depressive and anxious, intrusive thoughts: distinct or uniform phenomena? *Behaviour Research and Therapy, 23*, 383–393.

Clark, D. A., & Hemsley, D. R. (1985). Individual differences in the experience of depressive and anxious, intrusive thoughts. *Behaviour Research and Therapy, 23*, 625–633.

Conway, M., Csank, P. A. R., Holm, S. L., & Blake, C. K. (2000). On assessing individual differences in rumination on sadness. *Journal of Personality Assessment, 75*, 404–425.

DeRubeis, R. J., & Crits-Christoph, P. (1998). Empirically supported individual and group psychological treatments for adult mental disorders. *Journal of Consulting and Clinical Psychology, 66*, 37–52.

Fenigstein, A., Scheier, M., & Buss, A. H. (1975). Public and private self-consciousness: assessment and theory. *Journal of Consulting and Clinical Psychology, 43*, 522–527.

Flavell, J. H. (1979). Metacognition and metacognitive monitoring: a new area of cognitive-developmental inquiry. *American Psychologist, 34*, 906–911.

Fresco, D. M., Frankel, A. N., Mennin, D. S., Turk, C. L., & Heimberg, R. G. (2002). Distinct and overlapping features of rumination and worry: the relationship of cognitive production to negative affective states. *Cognitive Therapy and Research, 26*, 179–188.

Goring, H. J., & Papageorgiou, C. (2008). Rumination and worry: factor analysis of self-report measures in depressed participants. *Cognitive Therapy and Research, 32*, 554–566.

Hong, R. Y. (2007). Worry and rumination: differential associations with anxious and depressive symptoms and coping behavior. *Behaviour Research and Therapy, 45*, 277–290.

Luminet, O. (2004). Measurement of depressive rumination and associated constructs. In C. Papageorgiou & A. Wells (eds), *Depressive Rumination: Nature, Theory and Treatment* (pp. 187–215). Chichester, UK: Wiley.

Lyubomirsky, S., & Tkach, C. (2004). The consequences of dysphoric rumination. In C. Papageorgiou & A. Wells (eds), *Depressive Rumination: Nature, Theory and Treatment* (pp. 21–41). Chichester, UK: Wiley.

Martin, L. L., & Tesser, A. (1989). Toward a motivational and structural theory of ruminative thought. In J. S. Uleman & J. A. Bargh (eds), *Unintended Thought* (pp. 306–326). New York: Guilford Press.

Martin, L. L., & Tesser, A. (1996). Some ruminative thoughts. In R. S. Wyer (ed.), *Advances in Social Cognition* (Vol. 9, pp. 1–47). Mahwah, NJ: Lawrence Erlbaum Associates.

Muris, P., Roelofs, J., Meesters, C., & Boomsma, P. (2004). Rumination and worry in nonclinical adolescents. *Cognitive Therapy and Research*, *28*, 539–554.

Nezu, A. M., Nezu, C. M., Trunzo, J. J., & McClure, K. S. (1998). Treatment maintenance for unipolar depression: relevant issues, literature review, and recommendations for research and clinical practice. *Clinical Psychology: Science and Practice*, *5*, 496–512.

Nolen-Hoeksema, S. (1991). Responses to depression and their effects on the duration of depressive episodes. *Journal of Abnormal Psychology*, *100*, 569–582.

Nolen-Hoeksema, S., & Morrow, J. (1991). A prospective study of depression and posttraumatic stress symptoms after a natural disaster: the 1989 Loma Prieta earthquake. *Journal of Personality and Social Psychology*, *61*, 115–121.

Nolen-Hoeksema, S., & Morrow, J. (1993). Effects of rumination and distraction on naturally occurring depressed mood. *Cognition and Emotion*, *7*, 561–570.

Nolen-Hoeksema, S., Parker, L. E., & Larson, J. (1994). Ruminative coping with depressed mood following loss. *Journal of Personality and Social Psychology*, *67*, 92–104.

Papageorgiou, C. (2006). Worry and rumination: styles of persistent negative thinking in anxiety and depression. In G. C. L. Davey & A. Wells (eds), *Worry and Its Psychological Disorders: Theory, Assessment and Ttreatment* (pp. 21–40). Chichester, UK: Wiley.

Papageorgiou, C., & Wells, A. (1998). Effects of attention training on hypochondriasis: a brief case series. *Psychological Medicine*, *28*, 193–200.

Papageorgiou, C., & Wells, A. (1999a). Process and metacognitive dimensions of depressive and anxious thoughts and relationships with emotional intensity. *Clinical Psychology and Psychotherapy*, *6*, 156–162.

Papageorgiou, C., & Wells, A. (1999b, November). Dimensions of depressive rumination and anxious worry: a comparative study. Paper presented at the 33rd Annual Convention of the Association for Advancement of Behavior Therapy, Toronto, Canada.

Papageorgiou, C., & Wells, A. (2000). Treatment of recurrent major depression with attention training. *Cognitive and Behavioral Practice*, *7*, 407–413.

Papageorgiou, C., & Wells, A. (2001a). Metacognitive beliefs about rumination in recurrent major depression. *Cognitive and Behavioral Practice*, *8*, 160–164.

Papageorgiou, C., & Wells, A. (2001b). Positive beliefs about depressive rumination: development and preliminary validation of a self-report scale. *Behavior Therapy*, *32*, 13–26.

Papageorgiou, C., & Wells, A. (2001c, November). Metacognitive vulnerability to depression: a prospective study. Paper presented at the 35th Annual Convention of the Association for Advancement of Behavior Therapy, Philadelphia, USA.

Papageorgiou, C., & Wells, A. (2003). An empirical test of a clinical metacognitive model of rumination and depression. *Cognitive Therapy and Research*, *27*, 261–273.

Papageorgiou, C., & Wells, A. (2004). Nature, functions, and beliefs about depressive rumination. In C. Papageorgiou & A. Wells (eds), *Depressive Rumination: Nature, Theory and Treatment* (pp. 3–20). Chichester, UK: Wiley.

Papageorgiou, C., Wells, A., & Meina, L. J. *Development and Preliminary Validation of the Negative Beliefs About Rumination Scale.* Manuscript in preparation.

Pyszczynski, T., & Greenberg, J. (1987). Self-regulatory perseveration and the depressive self-focusing style: a self-awareness theory of reactive depression. *Psychological Bulletin, 102,* 122–138.

Pyszczynski, T., Greenberg, J., Hamilton, J. H., & Nix, G. (1991). On the relationship between self-focused attention and psychological disorder: a critical reappraisal. *Psychological Bulletin, 110,* 538–543.

Rippere, V. (1977). 'What's the thing to do when you're feeling depressed?': a pilot study. *Behaviour Research and Therapy, 15,* 185–191.

Robinson, S. M., & Alloy, L. B. (2003). Negative cognitive styles and stress-reactive rumination interact to predict depression: a prospective study. *Cognitive Therapy and Research, 27,* 275–291.

Roelofs, J., Papageorgiou, C., Gerber, R. D., Huibers, M., Peeters, F., & Arntz, A. (2007). On the links between self-discrepancies, rumination, metacognitions, and symptoms of depression in undergraduates. *Behaviour Research and Therapy, 45,* 1295–1305.

Sanderson, J., & Papageorgiou, C. *Metacognitive Beliefs About Depressive Rumination: Maintenance or Vulnerability?* Manuscript in preparation.

Shea, M. T., Elkin, I., Imber, S. D., Sotsky, S. M., Watkins, J. T., Collins, J. F., et al. (1992). Course of depressive symptoms over follow-up: findings from the NIMH treatment of depression collaborative research program. *Archives of General Psychiatry, 49,* 782–787.

Siegle, G. J., Sagrati, S., & Crawford, C. E. (1999, November). Effects of rumination and initial severity on response to cognitive therapy for depression. Paper presented at the 33rd Annual Convention of the Association for the Advancement of Behavior Therapy, Toronto, Canada.

Spasojevic, J., & Alloy, L. B. (2001). Rumination as a common mechanism relating depressive risk factors to depression. *Emotion, 1,* 25–37.

Treynor, W., Gonzalez, R., & Nolen-Hoeksema, S. (2003). Rumination reconsidered: a psychometric analysis. *Cognitive Therapy and Research, 27,* 247–259.

Wells, A. (1990). Panic disorder in association with relaxation induced anxiety: an attentional training approach to treatment. *Behavior Therapy, 21,* 273–280.

Wells, A. (1997). *Cognitive Therapy of Anxiety Disorders: A Practice Manual and Conceptual Guide.* Chichester, UK: Wiley.

Wells, A. (2000). *Emotional Disorders and Metacognition: Innovative Cognitive Therapy.* Chichester, UK: Wiley.

Wells, A. (2006). Detached mindfulness in cognitive therapy: a metacognitive analysis and ten techniques. *Journal of Rational-Emotive and Cognitive-Behavior Therapy, 23,* 337–355.

Wells, A., & Matthews, G. (1994). *Attention and Emotion: A Clinical Perspective.* Hove, UK: Lawrence Erlbaum Associates.

Wells, A., & Matthews, G. (1996). Modelling cognition in emotional disorders: the S-REF model. *Behaviour Research and Therapy, 34,* 881–888.

Wells, A., & Papageorgiou, C. (2004). Metacognitive therapy for depressive rumination. In C. Papageorgiou & A. Wells (eds), *Depressive Rumination: Nature, Theory and Treatment* (pp. 259–273). Chichester, UK: Wiley.

Wells, A., White, J., & Carter, K. (1997). Attention training effects on anxiety and beliefs in panic and social phobia. *Clinical Psychology and Psychotherapy, 4,* 226–232.

Chapter 3

Mindfulness-Based Cognitive Therapy: preventing relapse in depression

Thorsten Barnhofer and Melanie J. V. Fennell

Introduction

Major depression is a disabling emotional disorder, affecting all aspects of functioning. Negative thinking pervades the depressed person's views of the past, the self and the future; lack of interest and anhedonia reduce engagement in activities that used to be enjoyable; and physical symptoms, such as lack of energy and poor concentration, undermine the capacity to deal with everyday challenges. People experience depression as painfully discrepant from their usual (and desired) state, and struggle to escape it. Paradoxically, their attempts to overcome it often, in fact, keep it going. In particular, repetitive ruminative thinking, intended to help the sufferer to resolve the problem, actually contributes to further deteriorations in mood, establishing a vicious circle in which mood and thinking reciprocally feed each other.

The prevalence of depression in Western countries is high. Current estimates of 1-year prevalence in Europe and North America are 5–7 percent (Kessler et al., 2003; Paykel, Brugha, & Fryers, 2005), and demographic studies have shown consistent increases in rates over past decades (Compton, Conway, Stinson, & Grant, 2006). This is particularly concerning because, for most people, depression is recurrent (Kessler et al., 1994; Lavori et al., 1994). Thus, treatment must focus not only on alleviating current symptoms, but also on reducing the risk of relapse.

Mindfulness-Based Cognitive Therapy (MBCT) was specifically designed with this objective in mind. The program, developed by Segal, Williams, & Teasdale (2002), is based on Kabat-Zinn's 'Mindfulness-Based Stress Reduction' (1990). It combines intensive training in mindfulness meditation with interventions from cognitive therapy for depression (Beck, Rush, Shaw, & Emery, 1979). The principal aim is to reduce cognitive vulnerability to depression by helping participants to become more aware of and to respond differently to negative thoughts and emotions that might otherwise trigger downward spirals of thinking and mood.

The role of cognition in depression: development and maintenance

Cognitive vulnerability and differential activation

As noted above, the course of depression presents a worrying picture of relapse and recurrence. The risk of depression increases steeply with the number of previous episodes, from about 50 percent after one episode, to about 70 percent after a second, and about 90 percent after a third (American Psychiatric Association, 1994). At the same time, the role of major life events apparently weakens. That is, the association between life events and first episodes of depression is relatively strong, but it diminishes with further episodes (see Monroe & Harkness, 2005, for a recent review). It appears that, increasingly, depression occurs autonomously, or in response to minor or idiosyncratic stressors. Models explaining relapse and recurrence must take these changes into account.

Cognitive approaches are based on the observation that depression is characterized by negative biases in thinking, expressed in automatically occurring negative thoughts that have their roots in negative self-schemas and dysfunctional attitudes. Research has now demonstrated that, in people who have previously been depressed, such attitudes and schemas can easily be reactivated by minor changes in mood, a phenomenon referred to as 'cognitive reactivity'. This suggests that, with repeated experience of depression, mild negative mood *in itself* may become the trigger for a constellation of interrelated negative cognitions (for an overview, see Ingram, Miranda, & Segal, 1998). Once re-established, this processing mode increases the likelihood that negative cycles of cognition and mood will spiral downward into depression. Ease of reactivation is assumed to increase with each relapse, as associations between depressed mood and other aspects of functioning progressively strengthen (Segal, Williams, Teasdale, & Gemar, 1996). Equally, with each episode, the constellation's coherence increases, making it easier for activation of single elements to spread to the whole system.

The persistence of depression: the role of rumination and avoidance

Once negative thinking is reactivated, its further impact is crucially dependent on how the person responds to it. Rumination has been found to be a particularly important factor in perpetuating depression. Abstract-analytical, repetitive rumination represents an attempt to solve problems and reduce discrepancies between the current state and the desired (or ideal) state, and previously and currently depressed people report predominately positive beliefs about its usefulness as a coping strategy (Papageorgiou &

Wells, 2001). In fact, however, it causes further deteriorations in mood, increases negative biases in thinking, and undermines cognitive functions crucial for effective coping, including the ability to retrieve specific memories of autobiographical events and general problem-solving skills.

Avoidance also contributes to the persistence of depression (e.g., Hayes, Beevers, Feldman, Laurenceau, & Perlman, 2005). As mood worsens and belief in the value of rumination decreases, people often oscillate between rumination and attempts to avoid negative thoughts and states. Unfortunately, the effects of avoidance are equally negative. Attempts to suppress negative thoughts, for example, paradoxically increase their frequency (e.g., Lynch, Schneider, Rosenthal, & Cheavens, 2007), and avoidance also precludes active problem-solving. Thus both rumination and cognitive avoidance perpetuate negative mood states.

MBCT for depression

How does MBCT address cognitive vulnerability and maintaining processes?

MBCT was developed to target the processes described above. It teaches a core skill: the ability 'to recognize, and to disengage from mind states characterized by self-perpetuating patterns of ruminative, negative thought' (Segal et al., 2002, p. 75). In order to do this, participants must become aware of the subtle changes in mood and body state that trigger depressive thinking. Such thinking is usually emotionally charged and fueled by pressure to improve the situation. So disengagement requires a conscious, effortful change in perspective. Rather than seeing thoughts as reflections of objective truth which require a response, participants learn to understand them as passing mental events to which they can choose not to attend. Thus, MBCT teaches patients to take a different, decentered perspective on thinking and awareness itself. By systematically bringing mindful awareness to present moment experience, participants enter a mode of functioning that is incompatible with both rumination and avoidance. Segal et al. (2002) describe this as a change from 'doing' mode, in which the aim is to reduce discrepancies between current state and how things *should* be, to a mode of 'being' in which the person is in immediate and intimate contact with present-moment experience, just as it is. 'Doing' mode is extremely helpful in situations where goals can be attained through action, but with emotional problems it is often counterproductive. This may be because no immediate action is possible, as for example, because discrepancies relate to past events (e.g., 'If only I had . . .', 'Why didn't I . . .?'), or because goals are very general in nature (e.g., 'I want to feel better'). Ruminative attempts to problem-solve fail to reach their intended goals, while at the same time keeping the gap between how things are and how the person wants them to be (or thinks they should be) firmly in focus. Preoccupation and increasing depressed mood follow. In 'being' mode, in contrast, the focus is on accepting things as they are, rather than constantly monitoring, evaluating and attempting to change them. Thoughts and feelings are seen as part of changing moment-to-moment experience, and this leads to a sense of greater freedom and choice, and to possibilities of skillful responses rather than automatic, schema-driven reactions.

What is MBCT?

Mindfulness has been described as *'the awareness that emerges through paying attention on purpose, in the present moment, and non-judgmentally to the unfolding of experience moment to moment'* (Kabat-Zinn, 2003, p. 145). Thus, it is both a means of becoming aware of and entering 'being' mode, and a central part of 'being' mode itself. MBCT is first and foremost a skills-training program: formal meditation practice and exercises designed to bring mindful awareness into everyday life are essential components, learned during classes and practiced regularly at home. The focus during sessions is more experiential than didactic, and interactive teaching about cognitive vulnerability to depression and what maintains it. Each class begins with a 30–45-minute meditation practice led by the instructor, followed by an inquiry into participants' experiences. Discussion of homework follows, and then another practice or exercise. New homework is agreed before the session closes. The instructor's role is facilitative, inviting participants to explore their experience and bringing to what they say an attitude of curiosity, interest, acceptance and compassion. S/he allows difficult thoughts and feelings to be experienced and discussed without resorting to problem-solving or 'fixing'. Thus, the instructor embodies the very principles that participants learn to bring to their own meditation practice, including the ability to relate calmly and kindly to negative affect. For this reason, and because instructors practice the meditations as they lead them, an established mindfulness meditation practice is a prerequisite for teaching MBCT classes.

The eight-session program

The program described below follows the format devised by Segal et al. (2002) for recurrent depression. Readers should appreciate that this program is potentially open to modification in the light of experience (for example, some instructors now increase the length of classes from 2 to 2½ hours), or to suit the specific needs of particular patient groups (thus, for example, the psychoeducational focus would be different for a different diagnostic group, as might the precise nature of the meditation practices). However, elaboration of these issues is beyond the scope of this chapter.

Within the original 8-week program, each 2-hour class follows its own theme and curriculum. Class size varies according to facilities, but the norm is about 12 participants, currently in recovery, each of whom is seen in an individual, preclass interview before the start of the program. There are two overarching aims:

1   *To teach participants to relate differently to painful thoughts, feelings and sensations.* In the first four sessions, they discover, by intentionally focusing attention on specific aspects of experience, how often the mind wanders. They learn to notice and acknowledge the wanderings, and to return the mind again and again to its intended point of focus (for example, the breath). This means choosing to let go of thoughts and feelings that may appear compelling, rather than pursuing them. In sessions 5 to 8, the emphasis changes, from choosing to let go, to remaining with and responding differently to difficult thoughts and feelings, accepting their presence and bringing a gentle, investigative awareness to them, rather than either getting entangled in them or attempting to eliminate them.
2   *To help them to enrich the experience of living* by being in direct sensory contact with moment-by-moment experience, instead of being lost in their heads. This is done through in-session practices (for example, the raisin exercise in session 1) and through homework practices designed to carry mindfulness into everyday life (for example, detailed appreciation of every day activities, hearing and sight).

Session 1: automatic pilot

We often function on automatic pilot, barely aware of what we are doing. Doing things automatically is helpful because it is effortless, but on automatic pilot we fail to savor our experiences, and we are more likely to react in accordance with old scripts, losing options to respond to difficulties in new and more helpful ways. Automatic pilot is particularly risky for people vulnerable to depression, because it means that subtle changes in mood and thinking that could lead into an episode are less likely to be detected.

Session 1 aims to help participants realize how often we function on automatic pilot and to experience the effects of being mindfully aware. The instructor welcomes participants and establishes ground rules (confidentiality, etc.). Participants then introduce themselves to each other, first in pairs and then as a group. The theme of the class is illustrated through a simple eating meditation. Each participant is given a raisin, invited to imagine they have never seen such a thing before, and to explore it very slowly and with full attention – looking at it, exploring its texture, inhaling its smell, placing it on the tongue, slowly chewing it and fully experiencing its taste, and finally swallowing it. The exercise usually highlights: (a) how often eating, like other activities, is done automatically, without paying attention; and (b) how paying attention can change the nature of an experience.

The first formal meditation practice of the program follows, the 'body scan'. Participants are invited to explore sensations in their bodies with the same attentiveness they brought to the raisin. Awareness of the body is chosen as the starting point because sensations associated with emotion can feed negative cycles of mood and cognition, often without awareness, especially in patients who predominantly live in their heads. Participants lie down on their backs on mats, and first focus on the sensations of breathing. Then, step by step, they move their attention through the whole body, starting with the toes of the left foot, then the bottom of the left foot, the heel, the ankle, and so on. Participants are invited to bring awareness to each region of the body in turn, exploring whatever sensations they discover without judgment, and then 'letting go' of that region and moving on.

For home practice, they do the body scan daily with the guidance of a CD. Additionally, they choose a routine activity, such as brushing their teeth, and every day they practice bringing moment-to-moment awareness to it.

Session 2: dealing with barriers

When participants return for session 2 they have done the body scan for 1 week. This first intensive experience of meditation usually stimulates a large number of questions (e.g., 'Am I doing it right?') and comments (e.g., 'It really worked/did not work for me'). An important part of session 2 is devoted to addressing these reactions. However, rather than beginning with a homework review, the session starts with meditation practice (another body scan), and this will be the pattern for all sessions from now on. The inquiry that follows is focused closely on *this* practice (and thus on immediate experience), before broadening to consider the week as a whole. Segal et al. (2002) describe several difficulties that participants often raise, including experiencing painful sensations during the practice, uncertainty about whether they are 'doing it right', and feeling that conditions were not right for practicing. All of these arise from expectations about how the practice should be done, and what the results should be (e.g. relaxation). In responding, the instructor stresses the importance of 'just doing' the practice, remaining open to whatever arises, just as it is, rather than trying to achieve any particular goal.

The cognitive model is then introduced through an interactive exercise. Participants are asked to close their eyes and imagine themselves in the following scenario: 'You are walking down the street, and on the other side of the street you see somebody you know. You smile and wave. The person just doesn't seem to notice and walks by' (Segal et al., 2002, p. 142). The instructor invites participants to become aware of their responses to this scenario – thoughts, feelings and body sensations. Discussion shows how the same scenario can prompt a variety of reactions, and how emotions and body state (and indeed behavior) are influenced by the meaning the person attached to the experience (thoughts), which in turn may depend on their mood at the time. Thus, participants encounter the reciprocal relationship between thinking and emotion at the heart of the cognitive model.

During the next week, participants continue practicing the body scan and bringing mindfulness to a routine activity. Additionally, they take 10–15 minutes daily to sit silently and focus on the breath. Each day, they pay careful attention to one pleasant experience, and record it in detail. This task has a dual purpose: to recognize how the mind categorizes experiences as pleasant or unpleasant, and to increase awareness of day-to-day moments of pleasure which might otherwise be missed.

Session 3: mindfulness of the breath

Through the practices during weeks 1 and 2, participants begin to realize how busy and scattered the mind often is. They may also experience negative thoughts, feelings and body states more clearly or more strongly. The practice does not offer quick solutions to painful sensations, emotions or thoughts, and at this stage some participants may feel frustrated or impatient, spending much of their meditation time checking to see whether they feel better yet. The program teaches participants to respond to problems in a different way: instead of using rumination or avoidance to tackle problems, they are learning to become aware of difficult aspects of experience, to attend briefly to them, and to let them go. Session 3 emphasizes using awareness of the breath to gather and steady themselves, and, by focusing on its constantly changing flow, to connect with the present moment. In addition, it introduces a new focus for mindfulness: the body in movement (through yoga stretches and mindful walking).

Present moment awareness implies openness to the experience of sensations as they occur. Being with present moment experience means remaining in direct contact with thought, feeling and sensation rather than viewing these through the prism of concepts (ideas, preconceptions, judgments) that may themselves become the objects of mental activities (further thought and analysis). This new skill is practiced in the session's first meditation (attending to sounds as they arise, or to vision – the view from the window). As they do this, participants are invited to notice how quickly their minds attach labels to what they see or hear and begin to think about it, rather than simply noticing pure sound or sight.

Because of its constant presence, the breath provides a particularly powerful anchor for bringing attention into the present moment. This is explored in the session's main meditation practice: a 10-minute sequence of standing yoga stretches, followed by a 20–30-minute sitting meditation. For the sitting, participants adopt a relaxed, upright posture on a chair or a cushion, bring their attention to breathing, and sustain attention on the breath as best they can. Whenever they notice their minds wander, they gently bring them back to focus on breathing. Toward the end of the sitting period, they expand the attentional focus to include the body as a whole. The sitting practice teaches participants repeatedly to return to the breath, stabilizing their attention in the present moment. Mind-wandering is seen not as a mistake or break in meditation, but rather as an opportunity to become familiar with the behavior of the mind. Participants learn to recognize and identify recurrent patterns of thinking, as well as to relate in an open and observant way to sensations of physical discomfort and to negative emotions.

This first sitting meditation is the foundation for a sequence of other practices. Importantly, in session 3, participants first encounter the '3-minute breathing space', a short, portable practice which brings mindful awareness into everyday life. The breathing space includes three steps. First, participants open their awareness to current thoughts, feelings and body sensations. Secondly, they narrow their attentional focus to breathing. In the third and final step, attention is expanded to include the body as a whole, and participants are invited to take the same careful awareness into the next moments of their day.

As usual, home practice is reviewed and, later in the session, participants may also be introduced to mindful walking, pacing very slowly back and forth over a short distance while bringing 'raisin mind' to the sensations of walking.

For homework, participants alternate standing yoga stretches followed by sitting meditation (days 1, 3, and 5) and more yoga stretches done on the floor (days 2, 4, and 6), both with guidance from CDs. Additionally, they use the 3-minute breathing space daily at three prescheduled times and record one unpleasant experience every day.

Session 4: staying present

In sessions 1–3, participants learned to stabilize present-moment awareness by bringing attention to body sensations and breathing. Noticing the mind wandering provided opportunities to train flexible attention and to notice patterns of thinking. In people vulnerable to depression, becoming aware of the workings of the mind often means being confronted by painful thoughts, feelings or sensations. Session 4 turns to focus on these, and specifically on the patterns of thought that are characteristic of depression.

Up until now, the aim has been to learn to relate differently to painful cognitions by noticing them, acknowledging their presence, and gently but firmly returning attention to where the person intends it to be (the body, the breath). Now there is the beginning of a change of emphasis, learning to turn towards painful experiences and to explore them with gentleness, curiosity and interest, keeping them on the workbench of the mind, so to speak, and bringing awareness to them, rather than trying to avoid them or getting caught up in ruminations. This implies allowing things to be as they are, and remaining steady in contact with them, as opposed to trying to change them.

The session starts with a short hearing or seeing meditation, followed by 30–40 minutes' sitting meditation, focusing first on the breath and then on the body as a whole. The longer participants sit, the more likely they are to encounter uncomfortable sensations. They are offered the opportunity, if they wish, to explore such sensations rather than changing posture right away to alleviate them. Awareness then expands further, first returning to sounds, and then attending to thought itself. Finally, participants are invited to be aware of the flow of experience as a whole without focusing on any particular aspect of it.

After the homework review, the session focuses specifically on exploring the thinking patterns that characterize depression. Participants read the Automatic Thoughts Questionnaire (Hollon & Kendall, 1980), a list of negative thoughts common in depression, and the DSM-IV (American Psychiatric Association, 1994) diagnostic criteria for major depressive episode. They discover (often with surprise) that the thoughts they assumed were theirs alone are in fact shared, and that these thoughts are symptoms of depression, in just the same way that a high temperature is a symptom of flu.

Participants then watch the first half of a documentary about Kabat-Zinn's stress reduction program, which follows an 8-week MBSR course. Most people immediately see the connection between the physical pain for which this program was designed and their own emotional pain, and the video makes it clear that the course on which they are embarked is part of a broader movement. Afterwards, they can borrow copies of *Full Catastrophe Living* (Kabat-Zinn, 1990). The session closes with a breathing space.

For homework, the participants practice the 40-minute guided sitting meditation, the 3-minute breathing space (at prescheduled times, and when they feel stress or emotional pressure mounting).

Session 5: allowing/letting be

Participants have by now usually developed increased awareness of the activity of their minds. Using the breath and the sensations of the body as anchor, they have practiced coming back to present moment awareness. In session 5, this increased flexibility becomes the basis for developing a radically different relationship to experience: a relationship in which all experience is allowed and met with acceptance. The mind is normally reactive, wanting to hold on to pleasant experiences and to avoid negative experiences. In contrast, accepting unpleasant experiences allows participants to assess them accurately, to choose how best to respond, and to counteract automatic drifts into relapse-related habits of mind. In session 5, participants have a first opportunity to practice this new approach.

The session opens with a 30–40-minute sitting meditation focusing on the breath, body sensations, sounds, and finally thoughts. Participants are invited to notice if the mind is drawn repeatedly to uncomfortable thoughts, feelings or body sensations, and to bring awareness deliberately to these. If nothing has spontaneously arisen, they may, if they wish, deliberately call to mind something that troubles them. Once a difficulty has come into mind, the instruction is to become aware of how it expresses itself in the body, and to breathe into and out of wherever it manifests most strongly, opening to the sensations and allowing them to remain in awareness. If participants find themselves getting caught up in feelings and thoughts or wanting to avoid them, they can return to the breath to steady themselves. When the difficulty no longer calls for their attention, they return to the breath or the body as a whole. This stance of approach and acceptance is now incorporated into the 'breathing space', so that people have opportunities over the week to practice it with the difficult feelings and thoughts that naturally arise as they go about their daily lives.

The session closes with the second half of the Kabat-Zinn documentary, followed by a breathing space. For homework, participants alternate guided sitting meditation with sitting in stillness for 30–40 minutes. They use the breathing space (as above) both at regular intervals and in troubling situations, and indeed will continue to do so daily between sessions until the end of the course.

Session 6: thoughts are not facts

This session makes wholly explicit the essential aim of the whole program: to help participants to experience thoughts as transient mental events, to which they can choose to attend – or not – rather than as reflections of objective truth, or an integral part of themselves. This capacity for decentering from thoughts, no matter how emotionally charged or convincing, is essential to short-circuiting the spiral into clinical depression.

The session starts with a sitting meditation in which participants pay particular attention to noticing thoughts as they arise, and seeing them simply as events in the mind. They are offered analogies: clouds crossing the sky, images coming and going on a cinema screen while they sit in the audience and watch. Once again, towards the end of the meditation, they are asked to deliberately bring to mind a difficulty and to become aware of the thoughts that come with it and, more particularly, how it expresses itself in the body.

A small exercise follows, which highlights once again the impact of mood on thinking. Participants are invited to imagine their responses to two scenarios in which a colleague rushes past them and leaves the office. In the first scenario, they are feeling down because of a quarrel; in the second, they are feeling happy because they have just been praised for good work.

The breathing space is again practiced, and participants are reminded that a breathing space can be a first step when negative thoughts arise in daily life, offering a sense of greater choice and skillful action.

The session finishes with a reminder that the end of the course is approaching, and participants are given recordings of several shorter guided meditations to experiment with (along with familiar practices), as a first step to identifying a meditation practice they will be able to make part of their lives.

Session 7: how can I best take care of myself?

This session, too, starts with a 30–40-minute sitting meditation, focusing on breath, body, sounds and thoughts, and offering an opportunity intentionally to bring a difficulty to mind and explore it. Attention turns to considering how awareness can be used as a prelude to skillful action, particularly action that participants can take when depression threatens. This intervention acknowledges the demonstrated power of activity scheduling to alleviate depression (Beck et al., 1979).

Participants make a list of things that they do on a typical day, noting whether each activity lifts mood and energy ('nourishing activities') or dampens their mood and drains them ('depleting activities'). In pairs or small groups, they explore how their balance of nourishment and depletion might be improved, either by changing the pattern of activities (perhaps adding activities, however small, which give them a sense of pleasure or mastery), or approaching previously depleting activities with a different, mindful stance.

Participants move on to prepare for relapse, identifying their own personal relapse signature and devising action plans for how to respond. In small groups, they list warning signals, and plan what to do when relapse threatens. They are invited to use the breathing space as a first step when they notice signs of relapse, then to make conscious choices about what to do, and only then to take action.

For homework, participants choose from all the formal meditations they have experienced a form of practice that they intend to use on a daily basis. They add a question at the end of their practice of the breathing space in troubling situations: 'What can I now do to take care of myself?'

Session 8: using what has been learned to deal with future low mood

The eighth and last session looks back over the course and forward into the future, asking how new skills and understanding can be maintained. Coming full circle, the session starts with a body scan, now perhaps a rather different experience from 8 weeks ago. Participants then look back over the program, alone or in pairs. Why did they come? What did they hope for? What have they learned? What obstacles might prevent them from continuing to practice? To prompt reflection, they complete a short questionnaire, rating how important the experience has been, and identifying why. The challenge of keeping up the practice without the support of the weekly meetings is highlighted. Generally, daily practice is recommended, even if only very brief, so that their skills remain fresh. In order to strengthen motivation, each participant is asked to identify one positive reason for maintaining the practice and having relapse-prevention strategies in place ('What is important to you in your life, what do you most value, that this practice could help you with?'). When it is time to say good-bye, each receives a small object (marble, pebble, or bead), a symbol of the experiences they have shared, the hard work they have done, and a reminder to continue the practice and to care for themselves. The class finishes with a short meditation in which participants explore the object just as they explored the raisin at the very beginning.

Outcome data

Two randomized, controlled trials have evaluated the effectiveness of MBCT. In an initial multicenter trial by Teasdale et al. (2001), 145 recovered depressed patients were randomized to MBCT or treatment-as-usual and followed up over a period of 60 weeks. In patients with three or more previous episodes of depression, MBCT reduced relapse rate by about 50 percent. Ma and Teasdale (2004) replicated this finding in a smaller sample of 73 recovered patients, 55 of whom had suffered three or more previous episodes of depression.

The results from both of these trials support using MBCT to reduce risk of relapse in people with recurrent depression. The fact that MBCT reduced relapse rates in people with three or more episodes of depression, but did not produce significant effects in those with one or two previous episodes, is consistent with its focus on cognitive reactivity and rumination and with the theoretical assumption that, through associative learning, these factors become increasingly important contributors to risk of relapse.

References

American Psychiatric Association (1994). *Diagnostic and Statistical Manual of Mental Disorders* (4th edn). Washington, DC: Author.

Beck, A. T., Rush, J., Shaw, B. F., & Emery, G. (1979). *Cognitive Therapy of Depression*. New York: Guilford Press.

Compton, W. M., Conway, K. P., Stinson, F. S., & Grant, B. F. (2006). Changes in the prevalence of major depression and comorbid substance use disorders in the United States between 1991–1992 and 2001–2002. *American Journal of Psychiatry, 163*, 2141–2147.

Hayes, A. M., Beevers, C. G., Feldman, G. C., Laurenceau, J. P., & Perlman, C. (2005). Avoidance and processing as predictors of symptom change and positive growth in an integrative therapy for depression. *International Journal of Behavioral Medicine, 12*, 111–122.

Hollon, S. D., & Kendall, P. (1980). Cognitive self-statements in depression: development of an automatic thoughts questionnaire. *Cognitive Therapy and Research, 4*, 383–395.

Ingram, R. E., Miranda, J., & Segal, Z. V. (1998). *Cognitive Vulnerability to Depression*. New York: Guilford Press.

Kabat-Zinn, J. (1990). *Full Catastrophe Living*. New York: Dell.

Kabat-Zinn, J. (1994). *Wherever You Go, There You Are: Mindfulness Meditation in Everyday Life*. New York: Hyperion.

Kabat-Zinn, J. (2003). Mindfulness-based interventions in context: past, present and future. *Clinical Psychology – Science and Practice, 10*, 144–156.

Kessler, R. C., McGonagle, K. A., Zhao, S. Y., Nelson, C. B., Hughes, M., Eshleman, S., et al. (1994). Lifetime and 12-month prevalence of DSM-III-R psychiatric-disorders in the United-States – results from the National Comorbidity Survey. *Archives of General Psychiatry, 51*, 8–19.

Kessler, R. C., Berglund, P., Demler, O., Jin, R., Koretz, D., Merikangas, K. R., et al. (2003). The epidemiology of major depressive disorder: results from the National Comorbidity Survey Replication (NCS-R). *JAMA, 289*, 3095–3105.

Lavori, P. W., Keller, M. B., Mueller, T. I., Scheftner, W., Fawcett, J., & Coryell, W. (1994). Recurrence after recovery in unipolar MDD – an observational follow-up-study of clinical predictors and somatic treatment as a mediating factor. *International Journal of Methods in Psychiatric Research, 4*, 211–229.

Lynch, T. R., Schneider, K. G., Rosenthal, M. Z., & Cheavens, J. S. (2007). A mediational model of trait negative affectivity, dispositional thought suppression, and intrusive thoughts following laboratory stressors. *Behaviour Research and Therapy, 45*, 749–761.

Ma, H. S., & Teasdale, J. D. (2004). Mindfulness-based cognitive therapy for depression: replication and exploration of differential relapse prevention effects. *Journal of Consulting and Clinical Psychology, 72*, 31–40.

Monroe, S. M., & Harkness, K. L. (2005). Life stress, the 'Kindling' hypothesis, and the recurrence of depression: considerations from a life stress perspective. *Psychological Review, 112*, 417–445.

Papageorgiou, C., & Wells, A. (2001). Metacognitive beliefs about rumination in recurrent major depression. *Cognitive and Behavioral Practice, 8*, 160–164.

Paykel, E. S., Brugha, T., & Fryers, T. (2005). Size and burden of depressive disorders in Europe. *European Neuropsychopharmacology, 15*, 411–423.

Segal, Z. V., Williams, J. M., Teasdale, J. D., & Gemar, M. (1996). A cognitive science perspective on kindling and episode sensitization in recurrent affective disorder. *Psychological Medicine, 26*, 371–380.

Segal, Z. V., Williams, J. M. G., & Teasdale, J. D. (2002). *Mindfulness-Based Cognitive Therapy for Depression: A New Approach to Preventing Relapse.* New York: Guilford.

Teasdale, J. D., Moore, R. G., Hayhurst, H., Scott, J., Pope, M., & Paykel, E. S. (2001). How does cognitive therapy prevent relapse in residual depression? Evidence from a controlled trial. *Journal of Consulting and Clinical Psychology*, *69*, 347–357.

Chapter 4

Cognitive behavior therapy for social anxiety disorder

Michelle A. Blackmore and Richard G. Heimberg

The *Diagnostic and Statistical Manual of Mental Disorders*, fourth edition (DSM-IV), defines social anxiety disorder (also known as social phobia) as 'a marked or persistent fear of one or more social or performance situations' (American Psychiatric Association, 1994, p. 411). Social situations must invariably evoke anxiety or prompt avoidance in the individual, and he or she must realize the fear is excessive or unreasonable. Individuals with social anxiety disorder experience significant impairment in social, educational, and occupational functioning (Schneier et al., 1994). They are more likely to be divorced or never to have married (Wittchen, Fuetsch, Sonntag, Muller, & Liebowitz, 1999) and often have fewer friends than persons without the disorder (Whisman, Sheldon, & Goering, 2000). Impairment in occupational functioning includes more missed work days and reduced productivity than mentally healthy individuals (Stein, McQuaid, Laffaye, & Cahill, 1999). Socially anxious individuals also work at a level below their ability and have higher rates of unemployment (Wittchen et al., 1999). Subsequently, overall low life satisfaction is commonly associated with social anxiety (Hambrick, Turk, Heimberg, Schneier, & Liebowitz, 2003).

Socially anxious individuals endorsing fears across many social and performance situations (e.g., being assertive, speaking to persons of authority, initiating conversations) are characterized as having the generalized subtype of social anxiety disorder, whereas persons who fear a more limited set of situations (e.g., only fear public speaking) are referred to as having the nongeneralized subtype. Individuals with generalized and nongeneralized social anxiety disorder differ on dimensions of functional impairment and symptom severity (Heimberg, Holt, Schneier, Spitzer, & Liebowitz, 1993), although some researchers question the validity of dichotomizing the disorder along these lines (e.g., Vriends, Becker, Meyer, Michael, & Margraf, 2007). Common somatic symptoms associated with social anxiety include heart palpations, blushing, trembling, dry mouth, and perspiring. Persons with social anxiety may experience intense physical symptoms that meet criteria for a panic attack; however, unlike in panic disorder, the attacks are specifically associated with anticipation of social evaluation by others.

Social anxiety disorder is the fourth most common psychiatric disorder, with a reported 12-month prevalence of 6.8 percent (Kessler, Chiu, Demler, Merikangas, & Walters, 2005b) and a lifetime prevalence of 12.1 percent (Kessler et al., 2005a). Mean age of onset for the disorder ranges from 13 to 20 years of age, although many clients report struggling with fears of negative evaluation and shyness for as long as they can remember (Hazen & Stein, 1995). Epidemiological studies suggest women are more likely than men to have the disorder (Kessler et al., 2005a; Magee, Eaton, Wittchen, McGonagle, & Kessler, 1996), but relatively equal numbers of men and women seek treatment (Rapee, Sanderson, & Barlow, 1988). It may be that men are more likely to seek treatment given the degree to which social anxiety interferes with many gender-typical role behaviors expected of men (Turk et al., 1998).

Approximately 81 percent of persons with social anxiety disorder meet criteria for at least one additional Axis I disorder (Magee et al., 1996), most often other anxiety disorders (Kessler et al., 2005b). Comorbid diagnoses of depression and alcohol use disorders are also common and often associated with greater impairment than social anxiety disorder alone (e.g., see Erwin, Heimberg, Juster, & Mindlin, 2002). Avoidant personality disorder is the most commonly co-occurring Axis II disorder and shares many features with social anxiety, including extreme fear of negative evaluation. Indeed, approximately 60 percent of persons with generalized social anxiety disorder meet criteria for avoidant personality disorder and typically represent individuals with the most severe presentation of social anxiety and poorest global functioning (Heimberg, 1996).

Assessment of social anxiety disorder

Structured clinical interviews are useful tools in establishing the diagnosis and severity of social anxiety and other Axis I disorders. The Structured Clinical Interview for DSM-IV Axis I Disorders–Patient Edition (SCID) (First, Spitzer, Gibbon, & Williams, 1996) and the Anxiety Disorders Interview Schedule for DSM-IV: Lifetime Version (ADIS) (DiNardo, Brown, & Barlow, 1994) are two of the most commonly used semistructured interviews. Both measures require specialized training and are time-intensive; however, the SCID contains a screening module that directs the interviewer to the most relevant diagnostic modules and allows the clinician to 'skip out' of those less relevant. The ADIS asks a number of questions that go well beyond the basic DSM criteria and provide a more comprehensive picture of the client's symptoms, cognitions, and situational cues related to anxiety, all of which may be quite useful in treatment planning. Both the SCID and ADIS demonstrate strong psychometric properties, including high interrater reliability (T. Brown, DiNardo, Lehman, & Campbell, 2001; Ventura, Liberman, Green, Shaner, & Mintz, 1998).

Clinician-administered measures of social anxiety, such as the Liebowitz Social Anxiety Scale (LSAS) (Liebowitz, 1987) and the Brief Social Phobia Scale (BSPS) (Davidson et al., 1991), may be utilized to evaluate social anxiety-specific symptom severity and treatment progress. The LSAS is a 24-item, clinician-rated measure that assesses client fear and avoidance in performance and social interactions situations. The LSAS demonstrates high internal consistency and good convergent and discriminant validity, the ability to differentiate clients with social anxiety disorder from those with other anxiety disorders, and sensitivity to the effects of both cognitive-behavioral and pharmacological treatments (Fresco et al., 2001; Heimberg & Holaway, 2007; Heimberg et al., 1998, 1999). The BSPS is an 18-item scale that assesses fear and avoidance of seven social situations and physiological symptoms. The total scale demonstrates strong internal consistency, retest reliability, and sensitivity to pharmacotherapy effects (Davidson et al., 1997).

Self-report measures are another common and time-efficient tool in the assessment of social anxiety disorder and treatment change. Several of the more commonly used measures include the Brief Fear of Negative Evaluation Scale (Leary, 1983), the Social Interaction Anxiety Scale (Mattick & Clarke, 1998) and Social Phobia Scale (Mattick & Clarke, 1998), and the Social Phobia and Anxiety Inventory (Turner, Beidel, Dancu, & Stanley, 1989). Behavioral tests, in which clients role-play feared social situations, can also be extremely helpful in judging client progress, as clients with social anxiety disorder are known to underestimate the quality of their social behavior (e.g., Rapee & Lim, 1992).

Cognitive-behavioral conceptualizations of social anxiety disorder

Cognitive-behavioral conceptualizations of social anxiety disorder identify fear of negative evaluation as a central concern (e.g., Clark & Wells, 1995; Rapee & Heimberg, 1997). Research suggests that socially anxious individuals demonstrate biased attention toward social-evaluative threats (see Heinrichs & Hofmann, 2001) and often interpret ambiguous social feedback as negative, while at the same time ignoring the presence of more positive alternatives. This may be exacerbated by the physiological arousal typically experienced in anxiety-provoking situations (e.g., heart palpitations, blushing, trembling). Socially anxious individuals not only overestimate the visibility of these symptoms (Alden & Wallace, 1995), but also interpret them as confirmation that the situation is dangerous and that others will evaluate them negatively (Roth, Antony, & Swinson, 2001). Such biases often lead socially anxious individuals to engage in safety behaviors to avoid feared outcomes (e.g., limit conversational responding), and these behaviors may ultimately interfere with social performance (Clark & Wells, 1995).

It is hypothesized that, in situations with the potential for negative evaluation, socially anxious individuals construct a mental representation of how they believe they appear to others (Rapee & Heimberg, 1997). This representation consists of negatively distorted images, based in various proportions on actual feedback from others, biased memory of events, and fears of negative evaluation. Socially anxious individuals vigilantly attend to this mental self-representation during anxiety-producing situations, as well as environmental, cognitive, behavioral, and affective cues. Negative interpretation of these cues feeds back into the individual's poor self-perception and belief that he or she will not meet perceived audience standards, thus resulting in greater distress. Anxiety is maintained because the perceived danger of the situation is 'confirmed', as is the individual's negative self-representation, leading to fear and avoidance of future situations.

Cognitive-behavioral treatment for social anxiety disorder

Cognitive-behavior therapy (CBT) has been subjected to the most thorough empirical evaluation and is considered the psychological treatment of choice for social anxiety disorder (Rodebaugh, Holaway, & Heimberg, 2004). CBT integrates diverse cognitive and behavioral techniques, but here we focus on treatments that combine cognitive restructuring and exposure to feared social situations. The aim of these treatments is to engage clients in feared situations, challenge irrational, maladaptive beliefs, and provide opportunities for new learning experiences. During exposures, clients attempt to identify and challenge unrealistic automatic thoughts and practice new responses to feared situations. Although there is some expectation that the client will habituate to the situation, the goal is often more to learn to tolerate the experience of anxiety while engaging in behavior in furtherance of personal goals. Social skills training and applied relaxation are other techniques that may be utilized to enhance skill sets and provide the client with additional tools for coping with anxiety.

Efficacy for CBT has been demonstrated in numerous clinical trials and meta-analyses. In two meta-analyses comparing cognitive restructuring alone, exposure alone, cognitive restructuring plus exposure, and social skills training alone, cognitive restructuring plus exposure was the only active treatment superior to all control conditions (Fedoroff & Taylor, 2001; Taylor, 1996). In these reviews, cognitive restructuring appeared to enhance durability of gains, as exposure alone was associated with deterioration of gains following treatment. Individual trials have shown support for both individual and group CBT. For example, cognitively focused individual treatment based on the model of Clark and Wells (1995) has demonstrated superior efficacy to applied relaxation and a wait-list control (Clark et al., 2006). It has also proven superior to fluoxetine plus self-exposure instructions and placebo plus self-exposure instructions, with gains maintained at 1-year follow-up (Clark et al., 2003). This treatment helps clients shift to an external focus of attention (rather than internal self-focus) and to reduce reliance on safety behaviors. Video feedback and exposure tasks are used to restructure distorted cognitions.

Cognitive-behavioral group therapy (CBGT), originally developed by our group (Heimberg & Becker, 2002), has also received strong empirical support. CBGT has proven superior to educational-supportive group therapy, a credible placebo treatment (Heimberg et al., 1990, 1998), and produced durable treatment gains over extended follow-up periods (e.g., Heimberg, Salzman, Holt, & Blendell, 1993). CBGT has also demonstrated response rates equivalent to the monoamine oxidase inhibitor phenelzine after 12 weeks of treatment (Heimberg et al., 1998) and more durable gains at follow-up (Liebowitz et al., 1999). An intensive model of CBGT, based on a hybrid of the Heimberg and Clark treatment approaches, has also shown promising results compared to wait-list control (Mörtberg, Karlsson, Fyring, & Sundin, 2006). The intensive treatment consists of daily sessions for 2 weeks separated by 1 week of homework assignments. Ultimately, meta-analytic studies suggest that individual and group CBT show equivalent efficacy (Gould, Buckminster, Pollack, Otto, & Yap, 1997).

Individual CBT for social anxiety disorder

Our individual cognitive-behavioral treatment for social anxiety disorder is typically conducted in 16 weekly, 1-hour sessions. The treatment makes heavy use of a client workbook (Hope, Heimberg, Juster, & Turk, 2000) that reviews material discussed in each session and contains all necessary forms for treatment and homework assignments. Although guidelines have been established for following protocol (Hope, Heimberg, & Turk, 2006), therapists have some flexibility in determining the pace and organization of material presented. Writing down key concepts throughout treatment is helpful in tracking and processing information discussed, so a dry erase board or newsprint easel is often used in session. This process also assists in developing rapport as therapist and client actively work through the material together. Therapists are encouraged not to 'lecture' in session, but rather to engage the client through Socratic questioning and request the client to provide personal examples of experiences with social anxiety when applicable.

Clients are asked to review chapters in the client workbook (Hope et al., 2000) prior to each session so that any questions or reactions to the material can be discussed and workbook forms can be reviewed. No more than two chapters should be assigned each week to allow the client ample opportunity to process information from each session. In general, homework is reviewed at the beginning of each session and new homework is assigned at the end of each session. The five segments of treatment are summarized below.

Segment 1: psychoeducation

Chapters 1–4 of the client workbook consist of psychoeducation about social anxiety disorder and the cognitive-behavioral model, an overview of the treatment program, and discussion of the client's treatment goals. Establishing rapport is an essential component of segment 1.

Session 1

The first session focuses primarily on defining normal versus problematic social anxiety, the adaptive nature of anxiety, an overview of the treatment program, and the investment treatment will require. When explaining the continuum of social anxiety, factors such as number of situations that elicit anxiety, intensity and duration of anxious symptoms, and degree of distress and impairment are reviewed. Clients are encouraged to discuss personal experiences with anxiety and identify where they believe they fall on the anxiety continuum. This discussion leads into an overview of the treatment and research demonstrating meaningful changes made by individuals completing the program. Given research indicating the relationship of positive treatment expectancy to treatment outcome (e.g., Safren, Heimberg, & Juster, 1997), therapists should use this discussion as an opportunity to instill hope in the client and review the client's treatment goals. Therapists emphasize that clients are largely in control of their response to therapy and that investment of time and effort (e.g., attending sessions regularly, completing homework) and emotional energy (e.g., allowing oneself to experience anxiety during exposures) are required for successful treatment. The client should be given an opportunity to ask any questions or discuss any concerns he or she may have related to treatment at this time.

Session 2

In Session 2, the three components of anxiety (i.e., physiological, cognitive, behavioral) are presented. The therapist reviews bodily sensations often associated with anxiety (e.g., heart palpatations, upset stomach, sweating) and asks the client about physical symptoms he or she experiences when anxious. Discussion of the cognitive component involves identification of thoughts people often have about themselves during anxiety-producing situations (e.g., 'I'll sound stupid', 'Others will see my anxiety'). In reviewing the behavioral component of anxiety, avoidance and escape behaviors are described, and the function they serve in reducing anxiety in the short term but maintaining anxiety in the long term is explained. The interaction of the physiological, cognitive, and behavioral components is explained and the escalating spiral of anxiety that results is reviewed (e.g., trembling during a conversation might lead to the thought 'I look anxious', which may lead to the behavior of cutting the conversation short and walking away). Therapists typically use a hypothetical example to illustrate these components of anxiety before asking the client to discuss personal examples. Hypothetical examples are particularly useful in early sessions as they help clients look at situations more objectively, while at the same time limiting their fears of negative evaluation that may arise when discussing personal experiences. At the end of session, clients are assigned homework asking them to identify the three components of anxiety during an anxiety-producing situation in the next week.

Session 3

Session 3 begins with a description of factors that contribute to the development of social anxiety disorder. When reviewing the genetic contribution, the therapist emphasizes that genes do not *cause* social anxiety but rather contribute to a predisposition to it. The contribution of family environment (e.g., having an overprotective, anxious parent) and other important life experiences (e.g., being teased or bullied by peers) should then be discussed. At this point, explanation that social anxiety is *learned* through these experiences and therefore can be *changed* through new experiences is essential. Discussion of the influence of dysfunctional thoughts in the experience of anxiety can then be reviewed. Here, clients learn that their frequent negative thoughts originate from dysfunctional beliefs they have developed about themselves. These beliefs often increase anxiety, which, in turn, may interfere with their performance. For example, having the belief that 'nobody will like me' may increase heart rate and trembling in the presence of another person, and focusing on these symptoms may interfere with the ability to engage in conversation. Therapists provide rationale for the treatment components (i.e., cognitive restructuring, exposures, homework) in addressing these dysfunctional thinking patterns and ask clients for their reactions to starting the treatment program.

Session 4

In session 4, the client's fear and avoidance hierarchy, which will be used to guide in-session and *in vivo* exposure exercises, is developed. The therapist instructs the client on how to use the Subjective Units of Discomfort Scale

(SUDS) (Wolpe, 1973) as a measure of subjective anxiety. Avoidance ratings are also presented as a way to monitor the level of avoidance in anxiety-provoking situations. Self-monitoring is then presented; clients are asked to monitor their overall anxiety and overall depression daily, as well as their social anxiety in two anxiety-producing situations each week. Clients are encouraged to continue self-monitoring throughout treatment as a way to track their progress.

Segment 2: cognitive restructuring training

Chapters 5 and 6 of the client workbook focus on cognitive restructuring techniques. The segment is generally completed in two to three sessions, although some clients may have difficulty in mastering the cognitive concepts. In this case, Heimberg and Becker (2002) recommend moving forward in treatment and de-emphasizing the cognitive component of therapy while focusing more on repeated exposures. In general, exposures should not begin until cognitive restructuring techniques have been reviewed, so as to allow clients the opportunity to learn how to manage their anxiety and cope in anxiety-producing situations.

Session 5

Session 5 begins with discussion of the relationship between events, thoughts, and feelings and the idea that one's interpretation of a situation, not the situation itself, generates anxiety. Automatic thoughts are defined as irrational or maladaptive beliefs about the self, the world, and the future, and the emotions caused by these thoughts are explored. The client is asked to list automatic thoughts about starting treatment, allowing the client and therapist an opportunity to openly discuss those thoughts. Homework for this session includes monitoring automatic thoughts and the emotions they cause during the week.

Session 6

In session 6, the therapist presents the 'thinking errors' in automatic thoughts (e.g., all-or-nothing thinking, fortune telling, overgeneralization; Beck, 1995). The client is encouraged to identify thinking errors in the workbook examples, as well as identify personally relevant examples. Explanation on how to go about challenging automatic thoughts with disputing questions then follows (e.g., 'What evidence do I have that ____?', 'What is the worst that can happen?', 'Does ____ really mean that I am a ____?'). At this point, it is essential to emphasize the importance of not only asking but *answering* the disputing questions, in order to develop rational alternative thoughts. A 'rational response' is then created by summarizing the key points uncovered through the challenging of automatic thoughts.

The rational response should be realistic, concise, and used to combat automatic thoughts as they occur. Homework involves practicing the techniques learned in this session during an anxiety-producing situation. The therapist also informs the client that exposures will begin the following week and addresses any concerns that arise.

Segment 3: exposure

Segment 3 focuses on in-session and *in vivo* exposures and covers Chapters 7–11 in the client workbook. In-session exposures typically begin in session 7 and should not begin any later than session 8. The rationale for exposures and the format for exposure sessions are presented in Chapter 7 (see Table 4.1). Chapter 8 discusses the ongoing routine of in-session and *in vivo* exposures. Chapters 9–11 address some of the more commonly feared social situations (observational fears, interaction fears, public-speaking fears) and are assigned as appropriate for a given client. From this point forward, an exposure should be attempted in most every session, and weekly exposure homework should be assigned.

Sessions 7–11+

The first in-session exposure should consist of a situation that elicits a moderate amount of anxiety for the client (i.e., SUDS ~ 50) so as to be

Table 4.1 Outline of exposure session for social anxiety disorder

1. Review homework
2. Complete in-session exposure
   a. Exposure preparation
       1) Choose situation and discuss details
       2) Identify automatic thoughts and thinking errors
       3) Challenge automatic thoughts
       4) Develop rational response
       5) Establish behavioral goals
   b. Conduct exposure (~10 minutes)
       1) Request SUDS and rational response every minute
       2) Track progress of behavioral goals
   c. Debriefing
       1) Review completion of behavioral goals
       2) Review expected and unexpected automatic thoughts
       3) Discuss usefulness of rational response
       4) Interpret SUDS pattern
       5) Discuss client, therapist, and role-player feedback
       6) Summarize what was learned from exposure
3. Assign homework
   a. Choose similar out-of-session exposure
   b. Continued self-monitoring

challenging but not overwhelming. The therapist and client should come to an agreement on an appropriate exposure and briefly discuss some of the exposure details (e.g., setting and circumstances, roles to be played). Prior to beginning the exposure, the therapist guides the client through cognitive preparation. First, the client is asked to imagine the upcoming exposure and identify any automatic thoughts elicited by the situation. One or two automatic thoughts are chosen for further examination. With therapist assistance, the client then identifies the emotions caused by the automatic thoughts, identifies the thinking errors inherent in the thoughts, challenges the thoughts with disputing questions, and develops a rational response. The rational response is then written down for easy reference during the exposure. The client is then asked to set achievable behavioral goals that are objective and observable (e.g., ask two questions, complete the role play). Often clients will be tempted to set nonbehavioral goals that are unrealistic and subjective (e.g., do not get anxious, be confident). The therapist should explain that nonbehavioral goals are difficult to evaluate and often not under the client's control. Once determined, the behavioral goals should be written down and placed where the client can easily refer to them during the exposure.

When cognitive preparation is complete, the exposure is ready to begin. Props can be used (e.g., notes for presentation, food to eat) and furniture rearranged to make the exposure as realistic as possible. Clients are encouraged to throw themselves into the role play as completely as possible and not interrupt the role play once it begins. Before, after, and every minute during the exposure, the therapist will request the client's SUDS ratings to monitor anxiety, as well as ask the client to quickly state his or her rational response. The length of the exposure should be approximately 10 minutes, and it should last until anxiety decreases or plateaus and the behavioral goals have been met.

An essential component of exposure exercises is the debriefing afterwards. Debriefing consists of congratulating the client for completing the exposure, reviewing the predetermined behavioral goals, discussing any unexpected automatic thoughts and the usefulness of the rational response, and finally, reviewing what was learned from the exposure that can be generalized to the client's real-world experiences. Clients should be asked whether they met their behavioral goals rather than how they think they did, as this more general question may lead them to disqualify the more positive aspects of their performance. Therapists and role-players are encouraged to offer input on goal attainment and provide feedback addressing any questions or concerns from the client.

When providing feedback, therapists and other role-players should aim to be realistic but also offer evidence against the client's negative beliefs (e.g., client showed some anxiety but the speech was clear and articulate). If clients are persistently negative about their performance during debriefing, therapists should help them identify and challenge any automatic thought or belief related to their performance. Additionally, clients should be reminded that repeated exposures are often necessary when conquering one's fears. SUDS ratings should then be reviewed. If SUDS decreased over time, the therapist can identify the process of habituation; if SUDS remained high throughout the entire exposure, the therapist can point out that the client was able to meet his or her goals even while highly anxious. If a spike of anxiety was noted during the exposure, it is worthwhile investigating what automatic thoughts might have led to that heightened anxiety. For homework after each session, the client is asked to complete the exposure process again by engaging in a similar situation outside of session, using a step-by-step guide from the client workbook.

Segment 4: advanced cognitive restructuring

Session 12+

Segment 4 includes Chapter 12 of the client workbook and reviews how to uncover and address core beliefs using more advanced cognitive restructuring techniques. The downward arrow technique helps clients go beyond superficial automatic thoughts to their core beliefs about themselves, other people, the world, and the future. Therapists may find it helpful to review automatic thoughts identified by the client in previous assignments and then systematically question those thoughts to uncover the client's core beliefs. Remaining exposure sessions target these core beliefs, providing an opportunity for the client to practice the downward arrow technique when addressing these beliefs.

Segment 5: consolidating gains and termination

Sessions 14–16

Segment 5 begins as session 16 approaches and includes Chapter 13 of the client workbook. This segment focuses on summarizing treatment gains, discussing termination, and outlining future goals. In the final session of treatment, the therapist and client review what the client has learned from treatment (e.g., challenging automatic thoughts, importance of ongoing exposures) and process emotions related to termination. At this time, the therapist may find it helpful to have the client update ratings on their fear and avoidance hierarchy as a way to evaluate the client's progress and identify areas to target in the client's ongoing efforts to master social anxiety. A plan should then be created to assist in relapse prevention (e.g., continued exposures, reviewing workbook, booster sessions). Clients may report disappointment that they continue to have some anxiety in social situations. In this case, they should be reminded that the goals of treatment are not to eliminate anxiety but to experience meaningful reduction or tolerance of anxiety, while becoming more confident in and less avoidant of social settings. Nevertheless, some clients may continue to have anxiety and avoidance severe enough to necessitate continued treatment, with additional cognitive restructuring and exposure exercises.

Predictors of treatment outcome

Several factors have been identified as important predictors in CBT outcomes. First, the client's ability and willingness to engage in exposures during session or for homework is important to assess. Research indicates that compliance with homework involving the exposure and cognitive restructuring components of CBT predicts more positive treatment outcome (Leung & Heimberg, 1996). Client safety behaviors also should be identified and closely monitored throughout treatment, as they diminish the efficacy of exposures and limit treatment gains (Morgan & Raffle, 1999). Managing a client's treatment expectancy may further enhance posttreatment outcome, as higher expectancy of treatment efficacy has been associated with greater improvement and maintenance of therapy gains (Safren et al., 1997).

Severity of social anxiety symptoms and comorbid conditions should also be considered prior to beginning treatment. Individuals with generalized social anxiety disorder are typically more impaired before and after treatment, although the amount of change compared to persons with the non-generalized subtype has been relatively equivalent (E. Brown, Heimberg, & Juster, 1995). Although comorbid anxiety disorders do not appear to affect client response to CBT, individuals with comorbid mood disorders are often more impaired before and after treatment; they do improve at a rate similar to nondepressed clients, but they may require extended treatment (Erwin et al., 2002). Trait anger is another predictor of CBT outcome; higher levels of anger are associated with early termination and poorer response among treatment completers (Erwin, Heimberg, Schneier, & Liebowitz, 2003). Mixed results have been found for comorbid personality disorders. For example, comorbid avoidant personality disorder has been associated with worse treatment response in one study (Feske, Perry, Chambless, Renneberg, & Goldstein, 1996) but minimally so in another (E. Brown et al., 1995). Ultimately, treatment management should take into consideration the complexity of the individual case, as well as client motivation and readiness for treatment.

References

Alden, L. E., & Wallace, S. T. (1995). Social phobia and social appraisal in successful and unsuccessful social interactions. *Behaviour Research and Therapy*, *33*, 497–505.

American Psychiatric Association (1994). *Diagnostic and Statistical Manual of Mental Disorders* (4th edn). Washington, DC: Author.

Beck, J. S. (1995). *Cognitive Therapy: Basics and Beyond.* New York: Guilford Press.

Brown, E. J., Heimberg, R. G., & Juster, H. R. (1995). Social phobia subtype and avoidant personality disorder: effect on severity of social phobia, impairment, and outcome of cognitive-behavioral treatment. *Behavior Therapy, 26,* 467–486.

Brown, T. A., DiNardo, P. A., Lehman, C. L., & Campbell, L. A. (2001). Reliability of DSM-IV anxiety and mood disorders: implications for the classification of emotional disorders. *Journal of Abnormal Psychology, 110,* 49–58.

Clark, D. M., Ehlers, A., Hackmann, A., McManus, F., Fennell, M., Grey, N., et al. (2006). Cognitive therapy versus exposure and applied relaxation in social phobia: a randomized controlled trial. *Journal of Consulting and Clinical Psychology, 74,* 568–578.

Clark, D. M., Ehlers, A., McManus, F., Hackmann, A., Fennell, M., Campbell, H., et al. (2003). Cognitive therapy vs. fluoxetine in generalized social phobia: a randomized placebo controlled trial. *Journal of Consulting and Clinical Psychology, 71,* 1058–1067.

Clark, D. M., & Wells, A. (1995). A cognitive model of social phobia. In R. G. Heimberg, M. R. Liebowitz, D. A. Hope, & F. R. Schneier (eds), *Social Phobia: Diagnosis, Assessment, and Treatment* (pp. 69–93). New York: Guilford Press.

Davidson, J. R. T., Foa, E. B., Huppert, J. D., Keefe, F. J., Franklin, M. E., Compton, J. S., et al. (2004). Fluoxetine, comprehensive cognitive behavioral therapy, and placebo in generalized social phobia. *Archives of General Psychiatry, 61,* 1005–1013.

Davidson, J. R. T., Miner, C. M., DeVeaughGeiss, J., Tupler, L. A., Colket, J. T., & Potts, N. L. S. (1997). The Brief Social Phobia Scale: a psychometric evaluation. *Psychological Medicine, 27,* 161–166.

Davidson, J. R. T., Potts, N. L. S., Richichi, E. A., Ford, S. M., Krishnan, R. R., Smith, R. D., et al. (1991). The Brief Social Phobia Scale. *Journal of Clinical Psychiatry, 52,* 48–51.

DiNardo, P. A., Brown, T. A., & Barlow, D. H. (1994) *Anxiety Disorders Interview Schedule for DSM-IV: lifetime version (ADIS-IV-L).* New York: Oxford University Press.

Erwin, B. A., Heimberg, R. G., Juster, H. R., & Mindlin, M. (2002). Comorbid anxiety and mood disorders among persons with social anxiety disorder. *Behaviour Research and Therapy, 40,* 19–35.

Erwin, B. A., Heimberg, R. G., Schneier, F. R., & Liebowitz, M. R. (2003). Anger experience and expression in social anxiety disorder: pretreatment profile and predictors of attrition and response to cognitive-behavioral treatment. *Behavior Therapy, 34,* 331–350.

Fedoroff, I. C., & Taylor, S. T. (2001). Psychological and pharmacological treatments of social phobia: a meta-analysis. *Journal of Clinical Psychopharmacology, 21,* 311–324.

Feske, U., Perry, K. J., Chambless, D. L., Renneberg, B., & Goldstein, A. J. (1996). Avoidant personality disorder as a predictor for severity and treatment outcome among generalized social phobics. *Journal of Personality Disorders, 10,* 174–184.

First, M. B., Spitzer, R. L., Gibbon, M., & Williams, J. (1996). *Structured Clinical*

Interview for DSM-IV Axis I disorders – Patient Edition (SCID-I/P). New York: Biometrics Research Department.

Fresco, D. M., Coles, M. E., Heimberg, R. G., Liebowitz, M. R., Hami, S., Stein, M. B., et al. (2001). The Liebowitz Social Anxiety Scale: a comparison of the psychometric properties of self-report and clinician-administered formats. *Psychological Medicine, 31*, 1025–1035.

Gould, R. A., Buckminster, S., Pollack, M. H., Otto, M., & Yap, L. (1997). Cognitive-behavioral and pharmacological treatment for social phobia: a meta-analysis. *Clinical Psychology: Science and Practice, 4*, 291–306.

Hambrick, J. P., Turk, C. L., Heimberg, R. G., Schneier, F. R., & Liebowitz, M. R. (2003). The experience of disability and quality of life in social anxiety disorder. *Depression and Anxiety, 18*, 46–50.

Hazen, A. L., & Stein, M. B. (1995). Clinical phenomenology and comorbidity. In M. B. Stein (ed.), *Social Phobia: Clinical and Research Perspectives* (pp. 3–41). Washington, DC: American Psychiatric Press.

Heimberg, R. G. (1996). Social phobia, avoidant personality disorder and the multiaxial conceptualization of interpersonal anxiety. In P. Salkovskis (ed.), *Trends in Cognitive and Behavioural Therapies* (pp. 43–61). Chichester, UK: Wiley.

Heimberg, R. G., & Becker, R. E. (2002). *Cognitive-Behavioral Group Therapy for Social Phobia: Basic Mechanisms and Clinical Strategies*. New York: Guilford Press.

Heimberg, R. G., Dodge, C. S., Hope, D. A., Kennedy, C. R., Zollo, L., & Becker, R. E. (1990). Cognitive behavioral group treatment of social phobia: comparison to a credible placebo control. *Cognitive Therapy and Research, 14*, 1–23.

Heimberg, R. G., & Holaway, R. M. (2007). Examination of the known-groups validity of the Liebowitz Social Anxiety Scale. *Depression and Anxiety, 24*, 447–454.

Heimberg, R. G., Holt, C. S., Schneier, F. R., Spitzer, R. L., & Liebowitz, M. R. (1993). The issue of subtypes in the diagnosis of social phobia. *Journal of Anxiety Disorders, 7*, 249–269.

Heimberg, R. G., Horner, K. J., Juster, H. R., Safren, S. A., Brown, E. J., Schneier, F. R., et al. (1999). Psychometric properties of the Liebowitz Social Anxiety Scale. *Psychological Medicine, 29*, 199–212.

Heimberg, R. G., Liebowitz, M. R., Hope, D. A., Schneier, F. R., Holt, C. S., Welkowitz, L. A., et al. (1998). Cognitive-behavioral group treatment versus phenelzine in social phobia: 12 week outcome. *Archives of General Psychiatry, 55*, 1133–1141.

Heimberg, R. G., Salzman, D., Holt, C. S., & Blendell, K. (1993). Cognitive behavioral group treatment of social phobia: effectiveness at 5-year follow-up. *Cognitive Therapy and Research, 17*, 325–339.

Heinrichs, N., & Hofmann, S. G. (2001). Information processing in social phobia: a critical review. *Clinical Psychology Review, 21*, 751–770.

Hope, D. A., Heimberg, R. G., Juster, H., & Turk, C. L. (2000). *Managing Social Anxiety: A Cognitive-Behavioral Therapy Approach* (Client Workbook). New York: Oxford University Press.

Hope, D. A., Heimberg, R. G., & Turk, C. L. (2006). *Managing Social Anxiety: A*

Cognitive-Behavioral Therapy Approach (Therapist Guide). New York: Oxford University Press.

Kessler, R. C., Berglund, P. D., Demler, O., Olga, J. R., Merikangas, K. R., & Walters, E. E. (2005a). Lifetime prevalence and age-of-onset distributions of DSM-IV disorders in the National Comorbidity Survey Replication. *Archives of General Psychiatry*, *62*, 593–602.

Kessler, R. C., Chiu, W. T., Demler, O., Merikangas, K., & Walters, E. (2005b). Prevalence, severity, and comorbidity of 12-month DSM-IV disorders in the National Comorbidity Survey Replication. *Archives of General Psychiatry*, *62*, 617–627.

Leary, M. R. (1983). A brief version of the Fear of Negative Evaluation Scale. *Personality and Social Psychology Bulletin*, *9*, 371–375.

Leung, A. W., & Heimberg, R. G. (1996). Homework compliance, perceptions of control, and outcome of cognitive-behavioral treatment for social phobia. *Behaviour Research and Therapy*, *34*, 423–432.

Liebowitz, M. (1987). Social phobia. *Modern Problems of Pharmacopsychiatry*, *22*, 141–173.

Liebowitz, M. R., Heimberg, R. G., Schneier, F. R., Hope, D. A., Davies, S., Holt, C. S., et al. (1999). Cognitive-behavioral group therapy versus phenelzine in social phobia: long-term outcome. *Depression and Anxiety*, *10*, 89–98.

Magee, W. J., Eaton, W. W., Wittchen, H.-U., McGonagle, K. A., & Kessler, R. C. (1996). Agoraphobia, simple phobia, and social phobia in the National Comorbidity Survey. *Archives of General Psychiatry*, *53*, 159–168.

Mattick, R. P., & Clarke, J. C. (1998). Development and validation of measures of social phobia scrutiny fear and social interaction anxiety. *Behaviour Research and Therapy*, *36*, 455–470.

Morgan, H., & Raffle, C. (1999). Does reducing safety behaviours improve treatment response in patients with social phobia? *Australian and New Zealand Journal of Psychiatry*, *33*, 503–510.

Mörtberg, E., Karlsson, A., Fyring, C., & Sundin, O. (2006). Intensive cognitive-behavioral group treatment (CBGT) of social phobia: a randomized controlled study. *Journal of Anxiety Disorders*, *20*, 646–660.

Rapee, R. M., & Heimberg, R. G. (1997). A cognitive-behavioral model of anxiety in social phobia. *Behaviour Research and Therapy*, *35*, 741–756.

Rapee, R. M., & Lim, L. (1992). Discrepancy between self- and observer ratings of performance in social phobics. *Journal of Abnormal Psychology*, *101*, 728–731.

Rapee, R. M., Sanderson, W. C., & Barlow, D. H. (1988). Social phobia features across the DSM-III-R anxiety disorders. *Journal of Psychopathology and Behavioral Assessment*, *10*, 287–299.

Rodebaugh, T. L., Holaway, R. M., & Heimberg, R. G. (2004). The treatment of social anxiety disorder. *Clinical Psychology Review*, *24*, 883–908.

Roth, D. A., Antony, M. M., & Swinson, R. P. (2001). Interpretations for anxiety symptoms in social phobia. *Behaviour Research and Therapy*, *39*, 129–138.

Safren, S. A., Heimberg, R. G., & Juster, H. R. (1997). Clients' expectancies and their relationship to pretreatment symptomatology and outcome of cognitive-behavioral group treatment for social phobia. *Journal of Consulting and Clinical Psychology*, *65*, 694–698.

Schneier, F. R., Heckelman, L. R., Garfinkel, R., Campeas, R., Fallon, B. A.,

Gitow, A., et al. (1994). Functional impairment in social phobia. *Journal of Clinical Psychiatry*, *55*, 322–331.

Stein, M., McQuaid, J., Laffaye, C., & Cahill, M. (1999). Social phobia in the primary medical care setting. *Journal of Family Practice*, *49*, 514–519.

Taylor, S. (1996). Meta-analysis of cognitive-behavioral treatments for social phobia. *Journal of Behavior Therapy and Experimental Psychiatry*, *27*, 1–9.

Turk, C. L., Heimberg, R. G., Orsillo, S. M., Holt, C. S., Gitow, A., Street, L. L., et al. (1998). An investigation of gender differences in social phobia. *Journal of Anxiety Disorders*, *12*, 209–223.

Turner, S. M., Beidel, D. C., Dancu, C. V., & Stanley, M. A. (1989). An empirically derived inventory to measure social fears and anxiety: the Social Phobia and Anxiety Inventory. *Psychological Assessment*, *1*, 35–40.

Ventura, J., Liberman, R. P., Green, M. F., Shaner, A., & Mintz, J. (1998). Training and quality assurance with Structured Clinical Interview for DSM-IV (SCID-I/P). *Psychiatry Research*, *79*, 163–173.

Vriends, N., Becker, E. S., Meyer, A., Michael, T., & Margraf, J. (2007). Subtypes of social phobia: are they of any use? *Journal of Anxiety Disorders*, *21*, 59–75.

Whisman, M., Sheldon, C., & Goering, P. (2000). Psychiatric disorders and dissatisfaction with social relationships: does type of relationship matter? *Journal of Abnormal Psychology*, *109*, 803–808.

Wittchen, H., Fuetsch, M., Sonntag, H., Muller, N., & Liebowitz, M. (1999). Disability and quality of life in pure and comorbid social phobia: findings from a controlled study. *European Psychiatry*, *14*, 118–131.

Wolpe, J. (1973). *The Practice of Behavior Therapy*. New York: Pergamon Press.

Chapter 5

Cognitive behavioral therapy for posttraumatic stress disorder (PTSD)

Sheila A. M. Rauch and Edna B. Foa

Posttraumatic stress disorder (PTSD) is an anxiety disorder that develops following exposure to a traumatic event. Such an event is defined as involving actual or threatened death or injury, or threat to the personal integrity of oneself or others. In addition to exposure to a traumatic event, the survivor must react to the event with intense fear, horror or helplessness (American Psychiatric Association, 1994). The symptoms of PTSD fall into three clusters: re-experiencing, avoidance/numbing, and hyperarousal. The re-experiencing symptoms include recurrent distressing recollections of the traumatic experience, recurrent distressing dreams of the trauma, flashbacks, and intense emotional or physiological arousal when exposed to trauma reminders. Avoidance and numbing symptoms include avoidance of thoughts, feelings and situations that remind the survivor of the trauma; loss of interest; detachment from others; and a sense of foreshortened future. Hyperarousal symptoms include difficulty in falling or staying asleep; problems with concentration, anger and irritability; and exaggerated startle response. Prevalence estimates of PTSD among adults vary widely depending on the population examined and the methods of assessment (Rauch & Foa, 2003) with 5 percent to 8 percent reported in two large epidemiological studies (Kessler et al., 1995; Norris, 1992).

Prospective studies indicate that a majority of trauma survivors recover over time and do not develop chronic PTSD (e.g., Brewin et al., 1999; Riggs et al., 1995; Rothbaum et al., 1992). While most survivors report symptoms consistent with a PTSD diagnosis in the acute aftermath of trauma, these symptoms tend to decrease within a few months after the trauma (Brewin et al., 1999; Riggs et al., 1995; Rothbaum et al., 1992). Indeed, in one prospective study, while 94 percent met criteria for PTSD (except duration) at their initial assessment (within 2 weeks of assault), only 47 percent of sexual and nonsexual assault survivors met criteria for PTSD at 12 weeks post-assault (Rothbaum et al., 1992). Estimates of the prevalence of PTSD in the general population of the USA range from 1 to 9 percent; the frequency varies with many factors, including sensitivity of the assessment measure, gender, ethnicity, socioeconomic status, type of trauma, etc. (Breslau et al.,

1991, 1998; Davidson et al., 1991; Helzer et al., 1987; Kessler et al., 1995; Norris, 1992).

Comorbidity with PTSD is common. Among a sample of adults with PTSD, 62 percent met criteria for another diagnosis (Davidson et al., 1991). In the Epidemiological Catchment Area Study (Helzer et al., 1987), people with PTSD were twice as likely to have another disorder as people without PTSD. Risk was highest for obsessive compulsive disorder, dysthymia, and bipolar disorder. In the national comorbidity study, alcohol abuse/ dependence (52 percent), major depressive disorder (48 percent), substance abuse/dependence (35 percent), and simple phobia (31 percent) were the most common comorbid diagnoses (Kessler et al., 1995). It seems that in many cases the onset of the comorbid disorder succeeds the onset of PTSD (Kessler et al., 1995), but more research is needed to examine whether people with PTSD are at risk of the development of other disorders and what disorders are more likely to precede or succeed PTSD.

Research has demonstrated the efficacy of several cognitive behavioral programs in reducing PTSD and related symptoms. Since a complete review of this literature is beyond the scope of the current chapter, we will focus on: 1) descriptions of the CBT interventions with proven efficacy; 2) presentation of key studies that demonstrate the efficacy of these programs by comparing an active CBT to a control condition (wait-list, supportive counseling, or relaxation); and 3) studies that compare the relative efficacy of evidence-based treatment programs.

Exposure therapy

Exposure therapy is a general term for treatment programs that focus on the patient confronting feared memories and anxiety-provoking stimuli until anxiety is reduced. Prolonged exposure (PE) is one such program that has received extensive empirical support for its efficacy (Foa et al., 2007). Foa and Kozak (1986) proposed emotional processing theory to explain the psychopathology and treatment of anxiety disorders. According to this theory, anxiety disorders, including PTSD, are represented by pathological fear structures. Exposure therapy is effective because it modifies the pathological elements of cognitive fear structures (for review of evidence related to emotional processing theory, see Foa, Huppert, & Cahill, 2006; Rauch & Foa, 2006). These fear structures contain pathological associations between stimulus, response, and meaning elements that maintain anxiety and the symptoms of PTSD. During exposure therapy, the fear structure is activated in the presence of corrective information, allowing for modification of these pathological associations so that a new structure containing more realistic associations is formed. Such modifications lead to reduction in PTSD symptoms, including escape and avoidance behaviors. For example, for a patient who completes *in vivo* exposures of going to a mall that he avoids because it reminds him of crowds encountered in Iraq, successful completion of the exposure exercise provides him with the information that the mall is not dangerous and that he can handle the anxiety that occurs when he is reminded of combat. Indeed, as he remains in the situation and the anxiety habituates, he learns that anxiety does not remain forever.

While a complete description of therapy process is beyond the scope of this chapter, interested readers are referred to Foa et al. (2007). PE includes four components: psychoeducation, breathing retraining, imaginal exposure, and *in vivo* exposure. Psychoeducation focuses on providing information on common reactions to trauma and the rationale for exposure therapy. This information constitutes the foundation for the major components of the treatment: imaginal exposure (IE) (revisiting the trauma) and *in vivo* exposure (confrontation of situations that the patient avoids because they trigger the traumatic memory). Accordingly, most problems that may arise during treatment (i.e., difficulty following homework instruction) are addressed through the therapist and patient referring back to the rationale for the treatment and how to overcome the problems (see Foa et al., 2007; Hembree et al., 2003).

During common reactions, the therapist discusses with the patient the most common reactions to trauma in a conversational manner. These common reactions include discussion of all of the 17 symptoms of PTSD, common negative thoughts that may contribute to PTSD, depression, and suicidal ideation. The therapist briefly discusses all of these topics while guiding the patient to provide personal experiences that may be consistent with these reactions. The therapist has latitude to expand or contract the amount of discussion as fits with the patient's presenting symptoms. Through this procedure, the therapist is providing a framework for the patient to understand his/her PTSD symptoms. In addition, this conversation should also include that these reactions are the focus of treatment and what we expect to change most readily as the patient proceeds through the treatment.

During the rationale, the therapist focuses on the seven functions of exposure. In brief, as a patient engages in exposure to trauma memories or trauma-related situations, he/she is able to: 1) process the meaning of the trauma; 2) differentiate between the traumatic memory and the traumatic event itself, emphasizing that the traumatic event was dangerous but remembering the memory is not; 3) habituate the emotional responses that are connected to the memory; 4) disconfirm the expectation that exposure to trauma reminders will cause harmful consequences; 5) disconfirm the belief that anxiety will continue forever; 6) block the negative reinforcement that is associated with avoidance; 7) learn that he/she can successfully manage distress. The rationale is distributed throughout the first three sessions in order to allow for repetition and really allow the patient to 'buy-in' to the model. Further, as the patient begins to engage in exposure exercises, the therapist should continue to refer back to the rationale to point out consistencies between described process and how the therapy is actually unfolding. Finally, when difficulties arise, referring back to the rationale can provide the patient and therapist direction on how to proceed. For instance, if a patient continues to experience high levels of anxiety during an *in vivo* exposure exercise, the therapist may need to look for possible cognitive or other avoidance strategies that the patient may be doing that are not allowing for habituation to occur. For instance, if a patient is sitting in a restaurant as an exposure, but he is sitting facing the door and constantly scanning for safety, it is unlikely that significant habituation of anxiety will occur, as the patient will attribute his safety to his diligence in scanning rather than to the fact that restaurants are safe. In this case, referring back to the rationale in a discussion with the patient about why his anxiety remains high can allow for an explanation as well as suggest a course change (sit with your back to the door).

While not always a part of all exposure therapy protocols, PE includes breathing retraining to slow breathing and extend the exhale as a means of reducing anxious activation. This technique is presented at the end of the first session, in order to ensure that the patient leaves the session relatively calm after discussing his/her trauma history, including the trauma that is most directly associated with the current PTSD symptoms. Thus, while exposure therapy is not based on the idea that relief of PTSD symptoms will come immediately upon starting therapy, rapport and therapy motivation may be boosted in this first session as patients feel that their concerns are validated and will be addressed. This also is the first opportunity to provide exercises for the patient to complete between sessions. Such a practice serves to assist the patient in recognizing the therapy expectations in PE as well as for the therapist to begin to address obstacles to practice completion.

During IE, the patient revisits the trauma memory in imagination for a prolonged period of time (30–60 minutes per session). During IE, the patient is directed to close his/her eyes, and retell the memory in the present tense as though it is happening now. He/she is asked to include all the thoughts, feelings, and actions that occurred at the time of the trauma. The IE is repeated within the session (if possible in the time allowed), for homework, and also in additional sessions. During the IE, the therapist is directing the patient to remain at a optimal level of engagement. Specifically, the therapist does not want the patient so distressed that he/she is unable to process the information or dissociates. The therapist may provide encouragement or grounding if the patient is overengaging with the memory (i.e., you are doing a good job, you are here in my office, this is a memory and cannot hurt you now, etc.). However, the therapist also wants the patient to allow himself/herself to connect to the emotions of the memory and experience these feelings as though the trauma were happening now. The therapist may ask brief probes to assist the patient to include relevant information (i.e., what are you feeling?, what are you thinking?, how does that feel in your body?, etc.). In addition, the therapist is asking for the patient's distress level as they complete the IE. This can be used as a means of determining whether patients are progressing in therapy (reductions in anxiety across sessions). Following IE, the therapist engages in processing the exposure with a discussion of both what happened during the exposure (was there reduction in anxiety?, how did it compare with previous session?) and the problematic thoughts that may maintain PTSD symptoms and are apparent in the trauma narrative. For instance, a rape survivor who blames herself for a man raping her because she was drunk is likely to feel poorly about herself, contributing to the maintenance of PTSD symptoms. Challenging such problematic beliefs can help the patient see alternative interpretations of the situation that may be more helpful for him/her.

In vivo exposure involves repeated and prolonged exposure to objectively safe situations that are avoided due to trauma-related fear. As a first step for *in vivo* exposure, a hierarchy of trauma-related, avoided situations is created. These situations are rated on a scale of 0 (not at all anxious) to 100 (most anxiety ever experienced). *In vivo* exposure typically begins with moderately difficult items (ratings of about 50) and proceeds up the hierarchy to the more difficult items as the patient demonstrates reductions in anxiety to the lower level items. For each *in vivo* exposure, the patient is asked to remain in the situation for either 30–45 minutes or until the anxiety has reduced to half of its peak. For instance, a patient may have an *in vivo* exposure of going to a church. While in the church, her reported anxiety reaches a peak of 80 during the first 5 minutes. She is then asked to remain in the church until she has been there for 45 minutes or her anxiety falls to 40. While remaining in the situation is important, repeating the exposures many times (typically, we ask at least once per day for each *in vivo* exposure assigned) is also key to experiencing the benefits of *in vivo* exposure. The therapist knows when to move on to assign another situation when the patient is experiencing peak anxiety scores of 50 or lower in the situation.

Other exposure therapy programs have included different variations of IE and *in vivo* exposure. For example, Marks et al. (1998) segregated the first few sessions for IE and the last few sessions for *in vivo* exposure rather than simultaneously doing both. Other programs have focused exclusively on IE (i.e., Levitt & Cloitre, 2005; Tarrier et al., 1999).

Exposure therapy, including PE and several other exposure therapy programs, has been proven highly effective and superior to control conditions (i.e., wait-list, supportive counseling, and relaxation) in reducing PTSD following a variety of traumas in several randomized, controlled trials (e.g., Foa, Rothbaum, Riggs, & Murdock, 1991; Foa, Dancu, Hembree,

Jaycox, Meadows, & Street, 1999; Foa, Hembree, Cahill, Rauch, Riggs, & Feeny, 2005; Marks, Lovell, Noshirvani, Livanou, & Thrasher, 1998; Resick, Nishith, Weaver, Astin, & Feuer, 2002; Taylor, Thordarson, Maxfield, Federoff, Lovell, & Ogrodniczuk, 2003). In addition, exposure therapy has resulted in reduction of depressive symptoms, general anxiety, guilt, and anger (e.g., Cahill, Rauch, Hembree, & Foa, 2003; Foa et al., 1999, 2005; Resick et al., 2002; Tarrier et al., 1999). These changes are generally maintained at follow-up assessments up to 1-year following the end of treatment. Recently, PE has demonstrated efficacy when compared to present-centered therapy among women with PTSD related to child sexual abuse with significant reductions in PTSD compared to a wait-list control and significantly more women in PE (77 percent) no longer meeting diagnosis of PTSD than in the present-centered therapy (42 percent) condition at 6-month follow-up (McDonagh et al., 2005).

Similar results were found in a large randomized, controlled trial of female veterans (Schnurr et al., 2007). In this study, PE resulted in greater reductions in PTSD symptoms than did present-centered therapy, and significantly more women who received PE (41 percent) no longer met criteria for PTSD than in a present-centered therapy control (28 percent). Given the evidence supporting the efficacy of exposure therapy for PTSD, Rothbaum, Meadows, Resick, and Foy (2000) recommended exposure therapy as a first-line therapy for PTSD due to its demonstrated efficacy across a wide variety of studies and some evidence from comparative trials to suggest that it may be more efficient and/or effective than alternate CBT approaches (see 'Comparisons among treatments and combined treatments' below).

Eye Movement Desensitization and Reprocessing (EMDR)

EMDR was developed by Francine Shapiro (1995) and has been widely disseminated. Shapiro has proposed adaptive information processing as the model to describe the mechanism of action in EMDR. This model posits that disorder occurs when distressing or traumatic experiences are inadequately processed. Specifically, distressing or traumatic memories are stored as they are input, including distorted perceptions and thoughts. Further, recalling these memories while engaging in eye movements or other dual-attention tasks is hypothesized to enhance information processing and allow these memories to be adequately processed.

EMDR involves eight phases (Shapiro & Maxfield, 2002). In session 1, the patient is assessed and learns some breathing and relaxation strategies. Session 2 includes a preparation phase in which the patient is given appropriate expectations for the therapy. This session also begins the desensitization phase. During desensitization, the patient is asked to focus on the most distressing part of the memory while moving his/her eyes back and forth following the therapist's finger. Next, the patient is asked to voice any associations that came up and to focus on these associations for the next set of eye movements or other dual-attention task. When distress associated with the memory is dissipated, the installation phase begins. During this phase, the patient pairs a positive cognition with the original trauma memory while doing eye movements or another dual-attention task. At the end of each of these cycles of eye movements, the patient is asked to rate the believability of the positive cognition while holding the trauma memory in mind. Then, the body-scan phase begins when the positive cognitions are rated as believable and the patient focuses on any remaining physical distress while doing a dual-attention task. Finally, during the debriefing phase, any remaining anxiety is addressed with relaxation techniques. A re-evaluation phase occurs in subsequent sessions where the patient and therapist review the trauma material for remaining distress.

In a review of seven randomized, controlled studies of EMDR, Chemtob et al. (2000) conclude that EMDR is an efficacious treatment for PTSD, resulting in significantly larger reductions in PTSD severity than wait-list, routine-care or active controls (relaxation). However, dismantling studies conducted thus far do not find that the addition of the dual-attention task improves efficacy over conducting the intervention without a dual-attention task (Cahill et al., 1999). In addition, Cusack and Spates (1999) found no difference in outcome between standard EMDR and a modification of EMDR that does not include the cognitive elements. Together, these studies suggest that exposure may be the active element in EMDR.

Cognitive therapy

In cognitive therapy, sessions focus on the interpretation of events rather than the events themselves as the source of emotional reactions (Beck & Emery, 1985). Therefore, the rationale for cognitive therapy asserts that PTSD and other anxiety symptoms result from negative and unhelpful thoughts that fall into common dysfunctional patterns. For instance, over-generalization occurs when a person reacts to a new situation based upon a previous experience that does not fit. For example, a rape survivor who was assaulted in a park may come to believe that all parks are dangerous. She may experience extreme anxiety whenever she is in a park. In cognitive therapy, these unhelpful thought patterns are identified, challenged (e.g., collecting evidence, looking for alternative interpretations, etc.), and replaced by more helpful alternative thoughts. Thus, the patient and therapist would focus on information about the true risk associated with specific and parks in general. They may focus on how she is overestimating risk based on the rape. Indeed, they may even work on how to evaluate risk associated with particular parks in a way that more accurately reflects reality rather than overestimating danger.

Controlled trials of cognitive therapy in survivors of various types of trauma have demonstrated that cognitive therapy reduced the rates of PTSD after treatment more than in wait-list and relaxation controls (Frank, Anderson, Stewart, Dancu, Hughes, & West, 1988; Marks et al., 1998). In addition, cognitive therapy has demonstrated reductions in general anxiety and depressive symptoms (Marks et al., 1998; Tarrier et al., 1999). Marks et al. (1998) also found that reductions in PTSD and associated symptoms were maintained at 6-month follow-up.

Cognitive processing therapy (CPT)

While emphasizing cognitive therapy techniques, cognitive processing therapy (CPT) (Resick et al., 2002) includes both exposure and cognitive therapy. For exposure, the client writes a detailed account of the trauma, which is read to the therapist. The points in the narrative that hold significant meaning and anxiety for the client, called stuck points, are identified and cognitive techniques are used to closely pull apart the meaning and provide more helpful alternate cognitions. In addition, trauma-related beliefs about safety, trust, power/control, esteem, and intimacy are examined in sessions that focus on each specific type of cognition.

Resick et al. (2002) found that CPT reduced PTSD severity more than a minimal attention-control condition. In addition, CPT resulted in significant reductions in depressive symptoms and trauma-related guilt. These reductions were maintained at 9-month follow-up. CPT has also been found efficacious among veterans with military-related chronic PTSD, with significant reductions in PTSD symptoms over 12 weeks of treatment and maintenance of gains over a 1-month follow-up (Monson et al., 2006). A modification of CPT for sexual abuse survivors has been found effective in a sample of women, with significant reductions in PTSD and depressive symptoms as well as dissociative symptoms from pre- to post-treatment. Further, these gains were maintained through a 1-year follow-up (Chard, 2005).

Comparisons among treatments and combined treatments

Key studies comparing the previously discussed efficacious treatments for PTSD have found few differences in outcome between them. Further, combining these interventions does not appear to result in additional benefit. For instance, in a study comparing stress inoculation training (SIT), exposure therapy, and their combination in a female assault survivor sample with PTSD, the only significant difference at post-treatment was lower general anxiety in exposure therapy than with the combination of exposure therapy and SIT (Foa et al., 1999). No significant differences were found between exposure therapy and SIT. However, there was a trend for more clients in exposure therapy (52 percent) to obtain good end-state functioning (a composite of low scores on PTSD, depressive, and general anxiety symptoms) than with SIT (31 percent) or exposure therapy/SIT (27 percent). Together, these results suggest that caution should be used in combining interventions due to potential reduction of efficacy over the single interventions. It is possible that patients may become overburdened with information in the combination conditions and end up not truly practicing the elements as much as they do when they have a more focused intervention.

Marks et al. (1998) found that exposure therapy, cognitive therapy, and their combination all resulted in larger reductions in PTSD and related symptoms than did relaxation. However, no differences were apparent between treatments. Similarly, when Paunovic and Ost (2001) compared a variation of exposure therapy and exposure therapy/cognitive therapy in a sample of refugees with PTSD, both treatments were efficacious, but the combined treatment did not offer more benefit than exposure therapy alone. Finally, when comparing CPT, exposure therapy, and minimal attention control in sexual assault survivors, Resick et al. (2002) found that both treatments were superior to control, but no differences between treatments were found in depression or PTSD severity.

In studies comparing EMDR to other exposure therapies, similar results were found. In one recent study, Lee et al. (2002) randomly assigned 24 people with PTSD from multiple traumas to either a combined SIT and PE or EMDR. On the global PTSD measure, no significant difference between treatments was detected at post-treatment. However, at 3-month follow-up, EMDR was significantly lower on PTSD severity than the PE/SIT group. These results are consistent with the previously reported results suggesting that the addition of SIT to PE may reduce the efficacy of PE alone (Foa et al., 1999). Taylor et al. (2003) found that both EMDR and PE resulted in significant reduction in PTSD severity from pre- to post-treatment but that PE resulted in significantly larger reductions in avoidance and re-experiencing at post-treatment and 6-month follow-up than EMDR and relaxation. Further, EMDR was not significantly different from relaxation, which served as a control condition. Finally, Rothbaum et al. (2005) found that both PE and EMDR resulted in significantly larger reduction in PTSD severity, depression, dissociation, and state anxiety than in a wait-list control group, but no significant differences were detected between the treatments at post-treatment. At 6-month follow-up, significantly more patients who received PE reached the status of responders than did those who received PE.

Summary and future directions

Several CBTs have proven efficacy for the treatment of chronic PTSD, including exposure therapy, SIT, cognitive therapy, CPT, and EMDR.

Studies that have compared these efficacious treatments have not consistently demonstrated the superiority of one over another. In addition, cognitive-behavioral treatment packages that combine elements of exposure therapy with SIT or cognitive therapy also have demonstrated efficacy, but have not demonstrated superior outcome compared to the component treatments alone.

While several efficacious psychotherapy treatment choices are available, in all of the studies presented, it is apparent that there remains a significant minority of clients who continue to have PTSD or significant PTSD symptoms even after completing these efficacious treatment programs. Finding reliable predictors of who may become a nonresponder or partial responder is a critical focus of future interventions research. Further, determining whether these predictors differ by the intervention and whether individuals who do not respond to one intervention may respond to another is important. In addition to identifying who may not respond, future research efforts should also focus on augmentation of CBT strategies with other treatment modalities or even the development of new treatment programs to address these clients' needs.

Because of the associated expense and logistical issues in designing such 'nonresponder' trials, they have not been conducted. However, such designs are critical for our understanding of what to do with refractory or partial responding patients. Two studies to date have examined this issue in PTSD populations combining medication and psychotherapy. Rothbaum et al. (2006) used a randomized design to examine whether augmentation of SSRI treatment (sertraline) with PE would result in additional benefits for trauma survivors with chronic PTSD. For patients who did not fully respond to 10 weeks of sertraline, augmentation with 10 sessions of PE over 5 weeks resulted in significantly more additional reduction in PTSD severity than in those who continued on medication alone. A study examining the impact of augmentation with SSRI for partial responders to eight sessions of PE is currently under review (Simon et al., 2007).

Finally, although many of these therapies have been available for years, difficulty in disseminating these programs to therapists has led to problems in consumer accessibility (Cahill, Hembree, & Foa, 2006). Finding ways to disseminate these programs effectively and efficiently to mental health service providers is critical to the utility of CBT.

References

American Psychiatric Association (APA) (2005). *Diagnostic and Statistical Manual of Mental Disorders* (4th edn, text revised). Washington, DC: American Psychiatric Association Press.

Beck, A. T., & Emery, G. (1985). *Anxiety Disorders and Phobias: A Cognitive Perspective*. New York: Basic Books.

Breslau, N., Davis, G., Andreski, P., & Peterson, E. (1991). Traumatic events and posttraumatic stress disorder in an urban population of young adults. *Archives of General Psychiatry, 48*, 216–222.

Breslau, N., Kessler, R., Chilcoat, H., Schultz, L., Davis, G., & Andreski, P. (1998). Trauma and posttraumatic stress disorder in the community: the 1996 Detroit Area Survey of Trauma. *Archives of General Psychiatry, 55*, 626–632.

Brewin, C., Andrews, B., Rose, S., & Kirk, M. (1999). Acute stress disorder and posttraumatic stress disorder in victims of violent crime. *American Journal of Psychiatry, 156*, 360–366.

Cahill, S., Carrigan, M., & Frueh, B. (1999). Does EMDR work? and if so, why?: a critical review of controlled outcome and dismantling research. *Journal of Anxiety Disorders, 13*, 5–33.

Cahill, S. P., Hembree, E. A., & Foa, E. B. (2006). Dissemination of prolonged exposure therapy for posttraumatic stress disorder: successes and challenges. In Y. Neria, R. Gross, R. Marshall, & E. Susser (eds), *Mental Health in the Wake of Terrorist Attacks* (pp. 475–495). Cambridge: Cambridge University Press.

Cahill, S. P., Rauch, S. A. M., Hembree, E. A., & Foa, E. B. (2003). Effect of cognitive-behavioral treatments for PTSD on anger. *Journal of Cognitive Psychotherapy, 17*, 113–131.

Calhoun, K. S., & Resick, P. A. (1993). Posttraumatic stress disorder. In D. H. Barlow (ed.), *Clinical Handbook of Psychological Disorders* (pp. 48–98). New York: Guilford Press.

Chard, K. (2005). An evaluation of cognitive processing therapy for the treatment of posttraumatic stress disorder related to childhood sexual abuse. *Journal of Consulting and Clinical Psychology, 73*, 965–971.

Chemtob, C., Tolin, D., van der Kolk, B., & Pitman, R. (2000). Eye movement desensitization and reprocessing. In *Effective Treatments for PTSD: Practice Guidelines from the International Society for Traumatic Stress Studies* (pp. 139–154). New York: Guilford Press.

Cusack, K., & Spates, C. (1999). The cognitive dismantling of eye movement desensitization and reprocessing (EMDR) treatment of posttraumatic stress disorder (PTSD). *Journal of Anxiety Disorders, 13*, 87–99.

Davidson, J., Hughes, D., Blazer, D., & George, L. (1991). Post-traumatic stress disorder in the community: an epidemiological study. *Psychological Medicine, 21*, 713–721.

Foa, E. B., Dancu, C. V., Hembree, E. A., Jaycox, L. H., Meadows, E. A., & Street, G. P. (1999). A comparison of exposure therapy, stress inoculation training, and their combination for reducing posttraumatic stress disorder in female assault victims. *Journal of Consulting and Clinical Psychology, 67*, 194–200.

Foa, E. B., Hembree, E. A., Cahill, S. P., Rauch, S. A., Riggs, D. S., & Feeny, N. C. (2005). Prolonged exposure for PTSD with and without cognitive restructuring: Outcome at academic and community clinics. *Journal of Consulting and Clinical Psychology, 73*, 953–964.

Foa, E. B., Hembree, E. A., & Rothbaum, B. O. (2007). *Prolonged Exposure Therapy for PTSD: Emotional Processing of Traumatic Experiences Therapist Guide (Treatments That Work)*. New York: Oxford University Press.

Foa, E., Huppert, J., & Cahill, S. (2006). Emotional processing theory: an update.

In B. O. Rothbaum (ed.), *Pathological Anxiety: Emotional Processing in Etiology and Treatment* (pp. 3–24). New York: Guilford Press.

Foa, E., & Kozak, M. (1986). Emotional processing of fear: exposure to corrective information. *Psychological Bulletin, 99*, 20–35.

Foa, E. B., Rothbaum, B. O., Riggs, D., & Murdock, T. (1991). Treatment of posttraumatic stress disorder in rape victims: a comparison between cognitive-behavioral procedures and counseling. *Journal of Consulting and Clinical Psychology, 59*, 715–723.

Frank, E., Anderson, B., Stewart, B. D., Dancu, C., Hughes, C., & West, D. (1988). Efficacy of cognitive behavior therapy and systematic desensitization in the treatment of rape trauma. *Behavior Therapy, 19*, 403–420.

Helzer, J., Robins, L., & McEvoy, L. (1987). Post-traumatic stress disorder in the general population: findings of the Epidemiologic Catchment Area Survey. *New England Journal of Medicine, 317*, 1630–1634.

Hembree, E. A., Rauch, S. A. M., & Foa E. B. (2003). Beyond the manual: The insider's guide to prolonged exposure therapy for PTSD. *Cognitive and Behavioral Practice, 10*, 22–30.

Kessler, R., Sonnega, A., Bromet, E., & Hughes, M. (1995). Posttraumatic stress disorder in the National Comorbidity Survey. *Archives of General Psychiatry, 52*, 1048–1060.

Lee, C., Gavriel, H., Drummond, P., Richards, J., & Greenwald, R. (2002). Treatment of PTSD: stress inoculation training with prolonged exposure compared to EMDR. *Journal of Clinical Psychology, 58*, 1071–1089.

Levitt, J., & Cloitre, M. (2005). A clinician's guide to STAIR/MPE: treatment for PTSD related to childhood abuse. *Cognitive and Behavioral Practice, 12*, 40–52.

Marks, I., Lovell, K., Noshirvani, H., Livanou, M., & Thrasher, S. (1998). Treatment of post-traumatic stress disorder by exposure and/or cognitive restructuring: a controlled study. *Archives of General Psychiatry, 55*, 317–325.

McDonagh, A., Friedman, M., McHugo, G., Ford, J., Sengupta, A., Mueser, K., et al. (2005). Randomized trial of cognitive-behavioral therapy for chronic post-traumatic stress disorder in adult female survivors of childhood sexual abuse. *Journal of Consulting and Clinical Psychology, 73*, 515–524.

Meichenbaum, D. (1974). Self instructional methods. In F. H. Kanfer & A. P. Goldstein (eds), *Helping People Change* (pp. 357–391). New York: Pergamon Press.

Monson, C., Schnurr, P., Resick, P., Friedman, M., Young-Xu, Y., & Stevens, S. (2006). Cognitive processing therapy for veterans with military-related post-traumatic stress disorder. *Journal of Consulting and Clinical Psychology, 74*, 898–907.

Norris, F. (1992). Epidemiology of trauma: frequency and impact of different potentially traumatic events on different demographic groups. *Journal of Consulting and Clinical Psychology, 60*, 409–418.

Paunovic, N., & Ost, L. G. (2001). Cognitive-behaviour therapy vs exposure therapy in the treatment of PTSD in refugees. *Behaviour Therapy and Researc, 39*, 1183–1197.

Rauch, S. A. M., & Foa, E. B. (2003). Posttraumatic stress disorder. In D. Nutt & J. Ballenger (eds), *Anxiety Disorders*. Oxford: Blackwell Science.

Rauch, S. A. M., & Foa, E. B. (2006). Emotional processing theory and exposure therapy for PTSD. *Journal of Contemporary Psychotherapy*, *36*, 61–65.

Resick, P. A., Nishith, P., Weaver, T. L., Astin, M. C., & Feuer, C. A. (2002). A comparison of cognitive-processing therapy with prolonged exposure and a waiting condition for the treatment of chronic posttraumatic stress disorder in female rape victims. *Journal of Consulting and Clinical Psychology*, *70*, 867–879.

Riggs, D., Rothbaum, B., & Foa, E. (1995). A prospective examination of symptoms of posttraumatic stress disorder in victims of nonsexual assault. *Journal of Interpersonal Violence*, *10*, 201–214.

Rothbaum, B. (2006). *Pathological Anxiety: Emotional Processing in Etiology and Treatment*. New York: Guilford Press.

Rothbaum, B., Astin, M., & Marsteller, F. (2005). Prolonged exposure versus eye movement desensitization and reprocessing (EMDR) for PTSD rape victims. *Journal of Traumatic Stress*, *18*, 607–616.

Rothbaum, B. O., Cahill, S. P., Foa, E. B., Davidson, J. R., Compton, J., Connor, K. M., et al. (2006). Augmentation of sertraline with prolonged exposure in the treatment of posttraumatic stress disorder. *Journal of Traumatic Stress*, *19*, 625–638.

Rothbaum, B., Foa, E., Riggs, D., & Murdock, T. (1992). A prospective examination of post-traumatic stress disorder in rape victims. *Journal of Traumatic Stress*, *5*, 455–475.

Rothbaum, B. O., Meadows, E. A., Resick, P. A., & Foy, D. W. (2000). Cognitive-behavioral therapy. In E. B. Foa, T. M. Keane, & M. J. Friedman (eds), *Effective Treatments for PTSD* (pp. 60–83). New York: Guilford Press.

Schnurr, P. P., Friedman, M. J., Engel, C. C., Foa, E. B., Shea, M. T., Chow, B. K., et al. (2007). Cognitive behavioral therapy for posttraumatic stress disorder in women: a randomized controlled trial. *JAMA*, *297*, 820–830.

Shapiro, F. (1995). *Eye Movement Desensitization and Reprocessing: Basic Principles, Protocols, and Procedures*. New York: Guilford Press.

Shapiro, F., & Maxfield, L. (2002). Eye movement desensitization and reprocessing (EMDR): information processing in the treatment of trauma. *Journal of Clinical Psychology*, *58*, 933–946.

Simon, N. S., Connor, K. M., Lang, A. J., Krulewicz, S., LeBeau, R. T., Rauch, S. A. M., et al. (2007). *Paroxetine-CR Augmentation for Posttraumatic Stress Disorder Refractory to Exposure Therapy*. Manuscript under review.

Tarrier, N., Pilgrim, H., Sommerfield, C., Faragher, B., Reynolds, M., Graham, E., & Barrowclough, C. (1999). A randomized trial of cognitive therapy and imaginal exposure in the treatment of chronic posttraumatic stress disorder. *Journal of Consulting and Clinical Psychology*, *67*, 13–18.

Taylor, S., Thordarson, D. S., Maxfield, L., Federoff, I. C., Lovell, K., & Ogrodniczuk, J. (2003). Efficacy, speed, and adverse effects of three PTSD treatments: exposure therapy, relaxation training, and EMDR. *Journal of Consulting and Clinical Psychology*, *71*, 330–338.

Chapter 6

Cognitive-behavioral approaches to health anxiety

Steven Taylor, Kelsey C. Collimore and Gordon J. G. Asmundson

Health anxiety arises when bodily changes or sensations are believed to be indicative of a serious disease. The magnitude of health anxiety can differ from person to person; as such, it is typically conceptualized along a continuum ranging from mild to severe (e.g., Taylor & Asmundson, 2004). Health anxiety can be adaptive because it motivates us to seek clinical care. However, it can become maladaptive when characterized by excessive worry and impaired functioning. In this chapter, we will discuss (a) diagnostic and descriptive features of health anxiety, (b) etiological factors contributing to health anxiety, (c) assessment strategies for treatment planning, (d) empirically supported treatments, and (e) a case example illustrating assessment and cognitive-behavioral treatment of severe health anxiety. We conclude with a summary and suggestions for future research.

Diagnostic and descriptive features

Clinically significant expressions of health anxiety are commonly referred to as health anxiety disorders. These include hypochondriasis (American Psychiatric Association (APA), 2000), symptom presentations failing to meet full diagnostic criteria for hypochondriasis, and disease phobia and delusional disorder, somatic type. Details of disease phobia and delusional disorder, somatic type, are discussed elsewhere (see Taylor & Asmundson, 2004). Hypochondriasis is defined by a preoccupation with fears of having, or the idea that one has, a serious disease, based on a misinterpretation of bodily sensations (APA, 2000). To be diagnosed with hypochondriasis, this preoccupation must persist despite appropriate medical evaluation and reassurance from physicians. Disease-related beliefs cannot be delusional or restricted to a specific concern about appearance, and they must be markedly distressing or associated with interference in daily functioning. The symptoms must persist for at least 6 months and cannot be better accounted for by another disorder. Hypochondriasis with poor insight is specified if, for most of the time, the individual does not recognize his or her concerns as excessive or unreasonable. Health anxiety can be clinically important even when people do not meet full diagnostic criteria for hypochondriasis (e.g., when a person has excessive health anxiety lasting less than 6 months, when excessive health anxiety is present but does not interfere significantly with daily functioning, or when a person is preoccupied with fears of having a disease but eventually responds to medical reassurance). This is often referred to as abridged hypochondriasis (Gureje et al., 1997). Because current findings suggest that the abridged form is no less disabling than the full disorder (Creed, 2006), we use the term 'excessive health anxiety' to represent full or abridged hypochondriasis in this chapter.

Excessive health anxiety is equally common among men and women (Creed & Barsky, 2004). Hypochondriasis has a lifetime prevalence of 1–5 percent (APA, 2000), and the abridged form is even more common. Current (i.e., past 12 months) prevalence rates vary among different samples, in the ranges 0.05–2.12 percent for the general population (Martin & Jacobi, 2006) and 2–7 percent for primary care outpatients. Onset generally occurs during early adulthood (APA, 2000), often when the person is under stress, seriously ill or recovering from serious illness, or has suffered the loss of a family member (Barsky & Klerman, 1983). Excessive health anxiety is often chronic and frequently comorbid with anxiety and mood disorders as well as somatization disorder (APA, 2000). It is noteworthy that there is controversy about the classification of the health anxiety disorders; specifically, it has been argued that they may be better classified as anxiety, mood, or personality disorders (e.g., Lesse, 1967; Mayou et al., 2005).

Cultural factors (e.g., socially transmitted beliefs) can influence how a person interprets bodily sensations and, thereby, can influence health anxiety. There is evidence of cross-cultural differences in which sensations are feared the most (e.g., Gureje, 2004), with some cultures appearing more concerned about gastrointestinal changes (e.g., the UK), cardiopulmonary sensations (e.g., Germany), and immunological symptoms (e.g., the USA; Escobar et al., 2001).

Etiology

A number of theories regarding the etiology of excessive health anxiety have been proposed (see Taylor & Asmundson, 2004). However, the cognitive-behavioral approach, which describes cognitive and behavioral processes underlying health anxiety, has received the most empirical support and has led to effective treatments (Salkovskis et al., 2003; Taylor & Asmundson, 2004). According to the cognitive-behavioral model, excessive health anxiety arises from and is maintained by dysfunctional beliefs about sickness and health, including beliefs that lead people to misinterpret the significance and overestimate the dangerousness of bodily changes and sensations. Bodily sensations are common occurrences in healthy people (Pennebaker, 1982) and may occur for a variety of reasons, such as benign perturbations, minor diseases, or autonomic arousal arising from stress. People with excessive health anxiety believe that bodily changes and sensations indicate some pending catastrophic consequences in the more distant future (Warwick & Salkovskis, 1990); for example, chest pain may be interpreted as evidence of poor cardiac health and approaching cardiac failure, or a lump under the skin may be taken as evidence of malignancy. Other common beliefs of people with excessive health anxiety are that they are healthy when they do not have any bodily sensations, that people do not recover from serious diseases, or that worrying about their health will keep them safe (see Taylor & Asmundson, 2004).

Consistent with the cognitive-behavioral model, research suggests that, relative to nonanxious controls, people with excessive health anxiety are more likely to report experiencing a lot of bodily sensations (Barsky et al., 1995) and to interpret these sensations as indicative of disease (Haenen et al., 1998). Findings also indicate selective processing and concern over health-related but not other information. For example, people with excessive health anxiety are more likely to attend to and recall health information (e.g., Owens et al., 2004; Pauli & Alpers, 2002). With increased self-focused attention, the intensity of perceived bodily sensations is amplified (Pennebaker, 1982). They are also more likely to overestimate the probability of contracting a disease and the seriousness of diseases (Ditto et al., 1988; Easterling & Leventhal, 1989), but do not believe they are at greater risk of being the victim of an assault or accident (Barsky et al., 2001; Haenen et al., 2000).

Dysfunctional beliefs persist in people with excessive health anxiety for many reasons. For example, they typically experience health-related 'false alarms', wherein their alarming bodily sensations turn out to be harmless. These experiences may disconfirm beliefs that health is at risk; however, they can also serve to confirm this belief. They may reason that just because a symptom turned out to be benign today does not rule out the risk that the same symptom could be due to a serious disease in the future.

Behaviors performed in order to alleviate concerns can also serve to perpetuate elevated levels of health anxiety. Common maladaptive coping behaviors include persistent reassurance seeking (from physicians or family), other forms of repetitive checking (e.g., bodily checking, searching the Internet for health information), and avoidance of behaviors that elicit bodily sensations (e.g., physical exertion). These behaviors persist because they are reinforced by reduced anxiety in the short term. In the long term, however, not only are they ineffective in producing lasting reductions in anxiety, but they actually serve to perpetuate health anxiety (Lucock et al., 1998). For example, reassurance seeking can prolong a

person's preoccupation with disease, expose them to frightening information about health conditions, reduce their sense of independence (e.g., by
repeatedly turning to others for help), and lead to iatrogenic effects (e.g.,
unnecessary medical tests; see Taylor & Asmundson, 2004, for details).

We (Taylor et al., 2006) recently estimated the relative effect of environmental and genetic factors implicated in health anxiety. Environmental
factors accounted for most of the individual differences in scores of health
anxiety (i.e., 63–90 percent of the variance) and genetic factors played a
modest role (i.e., 10–37 percent of the variance). Additional investigations
estimating the extent to which health anxiety is due to environmental or
genetic factors are currently underway. Environmental factors implicated
in the development of health anxiety include early learning experiences
(e.g., childhood history of disease, reinforcement or receiving special
attention when sick), which contribute to dysfunctional beliefs about the
dangerousness of bodily changes and that one's body is weak (e.g.,
Robbins & Kirmayer, 1996; Whitehead et al., 1994). Relevant genetic
factors have not yet been identified; however, these may include genes
associated with the modulation of emotional states, such as the serotonin
(5-HT) transporter gene.

Assessment for treatment planning

Assessment targets

Treatment planning for excessive health anxiety should always begin with a
careful and comprehensive assessment. The first two steps in assessment
involve (a) ruling out general medical conditions that might account for the
presenting problems, and (b) ruling in a DSM-IV-TR diagnosis of hypochondriasis or one of its abridged forms. These steps help to determine
whether it is appropriate to proceed with treatment and, if so, what tactics
and focus are most appropriate. Other steps in assessment aid in determining the predisposing, precipitating, perpetuating, and protective factors
underlying the person's concerns.

By the time people with excessive health anxiety see a mental health
professional, they have usually had many medical evaluations. These
evaluations are generally at the insistence of the patient, and the results
typically fail to identify a medical condition that could account for their
symptoms. While some doctors try to calm the patient by providing
unnecessary medical tests, these tests are not helpful and may serve to
perpetuate health anxiety. Repeatedly testing the patient can reinforce
beliefs that they have a serious disease and can lead to iatrogenic effects
(e.g., pain due to exploratory surgeries). The cognitive-behavior therapist
can use this information to rule out the presence of general medical
conditions, and to advise involved physicians on the effects that repeated

medical testing has on the patient. In some cases, patients present with both a general medical condition and excessive health anxiety. Under these circumstances, a health anxiety disorder is diagnosed when the medical condition does not fully account for presenting concerns about disease or bodily sensations (APA, 2000).

Given that disease-related fears and beliefs are common features of other psychiatric disorders (e.g., obsessive-compulsive disorder, panic disorder, major depressive disorder), it is also important to rule out these disorders during the assessment. If another psychiatric condition (with or without diseases-related fears and beliefs) is of greatest relevance to the patient, it should be made the primary focus of treatment. In this case, health-related fears and beliefs can be addressed in later treatment sessions if they persist after a course of treatment for the primary psychiatric condition.

Comprehensive assessment of health anxiety includes consideration of numerous other details. An evaluation of personal history helps to identify learning experiences that may have contributed to the development of health anxiety. Consideration of current living circumstances helps to determine stressors and relationships that may contribute to the maintenance of health anxiety. Evaluating why the patient is seeking treatment is important in order to address issues that can interfere with treatment adherence. Finally, it is important to explore the specific features of health anxiety (e.g., troubling bodily changes, disease fears, dysfunctional beliefs and strength of conviction, and avoidance or 'safety' behaviors) so that treatment plans can target those that are most salient.

Assessment methods

Several different assessment methods can be used for treatment planning. These include (a) hospital medical records (e.g., to chart the course of the patient's problems), (b) clinician-administered structured clinical interviews, (c) self-report questionnaires, and (d) prospective monitoring forms.

We recommend use of clinician-administered structured clinical interviews. For a more detailed assessment of the health anxiety disorders, the Health Anxiety Interview (HAI) (Taylor & Asmundson, 2004) can be used. However, because the HAI does not include an assessment of comorbid conditions, we suggest that it be supplemented with the Structured Clinical Interview for DSM-IV (SCID-IV) (First et al., 1996). The SCID provides a thorough assessment of a range of Axis I disorders, allowing for differential diagnosis and identification of comorbid conditions.

There are several self-report questionnaires that can be used to assess excessive health anxiety and related constructs. Although these measures provide supplementary information, they do not replace the need for structured interviews. The most commonly used self-report measures are reproduced in the appendices of Taylor and Asmundson (2004). These measures differ in breadth of assessment, time required for administration and scoring, availability of norms, and empirical support on their reliability and validity. Some measures are better suited for clinical purposes, whereas others are more suited for research purposes. The Whitely Index (Pilowsky, 1967) provides a brief assessment of health anxiety and can be used to monitor treatment progress. The Whitely Index is a good choice because norms and screening cut-off scores are available. For a more comprehensive assessment of the central facets of health anxiety, we recommend the Illness Attitudes Scale (IAS) (Kellner, 1986) or the Multidimensional Inventory of Hypochondriacal Traits (MIHT) (Longley et al., 2005). The IAS has generally good reliability and validity and norms are available. Factor analytic findings suggest that the IAS comprises four factors, including (a) fear of illness, disease, pain, and death; (b) symptoms interference with lifestyle; (c) treatment experience; and (d) disease conviction (Hadjistavro-poulos et al., 1999). The MIHT has comparable psychometric properties to the IAS, but less information is available on norms and cut-off scores. This measure comprises four factors, including (a) disease conviction, (b) worry about health, (c) reassurance-seeking to allay illness fears, and (d) somatic absorption with bodily sensations.

Prospective monitoring forms can be useful for gathering detailed information and to monitor the course of treatment. Prospective monitoring involves using daily diaries or checklists that provide information about episodes of health anxiety (e.g., health concerns and behaviors). Patients can be asked to complete daily monitoring forms for 1–2 weeks prior to treatment and on regular intervals (e.g., every 4 weeks) throughout treatment.

Empirically supported treatments

Psychosocial interventions

Several different types of psychosocial treatments have been developed for excessive health anxiety. The most promising are (a) psychoeducation, (b) exposure and response prevention, (c) cognitive-behavior therapy (CBT), and (d) behavioral stress management. These can be conducted either individually or in groups.

Psychoeducation involves providing patients with a cognitive-behavioral model in which health anxiety is explained in terms of the etiologic factors described above; for example, dysfunctional beliefs about health and disease, and maladaptive behaviors such as repeated checking or reassurance-seeking (for copies of psychoeducational handouts, see Asmundson & Taylor, 2005; Taylor & Asmundson, 2004). Several studies indicate that psychoeducation, compared to a wait-list control, is effective in treating hypochondriasis, with gains maintained at follow-ups of up to a year (Avia et al., 1996; Bouman, 2002; Lidbeck, 1997).

Exposure and response prevention involves, as the label suggests, exposure to fear-evoking stimuli (e.g., exposure to sick people by sitting in a hospital waiting area) combined with response prevention (e.g., refraining from seeking medical reassurance that one has not become ill as a result of sitting in the hospital waiting area). Uncontrolled studies indicate that exposure and response prevention can reduce health anxiety (e.g., Logsdail et al., 1991; Visser & Bouman, 1992). In a controlled study, Visser and Bouman (2001) found this treatment to be effective, and superior to a wait-list control, with gains maintained at 7-month follow-up.

CBT is a multicomponent intervention involving psychoeducation (as described above), cognitive restructuring of maladaptive beliefs, and behavioral exercises that may include exposure and response prevention. CBT has been shown to be effective in reducing health anxiety in many studies, with gains maintained at 1-year follow-up (e.g., Barsky & Ahern, 2004; Clark et al., 1998; Martinez & Botella, 2005). Barsky and Ahern's (2004) randomized, controlled study indicates that CBT is more efficacious in reducing health anxiety than the usual medical care offered by primary care physicians (Barsky & Ahern, 2004).

Behavioral stress management is based on the rationale that some people react to stress by becoming worried about their health. This intervention does not focus directly on health anxiety; instead, it is used to train patients to manage their stress and, in turn reduce arousal-related bodily sensations and thereby enhance their sense of health. This promising intervention has only been evaluated in one study. Clark et al. (1998) found that both behavioral stress management and CBT were effective, compared to the wait-list group. At post-treatment, CBT tended to be more effective, although there was little difference between the two at 12-month follow-up.

Pharmacotherapies

Case studies and a small number of trials suggest that various medications can be useful in reducing health anxiety, including imipramine, clomipramine, fluoxetine, fluvoxamine, paroxetine, and nefazodone (e.g., Fallon et al., 1996, 2003; Kjernisted et al., 2002; Oosterbaan et al., 2001). One controlled trial – the main results of which have so far been unpublished – found that fluoxetine was more effective than placebo in reducing health anxiety, with gains maintained at 9-month follow-up (B. A. Fallon, personal communication, 10 September 2002; see Fallon et al., 1996, for a preliminary report). In a study comparing paroxetine, CBT, and placebo, Greeven et al. (2007) found that medication and CBT were equally effective after 16 weeks of treatment, and both were more effective than placebo in reducing health anxiety.

Despite the promising effects of these drugs, there are several problems in using pharmacotherapy to treat excessive health anxiety. There are numerous case reports of health-anxious patients failing to benefit from one or more of these drugs (e.g., Stone, 1993; Viswanathan & Paradis, 1991). Some patients become preoccupied with side effects (Stone, 1993; Wesner & Noyes, 1991). In some cases, hypochondriacal symptoms worsen during drug treatment, as patients become alarmed by side effects such as gastro-intestinal discomfort (Fallon, 2001; Oosterbaan et al., 2001).

In summary, the available evidence suggests that various pharmaco-therapies show promise in the treatment of excessive health anxiety, at least in some cases. Unfortunately, there have been few controlled drugs studies and little is known about the long-term efficacy of medications.

Comparative efficacy of treatments

Only a handful of studies have directly compared two or more treatments for excessive health anxiety. Therefore, we conducted a meta-analysis in order to estimate the comparative efficacy of treatments (Taylor et al., 2005). Twenty-five trials from 15 studies contained sufficient data for the purpose of either (a) computing pre-post-effect sizes (Cohen's d) for treat-ment completers on self-report measures of health anxiety, or (b) assessing the proportion of treatment dropouts. Participants in these studies had either full or abridged hypochondriasis. Treatments included the psycho-social interventions described earlier in this chapter and various serotoner-gic medications (e.g., fluoxetine, fluvoxamine). Patients in drug trials were on medication at the time of the post-treatment assessment. Treatment durations were typically 6–12 weeks, and psychosocial treatments typically involved approximately 12 hours of therapy contact.

The effect sizes for the psychosocial and drug treatments were all larger than the effect size for wait-list controls. CBT and fluoxetine tended to yield the largest effects, and these were broadly similar to one another. CBT and behavioral stress management tended to have the lowest proportions of dropouts. For studies using mixed samples of full and abridged hypo-chondriasis, the results suggested that psychoeducation and CBT had similar effect sizes, which were larger than wait-list and medical care from a primary care physician. Other treatments were not examined for these mixed samples. Pretreatment-to-follow-up effect sizes for measures of hypochon-driasis could not be calculated for drug studies because follow-ups were not conducted in the trials included in the study. For those studies reporting follow-up data (3–12-month follow-up), results indicated that CBT had the largest effect sizes in studies of full hypochondriasis, and psychoeducation and CBT had the largest effects in studies of mixed full and abridged hypochondriasis. The findings suggest that CBT and fluoxetine are the most efficacious interventions for full hypochondriasis, whereas psychoeducation and CBT are efficacious for patients with abridged hypochondriasis.

Predictors of treatment outcome

Not all patients with excessive health anxiety benefit from drug or psycho-social treatments. Regardless of the type of treatment, the following are the most reliably identified predictors of good outcome, as obtained from a variety of sources (e.g., APA, 2000; Barsky et al., 1998; Hiller et al., 2002). Good treatment-outcome is predicted by health anxiety that is mild, short-lived, and not associated with complicating factors, such as personality disorders, comorbid general medical conditions, or contingencies ('second-ary gains'), that reinforce health anxiety or sick-role behavior (see Taylor & Asmundson, 2004, for a detailed review). Such findings suggest that it is important to find ways of improving treatment outcome for severe cases.

Research is also needed to determine which patients are more likely to benefit more from one treatment (e.g., pharmacotherapy) than another (e.g., CBT). If a patient has a strong preference for one type of treatment, she or he may be more likely to drop out when allocated to a nonpreferred treatment. Preliminary evidence suggests that most health-anxious people prefer CBT to medication (Walker et al., 1999).

Illustrative case example

Cases of excessive health anxiety are often complex, thereby making it challenging to describe fully the nature, assessment, and treatment within the confines of a short book chapter. The following is a synopsis of one of our CBT cases, which is discussed in further detail in Asmundson and Taylor (2007).

Sixty-nine-year-old Mr C. presented with a 2-year history of persistent bodily concerns and anxious and depressive symptoms. He described several bodily concerns, the most troubling being abdominal sensations, which he feared were indications of cancer. He also worried that he might succumb to kidney or liver failure as a result of the medications he had taken. Mr C.'s physical and emotional problems developed shortly after his wife died of pancreatic cancer. Her early symptoms consisted of abdominal pain, nausea, loss of appetite, unexplained weight loss, and jaundice. Shortly after her death, Mr C. isolated himself from others. Intensely grieving, he began to have recurrent bouts of abdominal discomfort and worried that he, too, might have cancer. He also noticed muscle stiffness and pain, which he feared were signs of some serious disease. Mr C.'s physical and emotional problems worsened 5 months later, when a close male friend died of complications associated with kidney failure. Mr C.'s grief worsened during the 7 months after his friend's death. Mr C.'s children and grandchildren readily came to his aid, offering him emotional and social support, and his depressive symptoms gradually abated over the course of the next 12 months. His health anxiety, however, persisted unabated.

Mr C. underwent numerous medical investigations. He was found to have borderline hypertension and gastritis. A small, benign kidney cyst was identified and removed. There was no evidence that the cyst caused any of his symptoms. There was no evidence of cancer, liver disease, or rheumatologic disease. The consensus of medical option was that Mr C. was in good health for his age. Regarding his general medical history, Mr C. said he rarely became ill; 'I never gave my health a second thought – I thought I'd always be healthy.' He could not recall ever having a serious medical condition, and could not recall any family members suffering from serious disease.

Mr C. was treated by his primary care physician with ranitidine for gastritis (150 mg, twice daily) and alprazolam for anxiety (0.25 mg, three times daily). He was prescribed paroxetine (10 mg/day) for depression, but it was discontinued because of side effects (jitteriness and gastrointestinal upset). He was also prescribed chlorthalidone (12.5 mg/day) for hypertension, but he quickly discontinued it because of side effects (nausea and dizziness). Mr C. became increasingly preoccupied by the idea that the medications might have somehow harmed his body. His primary care physician eventually persuaded Mr C. to see a cognitive-behavioral therapist.

When Mr C. presented to his first session with the therapist, he was agitated and repeatedly interrupted the therapist with questions about symptoms and treatments. These questions were clearly intended to elicit reassurance; for example, 'I get this dull, aching pain in my stomach. Do you think that could be serious?' Rather than getting sidetracked by these questions, the therapist replied with variants of the following response: 'I can see that you're really worried about your health. I'll be in a better position to answer all your questions once I've done a thorough assessment.' Although Mr C. expressed grave concerns with his health, he was able to acknowledge that his worries might be excessive. The initial diagnostic interview suggested that Mr C. had previously met DSM-IV diagnostic criteria for major depressive disorder, arising shortly after his wife's death, worsening after the death of his close friend, and then gradually abating. As Mr C.'s depression declined his health anxiety persisted, suggesting that the latter was not simply a feature of depression. This indicated a diagnosis of hypochondriasis.

The interview also revealed that Mr C. held the following beliefs: (a) 'If I experience symptoms [i.e., unpleasant bodily sensations], then I must be ill'; (b) 'Real symptoms aren't caused by anxiety or stress'; (c) 'Medications can seriously damage your body'; (d) 'If I have symptoms, then the best thing to do is to rest'; and (e) 'Repeated medical tests are required because doctors often fail to detect serious diseases.' The interview also revealed evidence of maladaptive behaviors, such as avoidance of physical exertion whenever he felt tired or in pain, focusing on his stomach whenever he felt queasy, checking and rechecking medical pamphlets for information on drug side effects, and seeking reassurance from doctors or family members about symptoms and side effects. His reassurance seeking from his primary care physician persisted to the point that the physician no longer returned Mr C.'s telephone calls. Mr C. was considering changing doctors because he worried that he was not receiving proper medical care.

The case formulation sought to delineate the predisposing, precipitating, perpetuating, and protective factors involved in Mr C.'s problems. The formulation for Mr C. is illustrated in Figure 6.1. The hypothesized predisposing factors involved a lack of knowledge about the bodily effects of stress, a lack of experience with bereavement, and a lack of experience in coping with grief. These factors, in aggregate, made it very difficult for Mr C. to deal with his losses.

Figure 6.1 suggests that many factors interacted in various ways to perpetuate or maintain Mr C.'s problems. His profound distress over the loss of his wife and close friend was associated with strong arousal-related sensations such as pain and nausea. Given (a) his lack of knowledge about the effects of stressors such as interpersonal loss in producing arousal-related bodily sensations, (b) his lack of experience of bereavement, and (c) that his arousal-related abdominal sensations resembled his wife's prodromal symptoms of pancreatic cancer, Mr C. drew the understandable but erroneous conclusion that his abdominal distress was a sign of cancer. Because Mr C. isolated himself in his house after the loss of his wife and friend, the reduction in external distractions increased the opportunity for him to notice and focus on bodily sensations such as stomach discomfort. Mr C.'s misinterpretation of his abdominal sensations made him anxious, and this in turn, exacerbated the sensations. His anxiety about his health prompted him to seek medical testing and reassurance, further exacerbating his health anxiety. His excessive health anxiety also led him to avoid physical exertion in an effort to avoid further exacerbating his abdominal and other unpleasant bodily sensations. This led to physical deconditioning, and this in turn, led to increased fatigue and muscle stiffness and pain.

Figure 6.1 suggests that the main protective factor for Mr C. appeared to be the social support of his children, grandchildren, and friends. At the urging of Mr C.'s primary care physician, his family encouraged Mr C. to socialize more often with them. This social support apparently prevented his depression from persisting. But, given the number of factors contributing to his misinterpretation of bodily sensations (Figure 6.1), social support (which unfortunately entailed reassurance) was insufficient to reduce his health anxiety.

The case formulation suggested that various cognitive-behavioral interventions might be useful, such as cognitive restructuring exercises to challenge directly dysfunctional beliefs, and behavioral exercises to teach him about the effects of stress or anxiety on bodily sensations, and how the odds of detecting an unpleasant bodily sensation are influenced by the tendency to focus on one's body or on one's external environment. Mr C. had difficulty

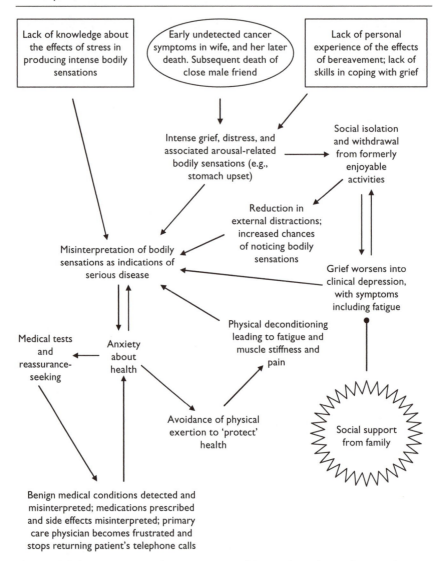

Figure 6.1 Relationships among elements in Mr C.'s case formulation. Boxes indicate predisposing factors, ellipse represents precipitating factor, and star represents protective factor. The remaining elements are involved in the perpetuation (maintenance) of Mr C.'s problems

in concentrating, was easily sidetracked, and repeatedly asked for reassurance on a range of different medical topics. This made it difficult to conduct cognitive restructuring. Therefore, the therapist simplified the treatment program to target Mr C.'s main problems. Treatment essentially consisted of (a) eliciting Mr C.'s primary concerns (i.e., distressing abdominal sensations) and providing education about the effects of stress and selective attention on the experience of bodily sensations (using handouts in Taylor & Asmundson, 2004), and (b) behavioral activation exercises (i.e., exercises that afforded a sense of enjoyment or mastery, scheduled at least daily). The latter activities helped prove to Mr C. that he was capable of physical activity and that this was good for his health (e.g., it reduced fatigue and muscle pain, and challenged the view that he was weak and would be damaged by physical activity). These activities also reduced abdominal distress, which would be expected if his stomach problems were stress-related rather than cancer-related. The exercises provided Mr C. with exposure to positively reinforcing activities, which further reduced his depressive symptoms. The physical aspects of the exercises were also useful in reducing his hypertension.

Mr C. was seen for 10 weekly, 50-minute sessions. In addition to the above-mentioned interventions, he was educated about the self-defeating effects of persistently seeking reassurance from physicians (e.g., the iatrogenic effects of repeated medical tests, along with the risk of exhausting and alienating one's doctor through repeated requests for reassurance). The therapist asked Mr C. to test for himself the effects of not seeking reassurance for a period of time (e.g., for a few days, to begin with) from health professionals and family members. He was also encouraged not to read medical texts or articles, either in print or on the Internet, because they fueled his health concerns. Mr C. agreed to refrain from talking about his bodily concerns with family members and from seeking reassurance from them. Mr C.'s daughter, who often drove him to appointments, was also interviewed by the therapist with Mr C.'s permission. She was provided with information about health anxiety (see Asmundson & Taylor, 2005, for educational materials for significant others). The treatment plan was explained to her and she readily agreed that it was important for her and the other family members to stop reinforcing Mr C.'s health preoccupation by offering needless reassurance. The family members agreed to refrain from offering reassurance. When Mr C. tried to elicit reassurance, he would receive replies such as 'Dad, you know it's against hospital rules for me to reassure you.' According to guidelines worked out by Mr C., his physician, and the therapist, if Mr C. felt especially ill, then he would seek medical attention.

Over the course of treatment, Mr C.'s unwanted bodily sensations and health anxiety abated, and his mood continued to improve. His family also noted an improvement in his physical and emotional well-being, and his primary care physician reported that Mr C.'s blood pressure had improved.

Summary

Health anxiety can be severe and disabling. It can occur as a secondary feature of many different disorders (e.g., anxiety disorder, mood disorders).

As a primary condition, it occurs in the full and milder (abridged) forms of hypochondriasis. Preliminary research suggests that genetic factors play a minor role in health anxiety and that learning experiences about health and disease are etiologically important. These experiences can give rise to dysfunctional beliefs which, in turn, can contribute to self-defeating behaviors such as excessive reassurance-seeking.

Before initiating treatment for health anxiety, it is important that the patient have a medication evaluation in order to rule out general medication conditions that could account for his or her problems. Other useful assessment methods include structured clinical interviews, self-report questionnaires, and prospective monitoring methods.

For mild forms of hypochondriasis, psychoeducation may be sufficient. For more severe conditions, such as full-blown hypochondriasis, cognitive-behavioral interventions and serotonergic medications are both promising. Numerous controlled studies support the long-term efficacy of CBT for full-blown hypochondriasis. Research indicates that the gains from CBT tend to be maintained at follow-up periods of a year or more. Although the current psychosocial and pharmacologic treatments are often effective, they are far from completely efficacious. Further research is needed to develop ways of increasing treatment acceptability and efficacy.

References

American Psychiatric Association (APA) (2000). *Diagnostic and Statistical Manual of Mental Disorders* (4th edn, text revised). Washington, DC: Author.

Asmundson, G. J. G., & Taylor, S. (2005). *It's Not All in Your Head: How Worrying About Your Health Could Be Making You Sick – and What You Can Do About It.* New York: Guilford.

Asmundson, G. J. G., & Taylor, S. (2007). Health anxiety and its disorders. In M. Hersen & J. Rosqvist (eds), *Handbook of Assessment, Case Conceptualization, and Treatment* (pp. 701–727). Chichester, UK: Wiley.

Avia, M. D., Ruiz, M. A., Olivares, M. E., Crespo, M., Guisado, A. B., Sanchez, A., et al. (1996). The meaning of psychological symptoms: effectiveness of a group intervention with hypochondriacal patients. *Behaviour Research and Therapy, 34,* 23–31.

Barsky, A. J., & Ahern, D. K. (2004). Cognitive behavior therapy for hypochondriasis: a randomized controlled trial. *JAMA, 291,* 1464–1470.

Barsky, A. J., Brener, J., Coeytaux, R. R., & Cleary, P. D. (1995). Accurate awareness of heartbeat in hypochondriacal and non-hypochondriacal patients. *Journal of Psychosomatic Research, 39,* 489–497.

Barsky, A. J., Ettner, S. L., Horsky, J., & Bates, D. W. (2001). Resource utilization of patients with hypochondriacal health anxiety and somatization. *Medical Care, 39,* 705–715.

Barsky, A. J., Fama, J. M., Bailey, E. D., & Ahern, D. K. (1998). A prospective 4- to 5-year study of DSM-III-R hypochondriasis. *Archives of General Psychiatry, 55,* 737–744.

Barsky, A. J., & Klerman, G. L. (1983). Overview: hypochondriasis, bodily complaints, and somatic styles. *American Journal of Psychiatry*, *140*, 273–283.

Bouman, T. K. (2002). A community-based psychoeducational group approach to hypochondriasis. *Psychotherapy and Psychosomatics*, *71*, 326–332.

Clark, D. M., Salkovskis, P. M., Hackmann, A., Wells, A., Fennell, M., Ludgate, J., et al. (1998). Two psychological treatments for hypochondriasis: a randomised controlled trial. *British Journal of Psychiatry*, *173*, 218–225.

Creed, F. (2006). Can DSM-V facilitate productive research into the somatoform disorders? *Journal of Psychosomatic Research*, *60*, 331–334.

Creed, F., & Barsky, A. (2004). A systematic review of the epidemiology of somatization disorder and hypochondriasis. *Journal of Psychosomatic Research*, *56*, 391–408.

Ditto, P. H., Jemmott, J. B., & Darley, J. M. (1988). Appraising the threat of illness: a mental representational approach. *Health Psychology*, *7*, 183–201.

Easterling, D. V., & Leventhal, H. (1989). Contribution of concrete cognition to emotion: neutral symptoms as elicitors of worry about cancer. *Journal of Applied Psychology*, *74*, 787–796.

Escobar, J. I., Allen, L. A., Hoyos Nervi, C., & Gara, M. A. (2001). General and cross-cultural considerations in a medical setting for patients presenting with medically unexplained symptoms. In G. J. G. Asmundson, S. Taylor, & B. J. Cox (eds), *Health Anxiety: Clinical and Research Perspectives on Hypochondriasis and Related Conditions* (pp. 220–245). New York: Wiley.

Fallon, B. A. (2001). Pharmacologic strategies for hypochondriasis. In V. Starcevic & D. R. Lipsett (eds), *Hypochondriasis: Modern Perspectives on an Ancient Malady* (pp. 329–351). New York: Oxford University Press.

Fallon, B. A., Qureshi, A. I., Schneier, F. R., Sanchez-Lacay, A., Vermes, D., Feinstein, R., et al. (2003). An open trial of fluvoxamine for hypochondriasis. *Psychosomatics*, *44*, 298–303.

Fallon, B. A., Schneier, F. R., Marshall, R., Campeas, R., Vermes, D., Goetz, D., et al. (1996). The pharmacotherapy of hypochondriasis. *Psychopharmacology Bulletin*, *32*, 607–611.

First, M. B., Spitzer, R. L., Gibbon, M., & Williams, J. B. W. (1996). *Structured Clinical Interview for DSM-IV*. New York: New York State Psychiatric Institute, Biometrics Research Department.

Greeven, A., van Balkom, A. J. L. M., Visser, S., Merkelbach, J. W., van Rood, Y. R., van Dyck, R., et al. (2007). Cogitive behavior therapy and paroxetine in the treatment of hypochondriasis: a randomized controlled trial. *American Journal of Psychiatry*, *164*, 91–99.

Gureje, O. (2004). What can we learn from a cross-national study of somatic distress? *Journal of Psychosomatic Research*, *56*, 409–412.

Gureje, O., Üstün, T. B., & Simon, G. E. (1997). The syndrome of hypochondriasis: a cross-national study in primary care. *Psychological Medicine*, *27*, 1001–1010.

Hadjistavropoulos, H. D., Frombach, I. K., & Asmundson, G. J. G. (1999). Exploratory and confirmatory factor analytic investigations of the Illness Attitudes Scale in a non-clinical sample. *Behaviour Research and Therapy*, *37*, 671–684.

Haenen, M. A., de Jong, P. J., Schmidt, A. J. M., Stevens, S., & Visser, L. (2000). Hypochondriacs' estimation of negative outcomes: domain-specificity and responsiveness to reassuring and alarming information. *Behaviour Research and Therapy*, *38*, 819–833.

Haenen, M. A., Schmidt, A. J. M., Schoenmakers, M., & van den Hout, M. A. (1998). Quantitative and qualitative aspects of cancer knowledge: comparing hypochondriacal subjects and healthy controls. *Psychology and Health*, *13*, 1005–1014.

Hiller, W., Leibbrand, R., Rief, W., & Fichter, M. M. (2002). Predictors of course and outcome in hypochondriasis after cognitive-behavioral treatment. *Psychotherapy and Psychosomatics*, *71*, 318–325.

Kellner, R. (1986). *Somatization and Hypochondriasis*. New York: Praeger.

Kjernisted, K. D., Enns, M. W., & Lander, M. (2002). An open-label clinical trial of nefazodone in hypochondriasis. *Psychosomatics*, *43*, 290–294.

Lesse, S. (1967). Hypochondriasis and psychosomatic disorders masking depression. *American Journal of Psychotherapy*, *21*, 607–620.

Lidbeck, J. (1997). Group therapy for somatization disorders in general practice: effectiveness of a short cognitive-behavioural treatment model. *Acta Psychiatrica Scandinavica*, *96*, 14–24.

Logsdail, S., Lovell, K., Warwick, H. M., & Marks, I. (1991). Behavioural treatment of AIDS-focused illness phobia. *British Journal of Psychiatry*, *159*, 422–425.

Longley, S. L., Watson, D., & Noyes, R. (2005). Assessment of the hypochondriasis domain: the Multidimensional Inventory of Hypochondriacal Traits (MIHT). *Psychological Assessment*, *17*, 3–14.

Lucock, M. P., White, C., Peake, M. D., & Morley, S. (1998). Biased perception and recall of reassurance in medical patients. *British Journal of Health Psychology*, *3*, 237–243.

Marks, I. (1987). *Fears, Phobias, and Rituals*. New York: Oxford University Press.

Martin, A., & Jacobi, F. (2006). Features of hypochondriasis and illness worry in the general population in Germany. *Psychosomatic Medicine*, *68*, 770–777.

Martinez, M. P., & Botella, C. (2005). An exploratory study of the efficacy of a cognitive-behavioral treatment for hypochondriasis using different measures of change. *Psychotherapy Research*, *15*, 392–408.

Mayou, R., Kirmayer, L. J., Simon, G., Kroenke, K., & Sharpe, M. (2005). Somatoform disorders: time for a new approach in DSM-V. *American Journal of Psychiatry*, *162*, 847–855.

Oosterbaan, D. B., van Balkom, A. J. L. M., van Boeijen, C. A., de Meij, T. G. J., & van Dyck, R. (2001). An open study of paroxetine in hypochondriasis. *Progress in Neuro-Psychopharmacology and Biological Psychiatry*, *25*, 1023–1033.

Owens, K. M. B., Asmundson, G. J. G., Hadjistavropoulos, T., & Owens, T. J. (2004). Attentional bias toward illness threat in individuals with elevated health anxiety. *Cognitive Therapy and Research*, *28*, 57–66.

Pauli, P., & Alpers, G. W. (2002). Memory bias in patients with hypochondriasis and somatoform pain disorder. *Journal of Psychosomatic Research*, *52*, 45–53.

Pennebaker, J. W. (1982). *The Psychology of Physical Symptoms*. New York: Springer.

Pilowsky, I. (1967). Dimensions of hypochondriasis. *British Journal of Psychiatry*, *113*, 89–93.

Robbins, J. M., & Kirmayer, L. J. (1996). Transient and persistent hypochondriacal worry in primary care. *Psychological Medicine, 26*, 575–589.

Salkovskis, P. M., Warwick, H. M., & Deale, A. C. (2003). Cognitive-behavioral treatment for severe and persistent health anxiety (hypochondriasis). *Brief Treatment and Crisis Intervention, 3*, 353–367.

Stone, A. B. (1993). Treatment of hypochondriasis with clomipramine. *Journal of Clinical Psychiatry, 54*, 200–201.

Taylor, S., & Asmundson, G. J. G. (2004). *Treating Health Anxiety: A Cognitive-Behavioral Approach*. New York: Guilford.

Taylor, S., Asmundson, G. J. G., & Coons, M. J. (2005). Current directions in the treatment of hypochondriasis. *Journal of Cognitive Psychotherapy, 19*, 291–310.

Taylor, S., Thordarson, D. S., Jang, K. L., & Asmundson, G. J. G. (2006). Genetic and environmental origins of health anxiety: a twin study. *World Psychiatry, 5*, 47–50.

Visser, S., & Bouman, T. K. (1992). Cognitive-behavioural approaches in the treatment of hypochondriasis: six single case cross-over studies. *Behaviour Research and Therapy, 30*, 301–306.

Visser, S., & Bouman, T. K. (2001). The treatment of hypochondriasis: exposure plus response prevention vs cognitive therapy. *Behaviour Research and Therapy, 39*, 423–442.

Viswanathan, R., & Paradis, C. (1991). Treatment of cancer phobia with fluoxetine. *American Journal of Psychiatry, 148*, 1090.

Walker, J., Vincent, N., Furer, P., Cox, B., & Kjernisted, K. (1999). Treatment preference in hypochondriasis. *Journal of Behavior Therapy and Experimental Psychiatry, 30*, 251–258.

Warwick, H. M., & Salkovskis, P. M. (1990). Hypochondriasis. *Behaviour Research and Therapy, 28*, 105–117.

Wesner, R. B., & Noyes, R. (1991). Imipramine: an effective treatment for illness phobia. *Journal of Affective Disorders, 22*, 43–48.

Whitehead, W. E., Crowell, M. D., Heller, B. R., Robinson, J. C., Schuster, M. M., & Horn, S. (1994). Modeling and reinforcement of the sick role during childhood predicts adult illness behavior. *Psychosomatic Medicine, 56*, 541–550.

Chapter 7

Body dysmorphic disorder: symptoms, models and treatment interventions

Fugen Neziroglu, Sony Khemlani-Patel and Matthew Jacofsky

Clinical features

Appearance concerns are commonplace in today's society. However, for some individuals, this preoccupation may reach a pathological degree. According to the *Diagnostic and Statistical Manual of Mental Disorders* (4th edn, text revised; DSM-IV-TR), body dysmorphic disorder (BDD) is characterized by an excessive preoccupation with an imaginary and/or a slight defect in one's appearance not accounted for by another disorder (e.g., anorexia nervosa). The preoccupation must cause marked distress and/or result in a significant decrease in functioning within major life domains (e.g., social, occupational, or academic functioning) (American Psychiatric Association, 2000).

Presently, BDD is classified among the somatoform disorders of the DSM-IV-TR. BDD patients presenting with beliefs reaching delusional proportions receive an additional diagnosis of 'delusional disorder, somatic type,' although the need for dual diagnosis is questionable (Phillips, 2004). Due to the nature of the disorder, it has been hypothesized that BDD may belong under the category of obsessive compulsive spectrum disorders (OCSD) (Hollander, Liebowitz, Winchel, Klumker, & Klein, 1989; McElroy, Phillips, & Keck, 1994; Neziroglu & Yaryura-Tobias, 1993a). Like other OCSDs, BDD involves the primary symptoms of obsessions and compulsions.

As in obsessive compulsive disorder (OCD), individuals with BDD experience intrusive/repetitive thoughts. However, the content of their beliefs centers on appearance concerns. This preoccupation may revolve around an imaginary defect in their appearance, excessive concern over a slight defect, or overall general ugliness. Common body parts of concern include facial features such as complexion, facial blemishes (e.g., acne, redness, etc.), nose, hair, hairline, body shape, size, muscularity, and asymmetry of body parts (McElroy, Phillips, Keck, Hudson, & Pope, 1993; Neziroglu & Yaryura-Tobias, 1993a; Phillips, 1996; Phillips, McElroy, Keck, Pope, & Hudson, 1993).

Moreover, individuals with BDD frequently experience ideas of reference, believing that others notice and comment on their appearance. The ideas of reference may be the result of a misinterpretation of other individuals' emotional expressions as negative (i.e., angry, contemptuous, etc.), thus leading to the development of biased assumptions about the individual's level of attractiveness, ugliness, and perceived desirability (Buhlmann, Etcoff, & Wilhelm, 2006; Buhlmann et al., 2004).

Like individuals with OCD, BDD individuals also engage in significant compulsive behaviors to help alleviate distress. Common compulsive or safety behaviors include, but are not limited to, mirror checking/avoidance, camouflaging, excessive grooming, excessive use of cosmetics, cosmetic and dermatological consulting and procedures, reassurance seeking about appearance, alternating body posture, skin picking, and comparing their particular perceived flaw with others.

Avoidance of social, occupational, and academic situations is very common and disabling (Perugi et al., 1997; Phillips, McElroy, Keck, Pope, & Hudson, 1993), leading to significant impairment in daily life, including poor employment history (50 percent employed; Perugi et al., 1997; Veale et al., 1996) and low marital rates (75 percent are single; Phillips et al., 1994). As a result, overall quality of life is found to be poor in BDD and does not seem to improve post-treatment (Khemlani-Patel, 2001; Phillips, Menard, Fay, & Pagano, 2005).

BDD patients pose a challenge to treat due to a high degree of comorbid conditions, including mood disorders (Neziroglu & Yaryura-Tobias, 1993b; Phillips, 1991; Phillips et al., 1993), anxiety disorders (Brawman-Mintzer et al., 1995; Phillips et al., 1993; Wilhelm, Otto, Zucker, & Pollack, 1997) and personality disorders (Cohen, Kingston, Bell, Kwon, Aronowitz, & Hollander, 2000; Neziroglu, McKay, Todaro, & Yaryura-Tobias, 1996; Phillips & McElroy, 2000). Major depression seems to be the most common comorbid condition with rates of depression ranging from 71 percent (Neziroglu et al., 1996) to 78 percent for a lifetime occurrence (Gunstad & Phillips, 2003). Interestingly, one recent comorbidity study found that comorbid depression tended to occur after the onset of BDD, suggesting that depression is a complication of BDD (Gunstad & Phillips, 2003). Rates for comorbidity between OCD and BDD range from 16 percent (Bienvenu et al., 2000) to 37 percent of OCD patients meeting criteria for BDD (Hollander, Cohen, & Simeon, 1993).

Subsequently, suicide rates in BDD can be troubling, with 22–24 percent of patients attempting suicide (Phillips & Diaz, 1997; Veale et al., 1996), and up to 45–70 percent (Perugi et al., 1997; Phillips, McElroy, Keck, Hudson, & Pope, 1994) experiencing suicidal ideation during the course of the illness. One prospective study found that the completed suicide rate for BDD is much higher than the general population, perhaps due to poor psychosocial and occupational functioning as well as high comorbidity in this population (Phillips & Menard, 2006). In addition, BDD individuals are more likely to have been sexually and emotionally abused than OCD patients and the general population (Neziroglu, Khemlani-Patel & Yaryura-Tobias, 2006).

Cognitive-behavioral model (CBT) of BDD based on conditioning

Although the etiology of BDD is unknown, several models attempt to explain this disorder. Current models of BDD include the notion of esthetic sensitivity and information processing (Veale, Ennis, & Lambrou, 2002), the neurobiological model (Feusner, Yaryura-Tobias, & Saxena, 2008; Saxena & Feusner, 2006; Yaryura-Tobias, Neziroglu, Chang, Lee, Pinto & Donohue, 2002; Yaryura-Tobias, Neziroglu, & Torres-Gallegos, 2002), and the neuroanatomical model (Rauch et al., 2003). Despite the usefulness and importance of each of these separate and at times overlapping models, a thorough explanation of each is beyond the scope of this chapter.

The model put forth by Neziroglu and colleagues (Neziroglu et al., 2004, 2008) is a cognitive behavioral account of BDD. This model is similar to Cash's (1997, 2002) general CBT model of body image disturbance. Cognitive-behavioral explanations rest on the premise that individuals' thoughts, behaviors, and feelings contribute to the development and maintenance of a disorder. The predominant symptom profile of individuals with BDD includes a preoccupation with thoughts about specific aspects of one's appearance, various manifestations of emotional distress (e.g., anger, disgust, anxiety, etc.) and maladaptive behavior patterns.

The key components and hypothesized pathways of the Neziroglu and colleagues' CBT model for BDD are depicted in Figure 7.1, and they include: (1) a biological predisposition; (2) initial operant conditioning; (3) social learning; (4) classical/evaluative conditioning; (5) relational responding (based on relational frame theory); and (6) secondary operant conditioning. The following is a brief overview of the model. For a thorough explanation of each component, please refer to these recent publications: Neziroglu et al., 2004, 2008.

This model suggests that biological predisposition paired with early learning experiences (through both direct reinforcement of attractiveness as well as social learning) make individuals vulnerable to the classical and evaluative conditioning experiences that can lead to BDD symptomatology. Early learning experiences include positive and/or intermittent reinforcement for overall general appearance or for a particular body part or attribute such as height, cuteness, weight or body shape (Neziroglu et al., 2004; Rabinowitz, Neziroglu, & Roberts, 2007). Moreover, vicarious social learning occurs when observing others being rewarded or punished for a particular belief or behavior (Bandura, 1977). In the case of BDD, one

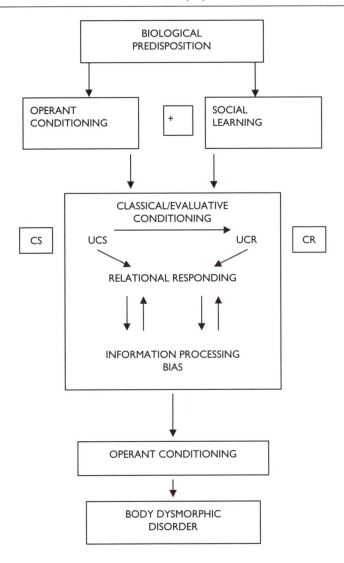

Figure 7.1 CBT working model

might observe the importance of appearance in the media or a family member's preoccupation with attractiveness. One's sociocultural and immediate environment can serve as opportunities for vicarious learning. Subsequently, the over-importance of and/or sensitivity to attractiveness serve as a potential risk factor for the development of BDD, and they lay down the framework for the specific beliefs, assumptions and values that are developed (Wilhelm & Neziroglu, 2002). Also, the authors believe that individuals with BDD may temperamentally be high in disgust sensitivity, thus representing an additional predisposition factor. More specifically, individuals with BDD may be more inclined to react with disgust to various disgust elicitors such as hygiene, sex, body envelope violations, sympathetic magic, animals, death, and foods (for a review of disgust sensitivity, see Rozin & Fallon, 1987).

Classical and evaluative conditioning experiences for BDD may include negative events involving one's physical appearances, such as being teased, being abused, or reaching puberty early. These events may serve as the unconditioned stimuli (UCS) leading to an unconditioned emotional response (UCR) such as anxiety, depression, disgust, or shame. The unconditioned stimulus (UCS) is evaluated to be negative or unpleasant, and therefore anything paired with it is also evaluated to be negative. For example, words used in the teasing (conditioned stimulus (CS): small) or a body part/aspect of appearance (CS: height), because of their pairing with the teasing, elicit the same negative affect (conditioned response (CR)). According to evaluative conditioning, any previously neutral body part or word (relational responding to the word 'small') can take on the same valence (negative reaction) as the UCS. Not only is the CS evaluated negatively but it also evokes the same response as the UCS; e.g., shame or disgust.

The next aspect of the model suggests that relational frame theory (RFT) may help us explain how certain thoughts elicit certain emotions and behaviors via relational responding. RFT (Hayes, Barnes-Holmes, & Roche, 2001) highlights the role of language and its impact on human emotions and cognitions, potentially contributing to human suffering. RFT suggests that conditioning and learning in humans are mediated by language by stimulating complex networks of associated ideas, images, and evaluations that play a significant role in the strengthening and development of beliefs.

Once established, BDD behaviors are maintained via negative reinforcement. Like the compulsive behavior seen in OCD, BDD individuals' compulsive behavior serves to reduce short-term distress by 'taking away' the negative emotional reaction (negative reinforcement) triggered by either an intrusive thought or contact with the perceived flaw. This relief represents a negative reinforcer in that it increases the probability that the avoidance behavior will be used again when in a similar situation.

Summary of the CBT model

The behavioral model of BDD developed by Neziroglu and colleagues suggests that a biological predisposition paired with early learning experiences makes individuals vulnerable to classical and evaluative conditioning experiences that can lead to BDD symptomatology. RFT may help us explain how certain thoughts elicit certain emotions and behaviors via relational responding. Once established, BDD behaviors are maintained by negative reinforcement.

Overview of BDD treatment interventions and effectiveness

Individuals with BDD are highly symptomatic and experience significant distress (Phillips, Siniscalchi, & McElroy, 2004). Moreover, they tend to have very poor psychosocial functioning and quality of life (Phillips et al., 2005), even for individuals receiving treatment (Phillips et al., 2005), thus representing a significant challenge even to seasoned practitioners (Rabinowitz et al., 2007).

Nonetheless, there is support for the effectiveness of cognitive-behavioral techniques, as well as pharmacological interventions in reducing symptoms and associated distress. Evidence for the effectiveness of CBT and pharmacological strategies comes from case studies, anecdotal accounts, and some empirical work (see Neziroglu et al., 2008; Neziroglu & Khemlani-Patel, 2002, 2003, for a thorough review of available treatment reports). Overall, these accounts usually report the use of both medication and cognitive-behavioral techniques in their treatment approach. A recent meta-analysis conducted by Williams, Hadjistavropoulos, and Sharpe (2006), examining both psychological and pharmacological treatment reports of BDD, revealed that cognitive-behavioral techniques were more effective than medication.

Despite support for the use of pharmacological strategies in the treatment of BDD, an explanation of the specific medications used, as well as information on dosages and augmentation strategies, is beyond the scope of this chapter. For additional information, see Hadley, Kim, Priday, and Hollander (2006) and Phillips and Hollander (2008) for a concise account of the pharmacological treatment of BDD. Subsequently, the remaining discussion will focus on specific CBT techniques often employed in treatment. Although cognitive and behavioral techniques are often used together, they will be presented separately for ease of comprehension.

Behavioral techniques

Exposure

Simply stated, exposure therapy guides the patient in systematically facing the situations that cause distress and/or lead to avoidance. Typical exposure exercises may include going to a shopping mall or a restaurant, or even, in a severe case, walking around the block, since avoidance of public places is common. At times, exposure may entail exposing patients to the very disastrous consequence they are afraid of. For example, a person with rosacea may purposely make themselves look red (i.e., apply blush) and then walk through the mall. Avoidance behaviors could also take the form of camouflaging. Again the therapist would need to expose the patient to him/herself or others without camouflaging and experience the disgust feelings. It may also be worthwhile to incorporate exposure to disgust elicitors in general to decrease disgust sensitivity if this has been found to be high in the particular individual.

The rationale behind exposure is that over time with repeated exposure to anxiety/disgusting situations, the individual will habituate to the associated negative emotions and the accompanying behaviors will be extinguished. Research in OCD has indicated that disgust reactions tend to habituate slower than those of anxiety (McKay, 2006). Repeated exposure also provides patients with the opportunity to test the validity of their beliefs. Patients' faulty beliefs may shift as a result of exposure exercises which do not support their initial beliefs (i.e., 'I can stand being around other people despite my appearance', or 'Everyone may not be staring at my large nose').

Several guidelines exist for carrying out successful exposure exercises. For BDD, appropriate pacing of exposure exercises, allowing patient control and input, and gradual increase in difficulty of exercises are both crucial components. Due to the distressing nature of exposures, we strongly advise in-session, therapist-assisted exposures as opposed to self-directed exposures. The use of imaginal exposure when feared situations are too anxiety producing may also be useful.

Response prevention

Response prevention refers to refraining purposely from engaging in a compulsive or safety-seeking behavior, and it is effective when used in conjunction with exposure. For example, a person would interact with others and not check himself in a mirror or fix his hair previous to the activity. Gradual reduction of compulsions is most palatable to patients. For example, patients may be asked to begin reducing make-up application one step at a time while continuing to engage in exposure exercises.

The purpose of response prevention is twofold. First, compulsions interfere with the process of habituation because they do not allow the person to be exposed to the distress- or disgust-eliciting stimuli or situations. Second, according to operant conditioning principles, the use of compulsive behavior actually maintains the behavior and obsessive thinking that treatment is aiming to decrease. Although compulsions may produce short-term relief, they result in long-term avoidance and distress.

Acceptance and commitment therapy

For those patients who are reluctant to enter exposure and response prevention treatment, it may be worthwhile to introduce acceptance and commitment therapy (ACT), which is derived from RFT. It is not within the scope of this chapter to discuss how ACT is derived from RFT (see Eifert & Forsyth, 2005), but it will suffice to say that language is what perpetuates our suffering. Because language allows us to attribute meaning to thoughts, it is possible to allow thoughts to enter our minds without giving them importance. ACT teaches patients how to accept their pain while simultaneously building a meaningful life based on personal values rather than symptoms. This is especially true for BDD individuals, who place great value on attractiveness to the exclusion of other values. One technique to tolerate pain is mindfulness meditation exercises aimed at awareness of one's thoughts, feelings, images, and memories without judgment or avoidance. Incorporating ACT into CBT treatment may be a valuable tool to target poor quality of life, high suicide rates, depression, and the immense suffering experienced by many BDD patients.

Mirror retraining

Mirror training is a strategy used to teach the individual to concentrate on the total physical appearance rather than selectively attending to the disliked body part (Wilhelm, 2006). It is not empirically supported but appears clinically to be of value to patients. Mirror training involves having patients look at themselves in the mirror and describe themselves in the most objective manner. For example, 'I have medium-length brown hair. My face is oval, my eyebrows are arched slightly, my eyes are brown and almond shape, etc.' The therapist coaches the patient to eliminate any subjective evaluations of the body and eliminate the usage of adjectives such as 'ugly, unattractive, grotesque, poor, bad, extremely big, etc.'

Cognitive techniques

The use of cognitive techniques is based on the premise that events in our environment do not necessarily lead directly to our emotional reactions and behavioral choices. Instead, what proponents of various cognitive treatment approaches, such as cognitive therapy and rational emotive behavioral therapy, suggest is that it is the individuals' unique idiosyncratic beliefs about the event's occurrence that lead to these reactions (Abrams & Ellis, 1994; Ellis, Gordon, Neenan, & Palmer, 1997). Unfortunately, at times, these beliefs may be characterized as being logically and empirically inconsistent, absolutist or dogmatic in nature, and interfering with individuals' ability to obtain desired goals, and may lead to inappropriate levels of disturbed emotions and maladaptive behavior choices (Walen, DiGiuseppe, & Dryden, 1992). Therefore, the main goal in using cognitive techniques is to assist patients to identify their dysfunctional beliefs and help replace them with more rational or adaptive alternatives.

In the case of BDD, patients often view situations in all-or-nothing and/ or perfectionist terms, and they engage in mind-reading, in which they believe they know what others are thinking in reference to them; catastrophizing, in which they may overestimate the importance of their perceived defect and the consequences it will have on their life (i.e., 'I will never be successful because of my nose'); and emotional reasoning (i.e., 'I feel ugly; therefore, I must be ugly').

It should be noted that rational alternative thoughts need to be realistic and acceptable to the patient and not necessarily overly 'positive', as this may actually have a counter-therapeutic effect by turning off the patient to their use or inadvertently reinforcing their faulty beliefs. Moreover, coping statements generated during therapy sessions should be used in addition to the thought-challenging homework exercises.

The following represents a possible therapeutic exchange during cognitive therapy:

Therapist: So you stated that while you were at the party you were very self-conscious about talking to Stephanie because you thought she would think you were bald.

Client: Yes, being bald makes me ugly, and I'd be rejected as usual.

Therapist: Where is the evidence that every girl will always reject you?

Client: Of course, they will. No girl wants a bald guy.

Therapist: How do you know no girl wants a bald guy?

Client: What do you mean? Everybody knows that. Bald guys don't get girls.

Therapist: Have you ever seen a bald guy with a girlfriend?

Client: Well, I guess so. My cousin Pete is bald and he actually has a very active dating life.

Therapist: Good. So is it possible that there are some girls out there that may not mind if you were bald?

Client: I guess it is possible. I still wish I did not have this problem.

Therapist: I know.

Although various methods may be used to gather evidence, as mentioned above, a hallmark technique of all cognitive approaches is Socratic questioning. Again the patient's original beliefs about the situation are not assumed to be accurate until proven so. Through the questioning of the original beliefs, the therapist and patient were able to come to a more realistic account of the impact of the patient's balding on his ability to attract a partner. It should be noted that although this technique may result in temporary relief, to be effective in terms of an actual shift in the patient's belief system, patients will need to challenge their beliefs constantly not only in session but between sessions as well. To this end, therapeutic homework in terms of thought-challenging assignments is often assigned between sessions to stress to the patient the importance of practice. The use of forms (e.g., dysfunctional thought record, REBT sheets, etc.) often facilitates this process.

Given the nature of BDD, an overwhelming majority of patients maintain a highly overvalued ideation (OVI) relevant to their beliefs about their flaws and poor levels of insight. Therapists must be realistic in their expectations as well as flexible and open to the possibility of modifying traditional cognitive techniques. Moreover, the therapist should avoid applying cognitive techniques aimed directly at challenging patients' beliefs about their particular flaw. Given the nature of BDD, these exchanges are often futile and at times actually have the paradoxical effect of strengthening the patient's already faulty belief. Subsequently, efforts should be directed at challenging core beliefs. Important beliefs to challenge are the following: how one's appearance interferes with functioning; how a narrow focus and conditional sense of self causes unnecessary distress; how perfection is neither achievable nor desirable; how perfectionism usually leads to unhappiness in many areas of one's life; and how faulty and/or extremely negative predictions are based on appearance; as well as patients' underestimation of their ability to tolerate and cope with various situations as a result of their perceived flaw. In addition, challenging the overemphasis on appearance as a value in people's life helps restructure their thinking. The over-importance patients place on the value of attractiveness is an extremely important target of treatment. Exploration of other values and the importance they give to them is a necessary component of treatment.

Hypothesis testing/behavioral experiments

As previously mentioned, not only do individuals with BDD have extreme beliefs about their appearance, but they also often believe that others share their unrealistic beliefs about them. Hypothesis testing is an important strategy in challenging the unrealistic belief attributed to others. Hypothesis testing refers to small 'experiments' used to challenge faulty beliefs (Swinson, Antony, Rachman, & Richter, 1998). For example, a BDD patient concerned that others are paying special attention to a flaw would be encouraged to interact with as many people as possible and to pay attention to how many people actually appear to notice the blemish. Although these types of exercises are similar to exposure exercises, hypothesis testing is more concerned with evaluating unrealistic predictions about others' behavior and reactions to the patient as opposed to the process of habituation described above.

Case example

David was a 21-year-old male student initially referred for a possible diagnosis of OCD. He had recently withdrawn from his college courses and returned home. His primary care physician had prescribed fluoxetine 20 mg and referred him for a psychiatric and psychological consultation. An initial evaluation revealed that his primary symptoms involved appearance preoccupations, suggesting that BDD was a more appropriate diagnosis. David was checking his appearance in mirrors for up to 5 hours a day, was avoiding college and most social activities, had begun using hair and cosmetic products, was picking skin blemishes, was washing his hands repeatedly, and appeared to be avoiding touching surfaces in public places. He had appeared increasingly agitated, tearful, and anxious, according to his parents. He had been sleeping much of the day and had experienced appetite changes. He reported that he believed he was rapidly balding, that he suffered from facial acne, and that his facial features were not in proportion to each other. His parents accompanied him to the consultation and reported that David had recently begun investigating hair replacement procedures. He was reluctant to enter psychological treatment but agreed to do so because he wanted to complete college. Upon the agreement to receive mental health treatment, his parents would allow him also to seek a dermatological consultation.

Information regarding his childhood revealed that he had suffered from mild OCD symptoms since the age of 9. His developmental and medical history was uneventful. David was diagnosed with BDD and major depression, severe, single episode. The clinician recommended a psychiatric consultation as well as an intensive outpatient cognitive behavioral treatment program.

Treatment planning

Treatment planning for David and most BDD patients involves some of the following considerations:

1   How severe are the symptoms and what are the most appropriate duration and frequency of treatment sessions?
2   Can the patient engage in psychological treatment without pharmacological intervention?
3   What is the patient's overall motivation level?
4   Does the patient have overvalued ideation or poor insight?
5   Will comorbid conditions need to be addressed first before the BDD?
6   Are suicidal ideation and intention present and how will they be managed?
7   Is there incorporation of treatment for other issues, such as the lack of daily life skills and social skills often seen in BDD?

In this particular case, due to the severity of symptoms and the time pressure to return to college, David was to engage in a daily treatment program. He denied suicidal ideation, so outpatient treatment would be sufficient. David appeared to have high overvalued ideation, comorbid depression, and symptoms which interfered with much of his day, suggesting that pharmacological intervention was necessary. Due to highly overvalued ideation and moderate motivation, a regime of cognitive therapy before proceeding with behavioral exercises would be most beneficial.

Sessions 1–4 or days 1 and 2 of intensive therapy

The goal of initial sessions is to gather more detailed background information, review the treatment plan, engage the patient in treatment, provide psychoeducation regarding BDD as well as the basic tenets of CBT, and develop a rudimentary anxiety hierarchy (see Table 7.1) for better understanding of the patient's daily behaviors and avoidance. Patients should also be administered structured, self-report and interview measures of BDD symptomatology and associated features, such as depression, suicidal thoughts, self-esteem, quality of life, and self-monitoring forms for frequency and intensity of ritualistic behaviors.

Family involvement, perhaps in joint sessions or separate sessions without the patient, is extremely valuable in the treatment process to teach family members how to set reasonable limits regarding reassurance seeking, healthy levels of support, managing their own frustration, and general education about BDD symptoms.

For patients insisting on cosmetic/dermatological procedures, we address that issue directly and suggest postponing that appointment for a pre-agreed time frame in order to give treatment a chance. If that is not agreed to by the patient, we request permission to stay involved in the process by speaking to the physician and/or accompany the patient to the consultation. We find that patients often misinterpret the information provided by a

Table 7.1 Hierarchy of skin concerns for case example

100	Going on a date
95	Being in a crowded bar with peers
90	Standing on a crowded subway train or bus
85	Sitting on a crowded subway train or bus
80	Touching handrail on stairs and then touching face without washing hands
75	Wearing 'unflattering' clothing that may accentuate acne (ex: the color red)
70	Going to the gym to exercise
60	Eating at a well-lit restaurant
50	Eating fried food or chocolate
45	Touching 'clean' surface and touching face
35	Asking receptionist a question
30	Eating at a quiet restaurant with low lighting
25	Sitting right next to someone in clinic waiting room
20	Sitting in the clinic waiting room

dermatologist or cosmetic surgeon. Accompanying the patient allows the subsequent sessions to focus on the patient's tendency to engage in biased thinking patterns and to discuss whether corrective procedures are 'necessary' versus 'preferred'. An increasing number of physicians are becoming aware of BDD and may assess the patient's distress and apparent insistence on cosmetic procedures and change their recommendations as a result.

Sessions 5–10 or days 3–5 of intensive therapy

Cognitive therapy for 6–12 initial sessions is often necessary, in most cases to be followed by formal behavior therapy. Motivation interviewing techniques also help the patient become invested in the treatment goals. Because behavioral change is often more rewarding than simply engaging in lengthy sessions of cognitive therapy, incorporating hypothesis testing, mirror retraining, and practice in decreasing compulsive behaviors helps keep patients engaged.

Session 11 and beyond

At this point, the therapist can systematically target items on the hierarchy in a graduated manner, starting with items that create mild/moderate discomfort. Exposure and response-prevention exercises in the beginning stages are primarily focused on facilitating normal daily activities, such as going to the mall, supermarkets, and other public situations while slowly decreasing the amount of camouflaging, make-up use, and other behaviors meant to disguise, alter, or hide the perceived defect.

David's exposure exercises consisted of first going to cleaner places, such as a bookstore and then touching his face. His therapist monitored David's anxiety rating, using the subjective units of distress scale (SUDS), which monitors anxiety ratings based on a self-report of anxiety on a scale of 1 to 10, with lower scores indicating lower anxiety. Ideally, for habituation to occur, an individual's SUDS rating should decrease approximately 70 percent from the beginning to end of an exercise. If a patient reports very low initial anxiety, the therapist should modify the current exposure. For example, the therapist could have asked David to touch the bathroom door or the escalator handle to elicit a higher initial SUDS rating.

As therapy progresses, therapists can deliberately exaggerate the perceived defect so that the individual is exposed to the fear of being judged or scrutinized by others. In David's case, the therapist used red lipstick to make marks on his face that were noticeable to others and then accompanied the patient to public situations. Since multiple appearance concerns are common in BDD, the therapist and patient can jointly decide which one to treat first. Some patients are more willing than others to begin addressing the worst fear first.

Maintenance of gains and relapse prevention

Research has shown that continued maintenance therapy is a crucial component of treatment (McKay, 1999) once a patient has achieved satisfactory progress. Multiple degrees of 'satisfactory progress' can be measured by decreases in self-report symptom measures, increase in daily functioning, involvement in social, occupational, and academic activities, and decrease in BDD thoughts and behaviors. We suggest a 1–2-year follow-up of sessions, with decreasing frequency as progress continues. This stage of treatment is also an opportunity to strengthen other life skills affected by the BDD, such as social skills and daily management of stress and increase in activity.

Special issues: treatment engagement, overvalued ideation, and quality of life

Patients may enter therapy for various reasons. One possible explanation, especially for those suffering from BDD, is symptom severity. Not only does symptom severity contribute to significant distress, but it also represents a potential obstacle to the individual's pursuit of an acceptable level of life satisfaction. Consequently, one of the primary goals of treatment is to assist the patient to acquire skills that will help reduce negative symptoms. Once the patient has experienced a reduction in symptoms and demonstrates a degree of self-efficacy in terms of applying these newly acquired skills, efforts may be directed toward increasing the patient's overall life satisfaction.

It should be noted that reducing symptoms and increasing quality of life are not necessarily a linear process. Negative symptomatology and quality of life may be viewed as two separate constructs. According to ACT, the goal is to teach patients to live a life according to their values despite their symptoms. This is not to say that negative symptoms do not have any effect on life satisfaction, or that one should not receive treatment, but rather that it should not be to the exclusion of living life. Indeed, as previously mentioned, BDD symptoms, whether they are behaviors or thoughts, represent obstacles that deprive individuals of the time that could be used to pursue more fulfilling activities.

Treatment engagement is difficult in BDD because patients lack insight and often believe that the actual defect is the true cause of their distress, and this makes patients more inclined to seek medical/plastic surgery interventions rather than mental health treatment. Establishing rapport and convincing patients that they need to correct their mental representations of their perceived flaw in order to have a satisfactory life are the primary and challenging treatment goal. Clinicians must validate the patient's concerns while simultaneously convincing them that there are other ways to combat their concerns besides medical alternatives. Perhaps the best way to achieve this balance is to focus on patients' dissatisfaction with their life and how to improve it. It is also helpful to teach the patient that mental representations of our body image involve perception, attitude and behaviors and demonstrate how we formulate images of ourselves that may be correct or incorrect, and how changes in our mental representations can be effective in reducing distress. Directly challenging patients' perception or opinion of their appearance is ineffective and can increase the likelihood of patients terminating treatment.

Summary and conclusions

Although presently there is no cure for BDD, available evidence suggests that CBT and pharmacological approaches are quite effective. While it is important that patient and therapist are optimistic about potential therapeutic gains, it is just as important to remain realistic in their expectations. Although improvement is possible for many BDD sufferers, more often than not they may still be considered impaired even with treatment. This point underscores the importance of constantly setting and reviewing realistic goals and expectations of treatment outcomes. Treatment for individuals with BDD will most likely be prolonged and require great flexibility on the part of both patients and clinicians. Subsequently, it is important to assess all aspects of the individual in order to determine when and which specific interventions should be employed. The use of a strong theoretical foundation may aid this process and in turn enhance treatment effectiveness and delivery.

References

Abrams, M., & Ellis, A. (1994). Rational emotive behaviour therapy in the treatment of stress. *British Journal of Guidance and Counseling, 22*, 39–50.

American Psychiatric Association (2000). *Diagnostic and Statistical Manual of Mental Disorders* (4th edn, text revised). Washington, DC: American Psychiatric Association.

Bandura, A. (1977). *Social Learning Theory*. Englewood Cliffs, NJ: Prentice-Hall.

Bienvenu, O. J., Samuels, J. F., Riddle, M. A., Hoehn-Saric, R., Liang, K.-.Y, Cullen, B. A. M., et al. (2000). The relationship of obsessive-compulsive disorder to possible spectrum disorders: results from a family study. *Biological Psychiatry, 48*, 287–293.

Brawman-Mintzer, O., Lydiard, R., Phillips, K. A., Morton, A., Czepowicz, V., Emmanuel, N., et al. (1995). Body dysmorphic disorder in patients with anxiety disorders and major depression: a comorbidity study. *American Journal of Psychiatry, 152*, 1665–1667.

Buhlmann, U., Etcoff, N. L., & Wilhelm, S. (2006). Emotion regulation bias for contempt and anger in body dysmorphic disorder. *Journal of Psychiatric Research, 40*, 105–111.

Buhlmann, U., McNally, R. J., Etcoff, N. L., Tuschen-Caffier, B., & Wilhelm, S. (2004). Emotion recognition deficits in body dysmorphic disorder. *Journal of Psychiatric Research*, *38*, 201–206.

Cash, T. F. (1997). *Body-Image Therapy: A Program for Self-Directed Change*. New York: Guilford Press.

Cash, T. F. (2002). Cognitive behavioral perspectives on body image. In T. F. Cash & T. Pruzinsky (eds), *Body Images: A Handbook of Theory, Research, and Clinical Practice* (pp. 38–46). New York: Guilford Press.

Cohen, L., Kingston, P., Bell, A., Kwon, J., Aronowitz, B., & Hollander, E. (2000). Comorbid personality impairment in body dysmorphic disorder. *Comprehensive Psychiatry*, *41*, 4–12.

Eifert, G. H., & Forsyth, J. P. (2005). *Acceptance and Commitment Therapy for Anxiety Disorders: A Practitioner's Treatment Guide to Using Mindfulness, Acceptance and Values-Based Behavior Change Strategies*. Oakland, CA: New Harbinger Press.

Ellis, A., Gordon, J., Neenan, M., & Palmer, S. (1997). *Stress Counseling: A Rational Emotive Behavior Approach*. New York: Springer.

Feusner, J. D., Yaryura-Tobias, J. A., & Saxena, S. (2008). The pathophysiology of body dysmorphic disorder. *Body Image: An International Journal*, *5*(1), 3–12.

Gunstad, J., & Phillips, K. A. (2003). Axis I comorbidity in body dysmorphic disorder. *Comprehensive Psychiatry*, *44*, 270–276.

Hadley, S., Kim, S., Priday, L., & Hollander, E. (2006). Pharmacologic treatment of body dysmorphic disorder. *Primary Psychiatry*, *13*, 61–69.

Hayes, S. C., Barnes-Holmes, D., & Roche, B. (eds) (2001). *Relational Frame Theory: A Post-Skinnerian Account of Human Language and Cognition*. New York: Plenum Press.

Hollander, E., Cohen, L., & Simeon, D. (1993). Body dysmorphic disorder. *Psychiatric Annals*, *23*, 359–364.

Hollander, E., Liebowitz, M., Winchel, R., Klumker, A., & Klein, D. (1989). Treatment of body dysmorphic disorder with serotonin reuptake blockers. *American Journal of Psychiatry*, *146*, 768–770.

Khemlani-Patel, S. (2001). Cognitive and behavior therapy for body dysmorphic disorder: a comparative investigation (Doctoral Dissertation, Hofstra University, 2001). *Dissertation Abstracts International: Section B: The Sciences and Engineering*, *62*, 1087.

McElroy, S., Phillips, K., & Keck, P. (1994). Obsessive compulsive spectrum disorders. *Journal of Clinical Psychiatry*, *55*, 33–51.

McElroy, S., Phillips, K., Keck, P., Hudson, J., & Pope, H. (1993). Body dysmorphic disorder: does it have a psychotic subtype? *Journal of Clinical Psychiatry*, *54*, 389–395.

McKay, D. (1999). Two-year follow-up of behavioral treatment and maintenance for body dysmorphic disorder. *Behavior Modification*, *23*, 620–629.

McKay, D. (2006). Treating disgust reactions in contamination-based obsessive-compulsive disorder. *Journal of Behavior Therapy and Experimental Psychiatry*, *37*, 53–59.

Neziroglu, F., & Khemlani-Patel, S. (2002). A review of cognitive and behavioral treatment for body dysmorphic disorder. *CNS Spectrums*, *7*, 464–471.

Neziroglu, F., & Khemlani-Patel, S. (2003). Therapeutic approaches to body dysmorphic disorder. *Brief Treatment and Crisis Intervention, 3*, 307–322.

Neziroglu, F., Khemlani-Patel, S., & Veale, D. (2008). Social learning theory and cognitive behavioral models of body dysmorphic disorder. *Body Image: An International Journal, 5*(1), 28–38.

Neziroglu, F., Khemlani-Patel, S., & Yaryura-Tobias, J. A. (2006). Rates of abuse in body dysmorphic disorder and obsessive compulsive disorder. *Body Image: An International Journal, 3*, 189–193.

Neziroglu, F., McKay, D., Todaro, J., & Yaryura-Tobias, J. A. (1996). Effect of cognitive behavior therapy on persons with body dysmorphic disorder and comorbid Axis II diagnosis. *Behavior Therapy, 27*, 67–77.

Neziroglu, F., Roberts, M., & Yaryura-Tobias, J. A. (2004). A behavioral model for body dysmorphic disorder. *Psychiatric Annals, 34*, 915–920.

Neziroglu, F., & Yaryura-Tobias, J. A. (1993a). Body dysmorphic disorder: phenomenology and case descriptions. *Behavioural Psychotherapy, 21*, 27–36.

Neziroglu, F., & Yaryura-Tobias, J. (1993b). Exposure, response prevention, and cognitive therapy in the treatment of body dysmorphic disorder. *Behavior Therapy, 24*, 431–438.

Perugi, G., Giannotti, D., Frare, F., Di Vaio, S., Valori, E., Maggi, L., et al. (1997). Prevalence, phenomenology and comorbidity of body dysmorphic disorder (dysmorphophobia) in a clinical population. *International Journal Clinical Practice, 1*, 77–82.

Phillips, K. A. (1991). Body dysmorphic disorder: the distress of imagined ugliness. *American Journal of Psychiatry, 148*, 1138–1149.

Phillips, K. A. (1996). Body dysmorphic disorder: diagnosis and treatment of imagined ugliness. *Journal of Clinical Psychiatry, 57*, 61–64.

Phillips, K. A. (2004). Psychosis in body dysmorphic disorder. *Journal of Psychiatric Research, 38*, 63–72.

Phillips, K. A., & Diaz, S. (1997). Gender differences in body dysmorphic disorder. *Journal of Nervous Mental Disorders, 185*, 570–577.

Phillips, K. A., & Hollander, E. (2008). Treating body dysmorphic disorder with medication: evidence, misconceptions, and a suggested approach. *Body Image: An International Journal, 5*(1), 13–27.

Phillips, K. A., & McElroy, S. (2000). Personality disorders and traits in patients with body dysmorphic disorder. *Comprehensive Psychiatry, 41*, 229–236.

Phillips, K. A., McElroy, S., Keck, P., Jr, Hudson, J., & Pope, H. (1994). A comparison of delusional and nondelusional body dysmorphic disorder in 100 cases. *Psychopharmacology Bulletin, 30*, 179–186.

Phillips, K. A., McElroy, S., Keck, P., Pope, H., & Hudson, J. (1993). Body dysmorphic disorder: 30 cases of imagined ugliness. *American Journal of Psychiatry, 150*, 302–308.

Phillips, K. A., & Menard, W. (2006). Suicidality in body dysmorphic disorder: a prospective study. *American Journal of Psychiatry, 163*, 128–1282.

Phillips, K. A., Menard, W., Fay, C., & Pagano, M. (2005). Psychosocial functioning and quality of life in body dysmorphic disorder. *Comprehensive Psychiatry, 46*, 254–260.

Phillips, K. A., Siniscalchi, J. M., & McElroy, S. L. (2004). Depression, anxiety, anger, and somatic symptoms in patients with body dysmorphic disorder. *Psychiatric Quarterly*, *75*, 309–320.

Rabinowitz, D., Neziroglu, F., & Roberts, M. (2007). Clinical application of a behavioral model for the treatment of body dysmorphic disorder. *Cognitive and Behavioral Practice*, *14*, 231–237.

Rauch, S. L., Shin, L. M., & Wright, C. I. (2003). Neuroimaging studies of amygdala function in anxiety disorders. *Annals of the New York Academy of Sciences*, *985*, 389–410.

Rozin, P., & Fallon, A. (1987). A perspective on disgust. *Psychological Review*, *94*, 23–41.

Saxena, S., & Feusner, J. (2006). Toward a neurobiology of body dysmorphic disorder. *Primary Psychiatry*, *13*, 41–50.

Swinson, R., Antony, M., Rachman, S., & Richter, M. (eds) (1998). *Obsessive-Compulsive Disorder: Theory, Research, and Treatment*. New York: Guilford Press.

Veale, D., Boocock, A., Gournay, K., Dryden, W., Shah, F., Willson, R., et al. (1996). Body dysmorphic disorder: a survey of fifty cases. *British Journal of Psychiatry*, *169*, 196–201.

Veale, D., Ennis, M., & Lambrou, C. (2002). Possible association of body dysmorphic disorder with an occupation or education in art and design. *American Journal of Psychiatry*, *159*, 1788–1790.

Walen, S., DiGiuseppe, R., & Dryden, W. (1992). *A Practitioner's Guide to Rational-Emotive Therapy* (2nd edn). New York: Oxford University Press.

Wilhelm, S. (2006). *Feeling Good About the Way You Look: A Program for Overcoming Body Image Problems*. New York: Guilford Press.

Wilhelm, S., & Neziroglu, F. (2002). Cognitive theory of body dysmorphic disorder. In R. Frost & G. Steketee (eds), *Cognitive Approaches to Obsessions and Compulsions: Theory, Assessment, and Treatment* (pp. 203–214). Amsterdam: Pergamon/Elsevier Science.

Wilhelm, S., Otto, M., Zucker, B., & Pollack, M. (1997). Prevalence of body dysmorphic disorder in patients with anxiety disorders. *Journal of Anxiety Disorders*, *11*, 499–502.

Williams, J., Hadjistavropoulos, T., & Sharpe, D. (2006). A meta-analysis of psychological and pharmacological treatments for body dysmorphic disorder. *Behaviour Research and Therapy*, *44*, 99–111.

Yaryura-Tobias, J. A., Neziroglu, F., Chang, R., Lee, S., Pinto, A., & Donohue, L. (2002). Computerized perceptual analysis of patients with body dysmorphic disorder. *CNS Spectrums*, *7*, 444–452.

Yaryura-Tobias, J. A., Neziroglu, F., & Torres-Gallegos, M. (2002). Neuroanatomical correlates and somatosensorial disturbances in body dysmorphic disorder. *CNS Spectrums*, *7*, 432–434.

Chapter 8

Cognitive-behavioral approaches to pathological gambling

Benjamin J. Morasco, David M. Ledgerwood,
Jeremiah Weinstock and Nancy M. Petry

Pathological gambling diagnostic issues and prevalence

The *Diagnostic and Statistical Manual of Mental Disorders* (4th edn; DSM-IV) defines pathological gambling (PG) as an impulse control disorder that involves persistent and recurrent gambling that is disruptive to one's personal, family or vocational life (American Psychiatric Association, 1994). To merit a diagnosis of PG, an individual must endorse at least 5 out of the 10 following diagnostic criteria: (1) preoccupation with gambling; (2) need to gamble with increasing amounts of money to maintain excitement; (3) repeated unsuccessful attempts to stop or reduce gambling; (4) restlessness and/or irritability when attempting to reduce or stop gambling; (5) gambling as a way to escape unpleasant emotions; (6) chasing loses; (7) lying to others to hide the extent of gambling; (8) committing illegal acts to finance gambling or repay debts; (9) placing a relationship, job, or educational or other opportunity in jeopardy by gambling; and (10) seeking assistance from others to relieve a dire financial situation caused by gambling.

PG has also been called *compulsive* or *disordered gambling*. Although not a formal diagnostic category, *problem gambling* is a term commonly used for individuals who meet some of the diagnostic criteria of PG, but who do not meet the full criteria for a diagnosis (Petry, 2005).

The prevalence of PG has been studied in several investigations. Shaffer and colleagues (1999) published a meta-analysis of North American prevalence studies conducted before 1997. They found lifetime PG prevalence among adults of 1.6 percent and problem gambling of 3.9 percent. Past-year prevalence rates were 1.1 percent for PG and 2.8 percent for problem gambling. These North American prevalence rates are similar to those reported in epidemiologic studies from around the world (Abbott & Volberg, 2000; Becona, 1993; Productivity Commission, 1999; Volberg et al., 2001; Wong & So, 2003). Recent surveys of the prevalence of lifetime PG in the USA range from 0.4 percent to 2.0 percent (Gerstein et al., 1999; Petry et al., 2005; Welte et al., 2001).

Assessment of gambling severity and treatment planning

The most commonly administered measure for assessing gambling severity is the South Oaks Gambling Screen (SOGS) (Lesieur & Blume, 1987). The SOGS is a 20-item, self-report questionnaire with scores ranging from 0 to 20. Scores of 3–4 indicate disordered or problem gambling, although some studies have used lower cut-off scores to suggest problem gambling. Scores of 5 or higher indicate probable pathological gambling.

The SOGS has good reliability and validity in clinical samples (Lesieur & Blume, 1987) and has been translated into more than 20 languages. It has been used extensively in research studies and is easy to administer and score, and its questions have high face validity. Disadvantages of the SOGS include that it has not been updated for DSM-IV criteria, was not developed as a diagnostic measure, places an overemphasis on financial problems, and has a high false-positive rate (Stinchfield, 2002).

The National Opinion Research Center DSM Screen for Gambling Problems (NODS) is a 17-item, interviewer-administered questionnaire (Gerstein et al., 1999). The NODS assesses past-year and lifetime gambling problems. Questions are consistent with DSM-IV criteria for PG. Although somewhat limited, psychometric data for the NODS are positive and the measure has demonstrated good reliability and validity (Gerstein et al., 1999; Hodgins et al., 2004).

Although the SOGS and NODS have demonstrated utility in classifying problem gambling and PG, they were not intended for diagnostic use. The Structured Clinical Interview for DSM-IV (SCID) (First, Spitzer, Gibbon, & Williams, 1996) was developed to assess psychological disorders. However, the psychometric properties of the SCID gambling subscale have not been rigorously evaluated. One structured interview that may aid in assessing PG is the Gambling Behavior Interview (GBI) (Stinchfield, Govoni, & Frisch, 2005). The GBI includes items that measure the 10 diagnostic criteria for PG as well as other questions of gambling severity. Initial psychometric data are strong (Stinchfield et al., 2005), but further psychometric studies are needed.

The Addiction Severity Index (ASI) (McLellan et al., 1985) is the most widely used measure for evaluating the severity of substance use problems. Given the high comorbidity between PG and other substance use disorders (Petry et al., 2005), a gambling scale for the ASI was developed (ASI-G) (Lesieur & Blume, 1992). The ASI-G has demonstrated adequate internal consistency and convergent validity with other measures of gambling severity, including a collateral informant and clinician-rated scales (Petry, 2003a). Although the ASI-G may not be used to diagnose PG, the measure provides a score of gambling severity.

In summary, psychological measures are available to assess PG prevalence rates, diagnoses, and gambling severity. Some measures have undergone rigorous psychometric evaluation, while others are in need of further testing. The development of additional screening measures for use in diverse clinical settings (e.g., primary care) are needed to accurately identify individuals in need of more comprehensive evaluation and/or treatment.

Etiology of PG

The development and course of PG is varied, multidimensional, and a product of the interaction between genetic, environmental, and individual factors. We review risk factors for PG and discuss principles of classical and operant conditioning that often maintain the behavior.

Genetic and biological factors

Twin studies indicate a link between PG and inherited genes. In a large study of male twins, genetic factors accounted for over 48 percent of the variance in the development of problem gambling (Eisen et al., 1998). More recently, a common genetic vulnerability was detected between PG and other psychiatric disorders such as alcohol dependence, major depression, and antisocial personality disorder (Potenza et al., 2005; Slutske et al., 2001). These findings suggest that numerous genes are involved with the development of the disorder. The mechanism by which genes increase the risk of PG has begun to receive empirical attention, and results suggest that the genes associated with the dopamine and serotonin neurotransmitter systems in the brain may be involved (Ibanez et al., 2003).

Environmental factors

EXPOSURE TO GAMBLING

Prevalence studies indicate that increased access to gambling is positively related to gambling participation and rates of PG (Shaffer et al., 1999). For example, Jacques and colleagues (2000) studied the prevalence of gambling-related problems in a city the year before and after a casino opened. Compared to a similar city without a casino, gambling behavior among individuals living in the city with the new casino increased dramatically.

Individual factors

GENDER

The development and course of PG varies significantly by gender. Prevalence studies find rates of PG three times higher in men than women (Petry et al., 2005). Additionally, men typically begin gambling earlier in life and go many years without experiencing problems associated with gambling. Women often begin gambling later in life, but progress to problems more quickly (Tavares et al., 2003). Preferred gambling activity also varies by gender, women often preferring slots and bingo to cards, sports, and betting on animals for men (Ladd & Petry, 2002). Despite differences in course and onset, severity of gambling problems generally does not differ between the men and women.

AGE

Age is inversely related to gambling problems. Lifetime prevalence rates of problem and PG in adolescents may be as high as 9.5 percent and 3.9 percent, respectively (Shaffer et al., 1999). These rates are significantly higher than those reported in the general population. Furthermore, the earlier one initiates gambling, the greater is the likelihood of progression to PG. For example, individuals who began betting in childhood and adolescence were significantly more likely to develop gambling-related problems than those who began betting as adults (Lynch, Maciejewski, & Potenza, 2004). Age of gambling initiation is also associated with poorer psychosocial functioning. In a study of 236 treatment-seeking pathological gamblers, Burge and colleagues (2006) found that gamblers who began betting during their pre- or early-adolescent years (mean age 10.5 years), compared to gamblers who began betting later in life (mean age 23.0 years), had increased severity of psychiatric, family/social, and substance abuse problems.

PSYCHIATRIC COMORBIDITY

PG frequently co-occurs with other psychiatric disorders, particularly substance use disorders (SUD). In a large nationally representative sample from the USA ($n = 43,093$), over 70 percent of pathological gamblers had an alcohol use disorder, 60 percent met criteria for nicotine dependence, and 30 percent had SUD (Petry et al., 2005). History of comorbid SUD is also associated with more severe gambling and other psychosocial concerns (Ladd & Petry, 2003).

PG is also closely tied with mood, especially because gambling to escape from problems or to allay dysphoric mood is one of the diagnostic criteria (American Psychiatric Association, 1994). In a national prevalence study in the USA, approximately half of pathological gamblers had a lifetime comorbid mood disorder (Petry et al., 2005). However, the course and onset of mood disorders in PG has received scant attention. In a study of 38 treatment-seeking pathological gamblers, gambling preceded depression in 86 percent of cases (McCormick et al., 1984). No matter the course or onset, depressive symptoms are typically present among individuals with PG.

HISTORY OF TRAUMA AND ABUSE

As in other addictions, pathological gamblers have high rates of trauma, abuse, and neglect compared to nonpathological gamblers (Scherrer et al., 2007). These developmental stressors are associated with earlier onset and increased gambling severity (Petry & Steinberg, 2005). Although these studies are unable to determine causality, gambling has been posited as a method for coping with trauma and abuse.

OTHER LIFE STRESSORS: SOCIOECONOMIC STATUS (SES) AND MARITAL STATUS

SES is often confounded with other variables that may be independently or interactively related to psychiatric disorders. For example, ethnic minorities are overrepresented in lower socioeconomic classes; therefore, whether increased risk of PG is related to ethnicity or SES is difficult to disentangle. PG is overrepresented in most non-Caucasian minorities in the USA (Gerstein et al., 1999). Less education is also associated with lower SES (as well as with non-majority ethnicity). A meta-analysis of 15 studies that reported income found that individuals with incomes under US$25,000 per year were likely to be overrepresented among the pathological gamblers (Shaffer et al., 1999). Therefore, the unique or shared risk these variables exert with respect to PG is difficult to ascertain; however, each is associated with PG.

Problem and pathological gamblers are more likely to be divorced or separated than nonproblem gamblers (Cunningham-Williams et al., 1998). Divorce or separation may result as a consequence of PG, or pathological gamblers may be less likely to marry due to an inability to form stable relationships, and thus they experience lower social support and greater distress.

Operant and classical conditioning

Due to its reinforcing nature, gambling often persists despite adverse consequences. This may be because gambling activities operate on a variable ratio scale of reinforcement, which is associated with the highest rates of maintenance in operant conditioning studies. Gambling is reinforcing for a variety of reasons. In a sample of treatment-seeking pathological gamblers ($n = 84$), over 80 percent of participants stated that gambling provided enhanced positive emotional states (e.g., excitement), and over half stated that they gamble to escape or disassociate (e.g., 'takes my mind off problems'; Morasco, Weinstock, Ledgerwood, & Petry, 2007). Many of the negative consequences associated with gambling are delayed or distal to the behavior (e.g., depressed due to losses, family problems, bankruptcy) and are not salient when the decision is made to gamble.

Classical conditioning applies to the maintenance of gambling, as many pathological gamblers have associated cues to gambling over time. These cues, such as mood states, gambling advertisements or payday, become paired with the behavior and its immediate and positive consequences. These cues may induce craving and/or a gambling episode (Tavares et al., 2005).

In conclusion, each of these factors is associated with an increased risk of the development of PG. While none alone is likely to be sufficient for the development of the disorder, the combination of factors across an individual's lifespan can spawn PG.

Treatment options for PG

Current treatments for PG include psychosocial and pharmacological interventions. While the study of gambling treatments has increased in the past two decades, efficacy research is still at a nascent stage. No one treatment is considered to be most efficacious, and no medications have been approved for treatment of PG by the US Food and Drug Administration. Nevertheless, several interventions have demonstrated promise.

Pharmacological treatments

Some research has evaluated medications to treat PG, and, to date, most studies have focused on opioid antagonists (Dannon et al., 2005; Kim et al., 2001) and antidepressants (Hollander et al., 1998; Kim et al., 2002). However, there is no approved medication for PG. Even if a medication is discovered that has benefits for treating PG, it is unlikely that medication would be provided in isolation. Rather, it would be administered with psychosocial therapies.

Psychosocial treatments

Gamblers Anonymous (GA), modeled after the 12-step approach of Alcoholics Anonymous, is the most frequent treatment for gambling problems in the USA and is available in many countries throughout the world. Despite its popularity, there are few empirical studies of the effectiveness of GA. The studies that have explored GA provide mixed results. Stewart and Brown (1988) studied 232 GA members throughout their fellowship. Only 8 percent of the participants maintained gambling abstinence for 1 year, and only 7 percent maintained abstinence for 2 years. Further, 22 percent of participants did not return to GA following their first meeting, and only 30 percent continued attending beyond the tenth meeting. Conversely, Petry (2003b) found that 48 percent of patients who chose to attend GA meetings maintained abstinence from gambling, compared with 36 percent of patients who did not attend GA. These findings suggest that GA may be particularly beneficial to those who choose to attend. However, patients who are motivated for change may work harder in treatment and subsequently avail themselves of additional treatment opportunities, such as GA.

Brief treatments rooted in motivational interviewing (MI) have been applied to problem and PG. Because the course of treatment is brief, MI sessions tend to focus on gambling frequency and consequences, and foster ways of coping with gambling urges or triggers. A few investigations have examined the efficacy of brief interventions (Dickerson et al., 1990; Hodgins et al., 2001). Hodgins and colleagues (2001) studied the efficacy of a single MI session combined with a self-help workbook, compared with self-help workbook only and wait-list control conditions. The self-help workbook alone did not lead to greater reductions in gambling compared with the wait-list group. However, the self-help workbook combined with the MI session resulted in the greatest reductions in PG symptoms. Follow-up assessments of patients in the active conditions found that MI was associated with greater reductions in gambling days, money lost, and gambling severity score, and that some benefits of the MI were apparent 24 months after the intervention (Hodgins et al., 2004).

The most frequently studied treatments for PG include those that incorporate cognitive and behavioral principles. As a group, these approaches are associated with the most evidence for efficacy. Early investigations were mostly uncontrolled and case studies of behavioral treatments. More recently, a greater emphasis has been placed on cognitive processes that mediate the relationship between gambling-related cues and subsequent gambling behavior. These cognitive and cognitive-behavioral therapies (CBT) differ from strictly behavioral approaches in their focus on internal processes. Most CBTs address the identification of gambling-related thought processes, affect, and cognitive distortions that increase one's vulnerability to gambling. Additionally, CBT approaches frequently utilize skill-building techniques geared toward relapse prevention, assertiveness and gambling refusal skills, problem-solving, and reinforcement of gambling-inconsistent activities and interests.

Several studies have demonstrated the efficacy of cognitive and CBT approaches in reducing PG symptoms (Echeburua, Baez, & Fernandez-Montalvo, 1996; Ladouceur et al., 2001, 2003; McConaghy, Blaszczynski, & Frankovia, 1991; Petry et al., 2006; Sylvain, Ladouceur, & Boisvert, 1997). Although these studies vary in their methodology, each supports the efficacy of CBT for treating PG. For example, Sylvain and colleagues (1997) randomly assigned pathological gamblers to either cognitive therapy or a wait-list control group. Therapy consisted of twice weekly 60–90-minute sessions (up to 30 hours of treatment) that focused on gambling-related cognitive distortions, problem-solving, social skills, and relapse prevention. Participants assigned to the cognitive therapy condition reported less gambling and fewer gambling-related difficulties, and reported feeling more in control than wait-list participants.

Members of our lab (Petry et al., 2006) recently conducted a large-scale investigation of CBT. In this study, 231 participants were randomly assigned to: (1) referral to GA; (2) referral to GA plus a CBT-oriented, self-directed treatment manual; or (3) referral to GA plus individual CBT. The individual CBT and treatment manual both consisted of eight sessions that covered identification of triggers, functional analysis of triggers and consequences of gambling, engaging in alternative activities, self-management of triggers, coping with urges to gamble, gambling refusal skills, irrational thinking related to gambling, and relapse prevention. Participants assigned to the manual group were instructed to cover each of the chapters on their own, while patients assigned to individual therapy met with a therapist to review the same topics once-weekly for 50 minutes over an 8-week period. Participants were assessed throughout treatment and afterward, even if they did not complete treatment. Outcomes included reductions in gambling disorder symptoms, number of days of gambling, and amount of money gambled. Participants who received individual CBT experienced significantly greater reductions in all three outcome measures and greater reductions in the amount of money wagered than patients who received the CBT workbook. Participants in individual CBT also experienced prolonged benefits of therapy that did not occur in the GA only and CBT workbook conditions.

In summary, several psychosocial treatments have been used to help gamblers reduce the frequency and severity of gambling. While CBT approaches appear to have the most efficacy, other approaches, including GA and brief MI, are promising. Perhaps most notable about the state of gambling treatment is that there are few methodologically rigorous investigations into treatment efficacy. However, the studies that have been done are largely positive. Future studies will improve our understanding of the effectiveness of these approaches.

Case example

In our study of CBT for PG, the first CBT session teaches the gambler to understand the pattern of his or her gambling behaviors and to identify triggers. Certain events, days and times, people, and emotions have been paired with gambling in the past and may now precipitate gambling episodes or urges, in a seemingly automatic manner. The most common triggers (Morasco et al., 2007) include unstructured or free time (weekends, days off), negative emotional states (depressed, anxious), reminders of gambling (seeing advertisements, watching sports), and access to money (payday, found money). Gamblers are asked to complete a worksheet (available in Petry, 2005) in the session indicating their triggers. They are asked to specify times when, people with whom, and events, moods and other activities in which they often gamble. In addition, they also indicate the converse – times, people, events and moods in which they *never* or rarely gamble. The therapist encourages the gamblers to spend more time in places where they do not gamble and with people with whom they do not gamble. A specific plan is developed for high-risk time(s) over the upcoming week, such as planning on going to the movies on Saturday evening, when they most often go to the casino.

Consider Judy, a 54-year-old wife seeking treatment for problems related to slot machine gambling. Judy began gambling 12 years ago. At first, she went with her friends, whenever their husbands were out of town. After several years of social gambling, Judy started going to the casino alone. Her husband Bob was traveling more after a promotion. Now that the kids were away at college, he spent little time at home. Judy was lonely, and an evening at the casino was a good way for her to have fun and feel 'alive'. Because her husband was also making more money, Judy felt she should be able to spend a little on herself for a change as well.

After about 3 years of increasingly frequent gambling, Judy was getting out of control. She was now going to the casino at least three nights a week. She sometimes stayed throughout the night, and when she was home, she suffered from insomnia. Judy had gotten several credit cards in her own name, some of which were now maxed out. She managed to pay the minimums on them each month, by taking cash from her husband and hiding from him where all the money was going. When he asked, she made up things that she had bought for the kids.

After several years of accumulating greater debt, Judy knew things were getting bad when she missed a few credit card payments and the collectors started calling the house. One day, her husband was home, sick with the flu, and he intercepted a credit card company call. While Judy tried to explain it as an oversight, it was too late; her husband had the statement resent, along with all the records from the year. She had no recourse but to tell him the truth. He insisted Judy come to gambling treatment.

While Judy presented to treatment with some remorse over the lost money, she was also angry at her husband for his perceived abandonment of her and their marriage. She saw gambling as something he owed her. She had spent her life raising their children and gave up her profession as an advertising executive to stay home with their family. It had been hard to make ends meet until the past 5 years or so, with Bob's new promotion. Throughout their entire marriage, she had never bought things for herself, and never asked for anything. She felt this was supposed to be her time in life, when she could relax and have a little fun. However, she and Bob had grown apart; they barely tolerated each other now. He got to travel the world, eat expensive dinners and stay at fancy hotels with his job – if she had to stay home, she might as well go to the casino.

In the first session, the therapist got a sense of Judy's life and her gambling history. She then introduced the session handout and explained triggers. Judy began to identify her triggers. Her top triggers related to unstructured free times – days that her husband traveled or was out late at business dinners. The therapist asked Judy to write those situations on the handout, and then she asked Judy whether she ever went to the casino even when her husband was home. Judy said that yes, she would sometimes head to the casino if they got in an argument, or if he was going to be home but watching a sports event all night. She added these events to the triggers list, under moods (interpersonal conflicts) and events (bored at home).

When the therapist asked Judy about days, times and moods when she *did not* feel like gambling, Judy indicated that if she had absolutely no money she would not go. They added that to the handout. They therapist also inquired whether there were ever times when her husband was away, but she *did not* go to the casino. Judy thought for a while and then stated that sometimes, such as two weeks ago, she did not go to the casino at all even though her husband was in Asia all week on business. The therapist asked Judy why it was she did not gamble that week. Judy answered that her sister was in town visiting and her sister hated gambling. The therapist replied, 'Let's put that on your list – spending time with your sister is something that helps you not to want to gamble. What kinds of things did you do with your sister? What other activities do you enjoy that don't involve gambling?' Those were additional activities that were listed on the 'Alternatives to gambling' section of the handout. Finally, the therapist asked Judy to consider her mood and frame of mind while her sister was visiting – did she want to gamble while her sister was there? Judy indicated that she had not thought about gambling at all during her sister's visit. While she thought about the money she owed and worried about how she would pay it off, she did not have any desire to gamble that week. Her nongambling moods, which she wrote on the handout, were 'having fun, spending time with someone I care about, keeping busy'.

The first session ended with the therapist asking Judy what she could do this upcoming week on Wednesday and Thursday evenings, the two days her husband would be away. Judy agreed to visit an elderly neighbor one night and to call her daughter at college the other.

The second session picks up directly from the first. In the beginning of the second and each subsequent session, the therapist asks about any gambling over the course of the week and provides praise and support for nongambling days. Even if no gambling had occurred, triggers that were encountered and managed should be reviewed, along with problem-solving related to other ways of managing triggers in the future. If gambling did occur, the gambling day(s) should be the focus of the second session, which delineates the concept of the functional analysis.

A functional analysis consists of breaking gambling episodes into their precipitants (or triggers), and evaluating both the positive and negative consequences of the episode. By the time they enter treatment, most gamblers can identify negative aspects of gambling, such as loss of money, guilt, troubles at work or home, and depressed or anxious mood. While negative aspects are often overwhelming when one presents for treatment, the positive effects are what maintain the gambling behavior (Morasco et al., 2007). At times, especially during desperation phases when gamblers seek treatment, the positive effects of gambling may be difficult to identify. They may include excitement, a dream of winning big and changing one's life, and relief from boredom or anxiety. As gamblers identify the reasons for gambling, they can begin to consider other methods for achieving these same goals, via more realistic and less harmful approaches.

In conducting a functional analysis, the therapist will have the gambler describe the most recent gambling experience. For example, Judy's most recent trip to the casino resulted from an argument with her husband over the gambling debt (a top trigger identified in the previous session). The positive or rewarding effects of gambling for Judy in response to that situation included the possibility of winning money and avoiding the situation. The negative effects were losing another $500, having to come clean to Bob, who may be even angrier, and increasing thoughts of guilt. While Bob went away for three days after her most recent casino trip, Judy aggravated and worried the whole time he was away about his lecturing to her about the money lost and her irresponsibility. On her way to the grocery store on the day of Bob's return, Judy suddenly changed directions and headed toward the casino rather than going home and making dinner. In this manner, the negative effects of gambling (more lost money, being untruthful, worry, guilt, and potential of an even larger argument) lead directly to triggers for gambling.

Re-evaluating several gambling episodes in this manner can help us to better understand the patterning and the automatic nature of gambling. The triggers lead to gambling, which may have some transient beneficial results, but, more likely than not, leads to longer-term negative consequences. These negative consequences are often consistent with the triggers that precipitate gambling, and the vicious cycle of addiction occurs.

This case example provides an overview of the first two sessions of a structured CBT for PG that has been shown to reduce the number of days gambled, dollars wagered, and gambling severity scores, and to increase the likelihood of gambling abstinence (Petry et al., 2006). Six other sessions are described in detail (Morasco et al., 2007; Petry, 2005), and include increasing pleasant activities, brainstorming, handling cravings or urges to gamble, assertiveness training, correcting irrational cognitions, and a termination session that summarizes gains made in treatment and includes relapse-prevention techniques.

Summary and future directions

Psychological treatments for PG are beginning to be developed, refined, and tested. Initial studies suggest that cognitive and CBT approaches to PG show promise in reducing the symptoms of PG, as well as related psychosocial concerns. Future studies are needed to compare different treatment approaches to identify the most effective form of treatment for this disorder. Additionally, dismantling studies are needed to identify the essential ingredients in treatment for PG. For example, in their study of 84 pathological gamblers undergoing CBT, Morasco and colleagues (2007) suggest that the session focused on identifying cognitive distortions that promote PG may not be necessary for all participants because few clients report that automatic or distorted thoughts serve as triggers to gamble. In contrast, other studies clearly support the utility of examining cognitions when treating PG (Ladouceur et al., 2001, 2003; Sylvain et al., 1997). Further studies are needed to examine the specific aspects of cognitive and CBT that are most useful in reducing gambling and gambling-related problems.

While the presence of a comorbid psychiatric disorder or SUD is common among pathological gamblers, it is not clear whether the presence of a comorbid condition confounds treatment. While Petry and colleagues (2006) found that severity of psychiatric symptoms at baseline was not associated with outcomes from CBT, additional treatment strategies, such as more intensive treatment, should be tested for individuals with comorbid conditions or severe psychopathology.

In summary, PG is found in about 1 percent of the adult population across the world. PG is associated with numerous adverse consequences and comorbid disorders. The etiology of PG is multifaceted, genetic factors, individual factors, and life experiences all exerting influence on development. There is also reason for optimism regarding mental health practitioners' ability to intervene to reduce the consequences of PG. Psychological interventions, particularly cognitive and cognitive-behavioral treatments, appear to be efficacious in reducing the frequency and severity of gambling and related concerns.

References

Abbott, M. W., & Volberg, R. A. (2000). *Taking the Pulse on Gambling and Problem Gambling in New Zealand: A Report on Phase One of the 1999 National Prevalence Survey: Selections from Report No. 3 of the New Zealand Gaming Survey.* Wellington, New Zealand: Department of Internal Affairs.

American Psychiatric Association (1994). *Diagnostic and Statistical Manual of Mental Disorders* (4th edn). Washington, DC: Author.

Becona, E. (1993). The prevalence of pathological gambling in Galicia (Spain). *Journal of Gambling Studies, 9*, 353–369.

Burge, A. N., Pietrzak, P. H., & Petry, N. M. (2006). Pre/early adolescent onset of gambling and psychosocial problems in treatment-seeking pathological gamblers. *Journal of Gambling Studies, 22*, 263–274.

Cunningham-Williams, R. M., Cottler, L. B., Compton, W. M., & Spitznagel, E. L. (1998). Taking chances: problem gamblers and mental health disorders: results from the St. Louis Epidemiological Catchment Area (ECA) Study. *American Journal of Public Health, 88*, 1093–1096.

Dannon, P. N., Lowengrub, K., Musin, E., Gonopolski, Y., & Kotler, M. (2005). Sustained-release bupropion versus naltrexone in the treatment of pathological gambling. *Journal of Clinical Psychopharmacology, 25*, 593–596.

Dickerson, M., Hinchy, J., & Legg-England, S. (1990). Minimal treatments and problem gamblers: a preliminary investigation. *Journal of Gambling Studies, 6*, 87–102.

Echeburua, E., Baez, C., & Fernandez-Montalvo, J. (1996). Comparative effectiveness of three therapeutic modalities in the psychological treatment of pathological gambling: long-term outcome. *Behavioural and Cognitive Psychotherapy, 24*, 51–72.

Eisen, S. A., Lin, N., Lyons, M. J., Scherer, J. F., Griffith, K., True, W. R., et al. (1998). Familial influences on gambling behavior: an analysis of 3359 twin pairs. *Addiction, 93*, 1375–1384.

First, M. B., Spitzer, R. L., Gibbon, M., & Williams, J. B. W. (1996). *Structured Clinical Interview for DSM-IV Axis I Disorders, Clinician Version*. Washington, DC: American Psychiatric Press.

Gerstein, D. R., Volberg, R. A., Toce, M. T., Harwood, H., Johnson, R. A., Buie, T., et al. (1999). *Gambling Impact and Behavior Study: Report to the National Gambling Impact Study Commission*. Chicago, IL: National Opinion Research Center.

Hodgins, D. C., Currie, S., & el-Guebaly, N. (2001). Motivational enhancement and self-help treatments for problem gambling. *Journal of Consulting and Clinical Psychology, 69*, 50–57.

Hodgins, D. C., Currie, S., el-Guebaly, N., & Peden, N. (2004). Brief motivational treatment for problem gambling: a 24-month follow-up. *Psychology of Addictive Behaviors, 18*, 293–296.

Hollander, E., DeCaria, C. M., Mari, E., Wong, C. M., Mosovich, S., Grossman, R., et al. (1998). Short-term single-blind fluvoxamine treatment of pathological gambling. *American Journal of Psychiatry, 155*, 1781–1783.

Ibanez, A., Blanco, C., de Castro, I. P., Fernandez-Piqueras, J., & Saiz-Ruiz, J. (2003). Genetics of pathological gambling. *Journal of Gambling Studies, 19*, 11–22.

Jacques, C., Ladouceur, R., & Ferland, F. (2000). Impact of availability on gambling: a longitudinal study. *Canadian Journal of Psychiatry, 45*, 810–812.

Kim, S. W., Grant, J. E., Adson, D. E., & Shin, Y. C. (2001). Double-blind naltrexone and placebo comparison study in the treatment of pathological gambling. *Biological Psychiatry, 49*, 914–921.

Kim, S. W., Grant, J. E., Adson, D. E., Shin, Y. C., & Zaninelli, R. (2002). A double-blind placebo-controlled study of the efficacy and safety of paroxetine in the treatment of pathological gambling. *Journal of Clinical Psychiatry*, *63*, 501–507.

Ladd, G. T., & Petry, N. M. (2002). Gender differences among pathological gamblers seeking treatment. *Clinical and Experimental Psychopharmacology*, *10*, 302–309.

Ladd, G. T., & Petry, N. M. (2003). A comparison of pathological gamblers with and without substance abuse treatment histories. *Experimental and Clinical Psychopharmacology*, *11*, 202–209.

Ladouceur, R., Sylvain, S., Boutin, C., Lachance, S., Doucet, C., Leblond, J., et al. (2001). Cognitive treatment of pathological gambling. *Journal of Nervous and Mental Disease*, *189*, 774–780.

Ladouceur, R., Sylvain, S., Boutin, C., Lachance, S., Doucet, C., & Leblond, J. (2003). Group therapy for pathological gamblers: a cognitive approach. *Behaviour Research and Therapy*, *41*, 587–596.

Lesieur, H. R., & Blume, S. B. (1987). The South Oaks Gambling Screen (the SOGS): a new instrument for the identification of pathological gamblers. *American Journal of Psychiatry*, *144*, 1184–1188.

Lesieur, H. R., & Blume, S. B. (1992). Modifying the Addiction Severity Index for use with pathological gamblers. *American Journal on Addictions*, *1*, 240–247.

Lynch, W. J., Maciejewski, P. K., & Potenza, M. N. (2004). Psychiatric correlates of gambling in adolescents and young adults grouped by age at gambling onset. *Archives of General Psychiatry*, *61*, 1116–1122.

McConaghy, N., Blaszczynski, A., & Frankova, A. (1991). Comparison of imaginal desensitization with other behavioral treatments of pathological gambling: a two- to nine-year follow-up. *British Journal of Psychiatry*, *159*, 390–393.

McCormick, R. A., Russo, A. M., Ramirez, L. F., & Taber, J. I. (1984). Affective disorders among pathological gamblers seeking treatment. *American Journal of Psychiatry*, *141*, 215–218.

McLellan, A. T., Luborsky, L., Cacciola, J., Griffith, J., Evans, F., Barr, H. L., et al. (1985). New data from the Addiction Severity Index: reliability and validity in three centers. *Journal of Nervous and Mental Disease*, *173*, 412–423.

Morasco, B. J., Weinstock, J., Ledgerwood, D. M., & Petry, N. M. (2007). Psychological factors that promote and inhibit pathological gambling. *Cognitive and Behavioral Practice*, *14*, 208–217.

Petry, N. M. (2003a). Validity of a gambling scale for the Addiction Severity Index. *Journal of Nervous and Mental Disease*, *191*, 399–407.

Petry, N. M. (2003b). Patterns and correlates of Gamblers Anonymous attendance in pathological gamblers seeking professional treatment. *Addictive Behaviors*, *28*, 1049–1062.

Petry, N. M. (2005). *Pathological Gambling: Etiology, Comorbidity, and Treatment*. Washington, DC: American Psychological Association.

Petry, N. M., Ammerman, Y., Bohl, J., Doersch, A., Gay, H., Kadden, R., et al. (2006). Cognitive-behavioral therapy for pathological gamblers. *Journal of Consulting and Clinical Psychology*, *74*, 555–567.

Petry, N. M., & Steinberg, K. L. (2005). Childhood maltreatment in male and female treatment-seeking pathological gamblers. *Psychology of Addictive Behaviors, 19*, 226–229.

Petry, N. M., Stinson, F. S., & Grant, B. F. (2005). Comorbidity of DSM-IV pathological gambling and psychiatric disorders: results from the National Epidemiologic Survey on Alcohol and Related Conditions. *Journal of Clinical Psychiatry, 66*, 564–574.

Potenza, M. N., Xian, H., Shah, H., Scherrer, J., & Eisen, S. A. (2005). Shared genetic contributions to pathological gambling and major depression in men. *Archives of General Psychiatry, 62*, 1015–1021.

Productivity Commission (1999). *Australia's gambling industries: Report No. 10* (Vol. 1). Canberra, Australia: Author.

Scherrer, J. F., Xian, H., Krygeil-Kapp, J. M., Waterman, B., Shah, K. R., Volberg, R., et al. (2007). Association between exposure to childhood and lifetime traumatic events and lifetime pathological gambling in a twin cohort. *Journal of Nervous and Mental Disease, 195*, 72–78.

Shaffer, H. J., Hall, M. N., & Vander Bilt, J. (1999). Estimating the prevalence of disordered gambling behavior in the United States and Canada: a research synthesis. *American Journal of Public Health, 89*, 1369–1376.

Slutske, W. S., Eisen, S., Xian, H., True, W. R., Lyons, M. J., Goldberg, J., et al. (2001). A twin study of the association between pathological gambling and antisocial personality disorder. *Journal of Abnormal Psychology, 110*, 297–308.

Stewart, R. M., & Brown, R. I. (1988). An outcome study of Gamblers Anonymous. *British Journal of Psychiatry, 152*, 284–288.

Stinchfield, R. (2002). Reliability, validity, and classification accuracy of the South Oaks Gambling Screen (SOGS). *Addictive Behaviors, 27*, 1–19.

Stinchfield, R., Govoni, R., & Frisch, G. R. (2005). DSM-IV diagnostic criteria for pathological gambling: reliability, validity, and classification accuracy. *American Journal on Addictions, 14*, 73–82.

Sylvain, C., Ladouceur, R., & Boisvert, J.-M. (1997). Cognitive and behavioral treatment of pathological gambling: a controlled study. *Journal of Consulting and Clinical Psychology, 65*, 727–732.

Tavares, H., Martins, S. S., Lobo, D. S. S., Silveira, C. M., Gentil, V., & Hodgins, D. C. (2003). Factors at play in faster progression for female pathological gamblers: an exploratory analysis. *Journal of Clinical Psychiatry, 64*, 433–438.

Tavares, H., Zilberman, M. L., Hodgins, D. C., & el-Guebaly, N. (2005). Comparison of cravings between pathological gamblers and alcoholics. *Alcoholism: Clinical and Experimental Research, 29*, 1427–1431.

Volberg, R. A., Abbott, M. W., Ronnberg, S., & Munck, I. M. (2001). Prevalence and risks of pathological gambling in Sweden. *Acta Psychiatrica Scandinavica, 104*, 250–256.

Welte, J. W., Barnes, G. M., Wieczorek, W. F., Tidwell, M.-C., & Parker, J. (2001). Gambling participation in the U.S. – results from a national survey. *Journal of Gambling Studies, 18*, 313–337.

Wong, I. L., & So, E. M. (2003). Prevalence estimates of problem and pathological gambling in Hong Kong. *American Journal of Psychiatry, 160*, 1353–1354.

Chapter 9

Cognitive-behaviour therapy in medical illness

Michael Kyrios

Introduction

Cognitive-behaviour therapy (CBT) is an established evidence-based treatment for mental health problems such as depression and anxiety (Nathan & Gorman, 1998), but CBT strategies also constitute a useful approach for dealing with a range of challenges to human functioning (e.g., time management, problem-solving). More recently, CBT has been applied in the health area, not only in dealing with mental health problems derived from the experience of physical illness, but also in improving the management of health problems that require adherence to medical treatments and lifestyle change regimes. This has been particularly evident in the area of chronic medical illness, where mental health problems are prevalent and known to harm quality of life and physical well-being, and where treatment adherence is usually necessary to maintain maximum function and long-term health outcomes. The present chapter reviews the literature on CBT interventions in medical illness, and covers a range of practical issues related to treatment. The techniques and strategies described are applicable to a range of common physical disorders and, although the chapter will focus mainly on diabetes, other medical conditions will be mentioned briefly.

Important issues in the treatment of medical illness

The higher prevalence of mental health problems in individuals with chronic medical problems relative to the general community has been supported by numerous studies in a range of medical conditions including cancer, heart disease, hypertension, lung disease, neurological conditions, kidney failure, rheumatoid arthritis, and diabetes (Honda & Goodwin, 2004; Kalender, Ozdemir, Dervisoglu, & Ozdemir, 2007; Sharpe, Sensky, Timberlake et al., 2001; Verhaak, Heijmans, Peters, & Rijken, 2005). For instance, in a large-scale, cross-sectional study, Verhaak et al. (2005) reported greater distress among chronically medically ill patients than in a community sample, but found no differences between specific medical conditions. Moreover, poorer physical condition and psychosocial stress (e.g., relationship, job-related and financial problems) were found to increase the likelihood of a mental disorder in the chronically ill. With specific reference to diabetes, elevated anxiety and depression levels, as well as higher prevalence rates for major depression and anxiety disorders, have been reported (de Groot et al., 2001; Egede, Zheng, & Simpson, 2002; Grigsby, Anderson, Freedland et al., 2002; Kyrios, Nankervis, Reddy, & Sorbello, 2006; Lustman, Griffith, & Clouse, 1988).

The nature of the relationship between mental health and physical condition appears to be complex. For instance, in the diabetes literature, depression can result from two possible pathways: (a) biochemical changes directly related to the illness or its treatment; and/or (b) the psychosocial demands or psychological factors related to the illness or its treatment (Talbot & Nouwen, 2000). Significant associations between depression and a variety of diabetes-related complications (e.g., retinopathy, nephropathy, neuropathy, macrovascular complications and sexual dysfunction) have been reported from a meta-analysis (de Groot, Anderson, Freedland et al., 2001). Individuals with diabetes who have a history of depression are more likely to develop diabetic complications than those without depression (Ciechanowski, Katon, Russo et al., 2000), as those with diabetes complications are more likely to be depressed (Rubin & Peyrot, 2002). The chances of becoming depressed increase as diabetes complications worsen, with a linear association between the number of complications and the degree of depression (Carnethon, Kinder, Fiar et al., 2003; de Groot et al., 2001). Overall, severe depression is associated with poorer health outcomes (e.g., higher morbidity and mortality rates, functional impairment) and worse psychological outcomes such as social isolation and hopelessness (Egede, 2002; Goldney, Phillips, Fisher, & Wilson, 2004). Hence, in treating medically ill patients, it is important to assess psychological distress and to prioritize the treatment of mental health problems as a potential way to improve longer-term health and quality-of-life outcomes.

Figure 9.1 illustrates the interrelationships between illness-related features and both psychological and behavioural factors. Mental health problems constitute an important consideration in maximizing treatment adherence in chronic medical illness. Depression and anxiety may interfere with the requirements for self-management in chronic medical illnesses. For instance, effective management of diabetes involves a lifelong commitment to diet, exercise, medication, glucose monitoring and, in the case of type 1 diabetes, insulin injections. This treatment regimen facilitates the maintenance of acceptable blood glucose levels, alleviates the probability of short- and long-term difficulties (e.g., fatigue, lethargy, concentration problems, irritability, complications), and maximizes quality of life. Depression, however, can decrease motivation for adherence to effective management strategies. The influence of depression in non-compliance with medical treatment

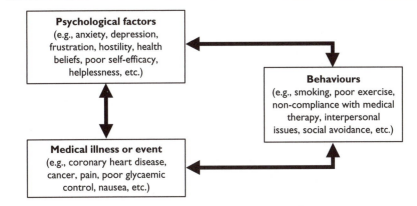

Figure 9.1 Relationships between illness-related, behavioural and psychological factors

has generally been supported (Ciechanowski et al., 2000; Di Matteo, Lepper, & Croghan, 2000). Significantly, average health-care costs in medical inpatients have been estimated as 46 per cent higher for depressed and anxious patients than for others (Creed, Morgan, Fiddler et al., 2002).

While several investigators suggest that factors such as disease duration are important in altering compliance and health outcomes in diabetes (Cleaver & Pallourios, 1994; Jacobson & Hauser, 1983), fluctuating glycaemic control or long-term complications can deplete emotional resolve and reduce self-efficacy, consequently lowering adherence (Rubin, Walen, & Ellis, 1990). Hence, successful treatment of chronic medical illnesses such as diabetes necessitates management of associated mental health problems, negative self-perceptions such as lowered self-efficacy, and fluctuations in treatment adherence. CBT interventions have been applied successfully to such issues.

Cognitive-behavioural models propose that it is not events or situations themselves that lead to maladaptive responses, such as psychological distress, but dysfunctional perceptions and subsequent consequences of reactions to those events or situations. Maladaptive responses reinforce dysfunctional cognitive styles or lead to unhelpful secondary appraisals and reactions. CBT is based on the premise that changing these maladaptive behaviours and dysfunctional cognitions will help alleviate distress and lead to more functional outcomes. Typically, patient problems are redefined in these terms, leading to the identification of changes that need to occur in behaviour and thinking in order to achieve specific identified goals (e.g., less frequent panic attacks in a cardiac patient, greater exercise adherence in a patient with diabetes, increases in activity levels and decreases in the focus on pain in an arthritic patient). Strategies are then developed in order to achieve the desired changes. CBT focuses on current problems, is time-limited, and emphasizes homework and out-of-session activities to reinforce within-session gains. CBT can be individualized, manualized or group-based. CBT programmes can be universal or focused on particular subgroups (e.g., depressed type 2 adolescents) or specific issues (e.g., poor glucose control). Further, CBT interventions can comprise active treatment, prevention or relapse prevention.

The main objectives of CBT include: (a) changing habitual behaviours and responses (i.e., by developing new helpful behaviours and phasing out unhelpful habitual responses to problematic situations; (b) increasing awareness and changing thinking in order to change responses to situations (e.g., by testing out old unhelpful and developing new helpful beliefs); (c) increased coping in feared situations by prolonged and repeated exposure to such situations, leading to habituation of anxiety reactions; and (d) improving life and coping skills (e.g., problem-solving, use of rewards, activity scheduling, time management, assertiveness, communication, adherence to desired treatment regimes, etc.).

There are multiple goals in most CBT programmes for medical illness with a range of problems and issues being targeted, including the following: (a) dealing with distress and symptoms of anxiety and depression; (b) improving how individuals cope with specific triggers of high arousal (situational factors, physiological factors); (c) decreasing maladaptive behavioural patterns (avoidance, inactivity and procrastination, non-adherence, safety mechanisms, reassurance-seeking, neutralizing, etc.); (d) increasing adaptive behaviours (e.g., treatment adherence, assertiveness); (e) improving cognitive patterns (e.g., increasing information and knowledge; decreasing distortions, biases, preoccupations, and catastrophizing; developing adaptive attitudes and beliefs); and (f) dealing with other issues, including co-morbidity (especially, anxiety and depression), lifestyle issues, family and personal issues (e.g., marital conflict, self-esteem), and skills deficits (self-efficacy, time management, problem-solving, assertiveness, anger management).

A range of intervention strategies are associated with CBT. Before presenting CBT tools that are useful in the management of medical conditions, the following section reviews outcome studies for specific illnesses.

A brief review of outcomes associated with CBT for medical illness

While there is a growing literature examining the effectiveness of CBT in medical illness, its quality and quantity vary across medical illnesses. Nonetheless, in general, psychological treatments have been shown to effect positive changes across various medical illnesses in a range of areas, including knowledge, adherence, mental health outcomes, coping strategies, quality of life, and illness-relevant physiological measures. However, while available evidence supports the effectiveness of CBT in improving psychological morbidity across a range of medical conditions, evidence for improving mortality is less consistent or unavailable. Universal and non-specific psychological interventions are less effective than focused pro-grammes, although they can constitute important public health interventions aimed at community change. Positive outcomes at the individual level are more likely with greater specificity regarding illness-relevant cognitive and behavioural factors. Patients who receive psychological therapy place fewer demands on medical services (Cummings, Dorken, & Henke, 1993) and cost savings estimated from 5 per cent to 80 per cent (Hunsley, 2003; Sobel, 2000).

From the diabetes area, CBT has consistently been shown to improve mental health or quality of life outcomes (Boyle, Allan, & Millar, 2004; Hains, Davies, Parton, & Silverman, 2000; Lustman & Clouse, 2002; van der Ven, Luback, Hogenelst et al., 2005), and to enhance treatment adherence (Méndez & Beléndez, 1997). A meta-analysis of group-based, diabetes self-management programmes that contain behavioural and cognitive change components (Deakin, McShane, Cade, & Williams, 2006) found evidence for significant reductions in physiological measures such as blood glucose control (including improvements in a physiological marker of long-term glycaemic control – HbA_{1c} levels), weight loss, and reduced systolic blood pressure. Lustman and Clouse (2002) undertook a follow-up study of CBT in depressed type 2 diabetic patients. HbA_{1c} levels were found to respond to CBT with a significant improvement at 6-month follow-up, compared to declines in glucose control for an educational programme. However, a systematic review and meta-analysis of randomized, control trials in type 2 diabetes concluded that, despite consistent significant improvements in psychological distress and long-term glycaemic control, weight control and short-term blood glucose concentration demonstrated only non-significant improvements (Ismail et al., 2004). Snoek and Skinner (2002) undertook a review of psychological treatments for problematic diabetes and concluded that CBT was effective in reducing depression and HbA_{1c}, stress management, eating disorders, and self-destructive behaviour in type 2 diabetes. Family therapy was also beneficial for the resolution of family conflict but did not necessarily affect glycaemic control.

Similar mixed results have emerged with other illnesses. For instance, some evaluations of psychological interventions with irritable bowel syndrome (IBS) report no significant effects in quality of life, depression, or anxiety (Bregenzer, Lange, Fürste et al., 2005; Larsson, Sundberg Hjelm, Karlbom et al., 2003), while others report improved coping (Maunder & Esplen, 2001; Mussell, Böcker, Nagel et al., 2003; Payne & Blanchard, 1995). With respect to physical outcomes, Payne and Blanchard (1995) reported that individualized CBT was associated with significant reductions in specific and overall gastrointestinal symptoms, which were maintained at 3-month follow-up, although group treatment did not differ from psychoeducation

(Blanchard, Lackner, Sanders et al., 2007). A large intervention study (Deter, Keller, von Wietershiem et al., 2007) found a significant decrease in days off work and frequency of hospital visits in psychotherapy and relaxation groups. Hence, psychological interventions can reduce health-care costs in IBS, despite ongoing psychological and physiological symptoms. Mixed results have also emerged from the rheumatoid arthritis area, where psychological interventions (e.g., relaxation, biofeedback, CBT) lead to positive results in a range of physical and functional areas compared with standard medical management (Astin, Beckner, Soeken et al., 2002; Sharpe et al., 2001, 2003). Evers, Kraaimaat, van Riel, and de Jong (2002) have also supported calls to customize CBT to individual needs in order to optimize its effectiveness.

In the cardiac area, psychological interventions have been shown to increase treatment adherence (Burke, Dunbar-Jacob, & Hill, 1997) and reduce medical costs compared with usual care and exercise (Blumenthal, Jiang, Babyak et al., 1997). However, findings of improvements in quality of life, levels of distress and depression, and cardiac events have been less consistent, possibly due to the heterogeneity of cardiac conditions and the lack of studies. Nonetheless, the principle of targeting specific groups with distinctive treatments may improve outcomes. For instance, Berkman, Blumenthal, Burg et al. (2003) examined whether mortality and recurrent infarction were reduced by treatment of depression and low perceived social support (LPSS) in patients enrolled within 28 days after myocardial infarction. Treatment consisted of CBT supplemented with antidepressants when indicated. Active treatment was more effective than treatment-as-usual for psychosocial outcomes at 6 months in depressed and LPSS groups. However, after an average follow-up of 29 months, there were no significant differences between usual care and active intervention due to the unexpected improvement in the usual care cohort.

Psychological interventions for cancer have become important given increasing numbers of patients with longer survival rates. Following a review, Fawzy, Fawzy, Arndt, and Pasnau (1995) concluded that structured interventions, consisting of health education, stress management and beha-vioural training, coping and problem-solving techniques, and psychosocial group support, offered the greatest potential benefit for patients in the early stages of treatment. They also supported the use of weekly group support for patients with advanced metastatic disease, with a focus on daily coping, pain management, and dealing with existential issues related to death and dying. Findings from evaluations of psychological interventions for cancer vary between components and cancer types. For instance, educational interventions (e.g., educational sessions, use of booklets, and audiovisual materials) are not considered sufficient to treat anxiety in cancer patients. However, psychological interventions to help patients deal with the demands of intensive medical treatments have been successful.

Behavioural treatments have been used to help reduce psychological stress and deal with the physical complications that stem from cancer and chemotherapy (e.g., anxiety, pain, nausea, vomiting). For instance, studies consistently support the use of relaxation and cognitive strategies in reducing the frequency, severity, and duration of anticipatory nausea following chemotherapy (Redd, Montgomery, & DuHamel, 2001).

The following sections examine a range of CBT interventions developed for chronic medical illnesses, and outline some specific tools and issues in relation to diabetes treatment.

Components and principles of CBT in treating chronic medical illness

The components of CBT vary between conditions, but include the following: (a) *psychoeducation*, whereby information about the disease, the process of coping, and available resources are provided; (b) *monitoring* of relevant health-related behaviours and cognitions; (c) *motivational interviewing* aimed at strengthening patients' commitment to change and treatment adherence; (d) *anxiety management techniques*, such as progressive muscle relaxation and controlled breathing, aimed at decreasing physiological arousal; (e) *cognitive and behavioural strategies* to identify and correct thoughts and behaviours contributing to the development and maintenance of negative mood states or other symptoms; (f) *relaxation and mindfulness-based techniques*, intended to decrease the degree of sympathetic arousal, and individuals' engagement and disturbance associated with events, thoughts, memories, mental images, and bodily sensations; (g) *interpersonal therapy*, which identifies and solves interpersonal problems; and (h) *skills training*, which seeks to help patients overcome deficits in areas such as problem-solving, anger/stress management, social skills, and communication.

Specific components are arranged in a variety of ways depending on the issues requiring attention (e.g., psychological adjustment and support, mental health, treatment adherence, management of physical well-being, etc.). Individualized focused treatments often lead to greater effects. For instance, CBT directly targeting cognitions associated with fears about loss of control and confidence in the management of complications may improve the effectiveness of anxiety management in diabetes (Boyle et al., 2004). There may be conflicts between patient-centred and clinician-centred goals. For instance, cancer patients may be more interested in discussing their fears of death and their experiences of chemotherapy-related nausea, whereas referral for psychological treatment may be related to panic attacks preceding chemotherapy or 'difficult' behaviour. Diabetic patients may be more concerned with discussing self-esteem than adhering to strict dietary, medication and blood glucose-testing regimes. There is firstly a need to undertake a thorough assessment of possible psychological issues and diagnoses, especially in light of findings that psychiatric and physical symptoms may mask each other. For instance, poorly controlled diabetes may present with fatigue or even hypoglycaemic attacks, which may be misdiagnosed as symptoms of depression or panic disorder, respectively. Alternatively, symptoms of depression may be masked by chronic hyperglycaemia. Most standardized measures of anxiety and depression are not sensitive to such distinctions. Furthermore, depressed or anxious affect is likely to be associated with cognitive features such as hopelessness, poor self-efficacy and low self-esteem. Furthermore, behavioural symptoms of psychological disorders are likely to be manifested in diverse ways for different individuals and medical conditions. In type 1 diabetes, depression may be manifested in low activity levels that lead to high blood glucose levels, while, in arthritis, patients' depression may be manifested in lower pain thresholds and greater reliance on pain medication. Initial sessions are likely to revolve around identification of such significant issues and developing treatment goals and priorities.

While it is important to identify and target specific maladaptive cognitions and behaviours, one also needs to consider the variance in patients' readiness and underlying motivations for change. It is generally agreed that there are six stages of change (Prochaska & DiClemente, 1983):

1   *Precontemplation*: During this stage, individuals are either preoccupied with their illness or deny the negative long-term health outcomes and the necessity for specific behavioural changes.
2   *Contemplation*: Patients become concerned about the long-term health consequences of their ongoing maladaptive adaptation and become aware of required behavioural and attitudinal changes.
3   *Preparation*: This is the 'turning point' where patients prepare for change by starting to make adaptive choices.
4   *Action*: During this stage, patients make changes they have chosen. Homework tasks are set and implemented. Support is usually required throughout this stage, as patients experience common feared short-term consequences of change (e.g., difficulties of organizing change, experiencing an immediate sense of loss over control, loss of current self-image, losing 'face', distress over losing predicted future outcomes, concerns about losing contact with one's usual social circle and activities, etc.). Therapists need to provide support and guidance or clear structure in order for required changes to occur. This is where CBT has many advantages over other treatment modalities, as it encompasses an inherent structure and tools to encourage graded change processes.
5   *Maintenance*: Patients attempt to maintain the changes they have made. While many adaptive behaviours are associated with contingencies that maintain them, use of self-rewards is helpful. Patients also need to be mindful of relapse risks and prevention strategies.

6   *Relapse*: During this stage, patients need to instigate the relapse plan that they have developed with their therapist. High-risk situations where relapse may be more likely are identified (e.g., during times of stress) and management strategies developed.

The central characteristic that drives change in individuals is their motivation. Motivation is defined as a patient's determination to change their behaviour, become actively involved in the treatment process, and make cogent adaptations for that process. As fears and uncertainties are associated with change, many patients experience a sense of ambivalence, but its resolution cannot be imposed on them. Motivational interviewing (MI) is a directive method that aims to elicit, explore, and resolve an individual's ambivalence regarding change (Rollnick & Miller, 1995). Miller, Rollnick, and colleagues (Miller & Rollnick, 2002; Miller, Rollnick, & Moyers, 1998) propose that the five basic principles of MI are as follows: (i) expressing empathy (e.g., 'I hear how difficult it has been for you'); (ii) avoiding arguments (therapists should avoid 'Yes, but . . .' responses); (iii) rolling with resistance (e.g., 'It sounds like it's still difficult to make a different decision'); (iv) supporting self-efficacy (e.g., 'That sounds like a good idea . . .', 'Let's see how that turns out . . .'); and (v) developing discrepancy (e.g., 'It sounds like you're saying option A has . . . advantages, while option B has . . . disadvantages'). It is particularly important to affirm patients' commitment to change by eliciting motivating statements relating to: (i) recognition of relevant issues ('You really have done well to acknowledge . . .'); (ii) expression of empathy and concerns ('That's a great insight . . .', 'You put that very well . . . I now understand'); (iii) expression of clear intentions (e.g., 'That's a very clear aim'); and (iv) expression of optimism for change (e.g., 'It's so helpful that you can be so positive'). Use of such counselling techniques may help enhance the therapeutic relationship, individuals' motivation to change, and agreement on the goals of therapy.

Motivation to change can be enhanced by systematically exploring the costs and benefits of continuing with particular dysfunctional behaviours or the consequences of failing to acquire new sets of functional behaviours. Patients tend to focus on the immediate costs associated with change, or overstate the benefits of and ignore the costs of continuing with current dysfunctional behavioural patterns. It is important to highlight the impact of continuing with unhelpful behaviours (e.g., interpersonal conflicts, immediate and long-term health costs, etc.). However, it is also imperative that there be acknowledgement of what patients feel they may lose if they stop current behaviours. Nonetheless, emphasis should be placed on helping patients become more aware of the real longer-term costs and benefits of change (e.g., the ability to enjoy greater quality of life for a longer time period). Once patients are convinced of the need for change, they are more likely to commit themselves to agreed courses of action, which may include a range of specific cognitive and behavioural strategies to target particular goals.

Monitoring in chronic medical illness

Assessment can include the use of monitoring strategies (e.g., diaries, structured monitoring sheets). The use of structured diaries is helpful in dealing with chronic medical illness where multiple factors are acting on patients. Such diaries increase awareness of illness-related factors, and behavioural and cognitive patterns that cause distress and decreased quality of life. Factors that require monitoring will vary from illness to illness. While activity, pain and mood levels may be relevant to conditions such as arthritis and migraines, physiological readings (e.g., blood glucose, blood pressure, and pulse), medication use (insulin doses, other medications), food and drink intake, exercise (type and amount), and mood ratings may be more relevant to diabetes. Table 9.1 outlines a typical monitoring sheet for someone with type 1 diabetes. The table illustrates the influence of maladaptive expectations about managing blood glucose control and mood problems. However, it also illustrates the usefulness of relaxation techniques and activity management in mood regulation and, ultimately, in enhancing an adaptive sense of control. In the initial stages of introducing the concept of monitoring, it is useful to keep such sheets simple. As patients build up a sense of confidence, more complex issues such as 'self-talk' can be introduced in order to consolidate links between behaviours, thoughts and feelings. At a later stage again, such sheets can incorporate planned activities.

CBT for diabetes

This section outlines two diabetes-related cases and possible psychological interventions. The first example is based on the case outlined in the monitoring sheet discussed above, while the second example summarizes a case described by Boyle et al. (2004).

Example 1

This 20-year-old man with type 1 diabetes presents with high anxiety and a sense of hopelessness based on a perfectionist drive for normal blood glucose levels, which, paradoxically, lead to erratic glycaemic control. Relaxation techniques and exercise were suggested for anxiety management and to distract him from negative ruminations. These also gave him a sense of adaptive control and undermined his hopelessness. A monitoring sheet was built up over three sessions and eventually provided evidence that

Table 9.1 Typical monitoring sheet examining health-related, mood and cognitive factors in diabetes

Day/ date	Time	Glucometer reading	Insulin dose (units)	Other medications	Food, drink	Activities (type, amount)	Blood pressure reading	Pulse	Mood rating 0 = most +ve, 10 = most −ve	Self-talk
Monday	8 am	10.5	8 Short-acting insulin (S)	Anti-hypertensive	2 pieces toast with sugar-free jam; coffee	Running late for work, no time to make lunch	190/120	65	Anxiety = 6 Hopeless = 8	Bad night. Blood sugars too high. Blood pressure out of control. Must get on top of everything today.
	1 pm		8 S		Ham sandwich (white bread and mayonnaise), apple pie, coffee, chocolate bar	Had quick lunch at work cafeteria			Anxiety = 8 Hopeless = 8	What's the point? I can't be bothered checking blood sugars. I'll have the pie and chocolate.
	5 pm	15.2	8 S		1 piece multigrain sourdough bread with cheese				Anxiety = 7 Hopeless = 8	Feel awful. I knew it would be a bad day. I just have myself to blame for making it worse. Feeling down.
	6 pm					Easy walk, 30 minutes			Anxiety = 3 Hopeless = 5	Feeling a bit better after walk. I should exercise more, even if I feel awful at the time.
	7 pm	5.5	11 S		Grilled fish, small potato, salad, 1 piece bread, cheese				Anxiety = 7 Hopeless = 6	Feeling in control again for the first time today. It's about time. I have to stay on top of it now; otherwise it will all have been in vain.
	9 pm	3.5			Apple, grapes				Anxiety = 8 Hopeless = 7	Blood sugars a bit low, but at least they are not still high. I'll have some grapes to get them up.
	10 pm	10.9	3 S 25 Long-acting insulin (L)	Anti-hypertensive		Relaxation tape	160/100	60	Anxiety = 4 Hopeless = 4	I'll never get control of these blood sugars! I've overshot again. Feeling stressed. I'll try relaxation.
	1 am	2.2			Sweets, banana				Anxiety = 9 Hopeless = 8	I'll never get it right. Why did I take the extra insulin? I'll be tired again tomorrow. It's just not fair.

safety behaviours (e.g., taking too much insulin, overeating) frequently drove the erratic blood glucose readings. He was eventually able to see the detrimental effects of his perfectionist expectations on driving such safety behaviours. A range of cognitive therapy techniques were used to deal with perfectionism. As part of the problem lay in the patient's inability to accept that he had diabetes, acceptance and mindfulness counselling techniques (Hayes, Follette, & Linehan, 2004) were used. The origins of his perfectionism were also explored, including high early parental expectations and a self-punitive approach to failing to meet such expectations in a range of areas in his life. MI counselling strategies were used to help the patient develop a formulation of his problems, which included self-imposed perfectionism as a core issue. As a result, he was able to commit himself to working on his perfectionism as a primary goal of psychological treatment. The Yerkes–Dodson Law was discussed as a way of demonstrating the relationship between self-imposed pressures and glycaemic control, and as a way of helping the patient understand that high degrees of perfectionism were detrimental to his overall health. He was eventually able to contemplate tolerating greater fluctuations in blood glucose readings. With medical advice, a number of behavioural experiments were set up whereby he was asked to tolerate higher blood glucose levels for longer periods of time than usual before instigating safety behaviours. He was also instructed to take lower doses of insulin than he had appraised himself as requiring during any hyperglycaemic episode, and to monitor the effects of the additional insulin after specified times. These interventions eventually led to better overall glycaemic control. Notably, these changes in attitude, behaviour, and glycaemic control were associated with reductions in levels of depression and hopelessness, and with greater adaptation in social, occupational and personal domains.

Example 2

Boyle et al. (2004) describe the case of a 37-year-old woman presenting with panic related to diabetes. A key feature was the misinterpretation of physical symptoms of anxiety as a sign of imminent hypoglycaemia, which she dreaded because of fears of loss of control and social humiliation. She would respond to these fears by using safety behaviour (in this case, eating inappropriately to increase blood glucose level). A CBT programme was designed to challenge the meaning of the feared panic sensations and to disprove predictions of loss of control and social humiliation in the context of experiencing hypoglycaemia. Two interventions were set up.

In the first intervention, the patient surrendered eating immediately after experiencing panic/hypoglycaemic symptoms and, instead, checked her blood glucose levels with a glucometer. A blood glucose cut-off point was established below which the patient was allowed additional food intake.

Symptoms experienced above that threshold were to be regarded as indicative of anxiety and managed with relaxation techniques. This intervention led to reductions in her belief that symptoms were due to hyperglycaemia and, to a lesser extent, reductions in the belief that loss of control would occur should a hypoglycaemic episode eventuate.

The second intervention closely targeted fears about loss of control and social humiliation in the context of experiencing hypoglycaemia. The patient was injected with enough insulin to allow a gradual blood glucose drop, which was monitored every 30 minutes, with cognitive ratings taken every 15 minutes on two beliefs, namely, that hypoglycaemia would lead to loss of control and the degree of confidence in recognizing and managing hypoglycaemia. The intervention led to marked reductions in these beliefs.

Overall, the interventions led to clinically reliable change in panic and anxiety, depression, and fear of hypoglycaemia, and 3-month follow-up scores on relevant measures were in the expected or normal range. Furthermore, blood glucose control had improved slightly and, importantly, had stabilized from previously erratic readings.

Conclusions

In recent years, cognitive and behavioural strategies have been applied to the health area, not only in dealing with mental health problems deriving from the experience of physical illness, but also in improving the management of health problems requiring adherence to lifestyle change regimes. This has been particularly evident in the area of chronic medical illness where mental health problems are prevalent and known to affect detrimentally quality of life and physical well-being, and where treatment adherence is necessary to maintain maximum function and long-term health outcomes.

CBT has consistently been shown to be effective in improving mental health functioning in individuals with medical illnesses. Less consistent, however, has been the establishment of improvements in health outcomes associated with CBT, although this varies from illness to illness. CBT programmes incorporating psychoeducation, modification of dysfunctional beliefs relating to self-efficacy and hopelessness, management of negative emotions, and enhancement of self-care practices have been shown to be beneficial. In particular, CBT that targets cognitions relating to specific aspects of presentation in medical illness may improve its effectiveness.

References

Astin, J. A., Beckner, W., Soeken, K., Hochberg, B., & Berman, B. (2002). Psychological interventions for rheumatoid arthritis: a meta-analysis of randomized controlled trials. *Arthritis and Rheumatism (Arthritis Care and Research)*, *47*, 291–302.

Berkman, L. F., Blumenthal, J., Burg, M., Carney, R. M., Catellier, D., Cowan, M. J., et al. (2003). Effects of treating depression and low perceived social support on clinical events after myocardial infarction: the Enhancing Recovery in Coronary Heart Disease Patients (ENRICHD) Randomized Trial. *JAMA*, *289*, 3106–3116.

Blanchard, E. B., Lackner, J. M., Sanders, K., Krasner, S., Keefer, L., Payne, A., et al. (2007). A controlled evaluation of group cognitive therapy in the treatment of irritable bowel syndrome. *Behaviour Research and Therapy*, *45*, 633–648.

Blumenthal, J. A., Jiang, W., Babyak, M. A., Krantz, D. S., Frid, D. J., Coleman, R. E., et al. (1997). Stress management and exercise training in cardiac patients with myocardial ischemia – effects on prognosis and evaluation of mechanisms. *Archives of Internal Medicine*, *157*, 2213–2223.

Boyle, S. Allan, C., & Millar, K. (2004). Cognitive-behavioural interventions in a patient with an anxiety disorder related to diabetes. *Behaviour Research and Therapy*, *42*, 357–366.

Bregenzer, N., Lange, A., Fürst, A., Gross, V., Schölmerich, J., Andus, T., et al. (2005). Patient education in inflammatory bowel disease does not influence patients knowledge and long-term psychosocial well-being. *Zeitschrift für Gastroenterologie*, *43*, 367–371.

Burke, L. E., Dunbar-Jacob, J. M., Hill, M. N. (1997). Compliance with cardio-vascular disease prevention strategies: a review of the research. *Annals of Behavioral Medicine*, *19*, 239–263.

Carnethon, M. R., Kinder, L. S., Fair, J. M., Stafford, R. S., & Fortmann, S. P. (2003). Symptoms of depression as a risk factor for incident diabetes: findings from the National Health and Nutrition Examination Epidemiologic Follow-up Study, 1971–1992. *American Journal of Epidemiology*, *158*, 416–423.

Ciechanowski, P. S., Katon, W. J., & Russo, J. E. (2000). Depression and diabetes: impact of depressive symptoms on adherence, function, and costs. *Archives of Internal Medicine*, *160*, 3278–3285.

Cleaver, G., & Pallourios, H. (1994). Diabetes mellitus: experiencing a chronic illness. *South African Journal of Psychology*, *24*, 175–183.

Creed, F., Morgan, R., Fiddler, M., Marshall, S., Guthrie, E., & House, A. (2002). Depression and anxiety impair health-related quality of life and are associated with increased costs in general medical inpatients. *Psychosomatics*, *43*, 302–309.

Cummings, N. A., Dorken, M. S., & Henke, C. (1993). *Medicaid, Managed Behavioral Health and Implications for Public Policy: Volume 2 Healthcare and Utilization Cost Series*. San Francisco: Foundation for Behavioral Health.

Deakin, T., McShane, D. T., Cade, J. E., & Williams, R. D. R. R. (2006). Group based training for self-management strategies in people with type 2 diabetes mellitus. *Cochrane Database of Systematic Reviews*, *2*.

de Groot, M., Anderson, R., Freedland, K. E., Clouse, R. E., & Lustman, P. J. (2001). Association of depression and diabetes complications: A meta-analysis. *Psychosomatic Medicine, 63*, 619–630.

Deter, H. C., Keller, W., von Wietersheim, J., Jantschiek, G., Duchmann, R., Zeitz, M., German Study Group on Psychosocial Intervention in Crohn's Disease (2007). Psychological treatment may reduce the need for healthcare in patients with Crohn's disease. *Inflammatory Bowel Diseases*, *13*, 745–752.

di Matteo, M. R., Lepper, H. S., & Croghan, T. W. (2000). Depression is a risk factor for non-compliance with medical treatment: meta-analysis of the effects of anxiety and depression on patient adherence. *Archives of Internal Medicine, 160*, 2101–2107.

Egede, L. E. (2002). Beliefs and attitudes of African Americans with type 2 diabetes toward depression. *Diabetes Educator, 28*, 258–268.

Egede, L. E., Zheng, D., & Simpson, K. (2002). Comorbid depression is associated with increased health care use and expenditures in individuals with diabetes. *Diabetes Care, 25*, 464–470.

Evers, A. W. M., Kraaimaat, F. W., Van Riel, P. L. C. M., & De Jong, A. J. L. (2002). Tailored cognitive-behavioral therapy in early rheumatoid arthritis for patients at risk: a randomized controlled trial. *Pain, 100*, 141–153.

Fawzy, F., Fawzy, N., Arndt, L., & Pasnau, R. (1995). Critical review of psycho-social interventions in cancer care. *Archives of General Psychiatry, 52*, 100–113.

Goldney, R. D., Phillips, P. J., Fisher, L. J., & Wilson, D. H. (2004). Diabetes, depression, and quality of life: a population study. *Diabetes Care, 27*, 1066–1070.

Grigsby, A. B., Anderson, R. J., Freedland, K. E., Clouse, R. E., & Lustman, P. J. (2002). Prevalence of anxiety in adults with diabetes: a systematic review. *Journal of Psychosomatic Research, 53*, 1053–1060.

Hains, A., Davies, W. H., Parton, E., & Silverman, A. H. (2000). Brief report: a cognitive-behavioral intervention for distressed adolescents with type 1 diabetes. *Journal of Pediatric Psychology, 26*, 61–66.

Hayes, S. C., Follette, V. M., & Linehan, M. M. (2004). *Mindfulness and Accept-ance: Expanding the Cognitive-Behavioral Tradition.* New York: Guilford Press.

Honda, K., & Goodwin, R. D. (2004). Cancer and mental disorders in a national community sample: findings from the National Comorbidity Survey. *Psychotherapy and Psychosomatics, 73*, 235–242.

Hunsley, J. (2003). Cost-effectiveness and medical cost-offset considerations in psychological service provision. *Canadian Psychology, 44*, 61–73.

Ismail, K., Winkley, K., & Rabe-Hesketh, S. (2004). Systematic review and meta-analysis of randomized controlled trials of psychological interventions to improve glycaemic control in patients with type 2 diabetes. *Lancet, 363*, 1589–1597.

Jacobson, A. M., & Hauser, S. T. (1983). Behavioral and psychological aspects of diabetes. In M. Ellenberg & H. Rifkin (eds), *Diabetes Mellitus: Theory and Practice* (3rd edn, pp. 1037–1049). New York: Medical Examination Publishing.

Kalender, B., Ozdemir, A. C., Dervisoglu, E., & Ozdemir, O. (2007). Quality of life in chronic kidney disease: effects of treatment modality, depression, malnutrition and inflammation. *International Journal of Clinical Practice, 61*, 569–576.

Kyrios, M., Nankervis, A., Reddy, P., & Sorbello, L. M. (2006). The relationship of depression to treatment adherence, quality of life and health outcomes in type 1 diabetes mellitus. *E-Journal of Applied Psychology (http://ojs.lib.swin.edu.au/index.php/ejap), 2*, 3–14.

Larsson, K., Sundberg Hjelm, M., Karlbom, U., Nordin, K., Anderberg, U. M., & Lööf, L. (2003). A group-based patient education programme for high-anxiety patients with Crohn's disease or ulcerative colitis. *Scandinavian Journal of Gastroenterology, 38*, 763–769.

Lustman, P. J., & Clouse, R. E. (2002). Treatment of depression in diabetes: impact on mood and medical outcome. *Journal of Psychosomatic Research, 53*, 917–924.

Lustman, P. J., Griffith, L. S., & Clouse, R. E. (1988). Depression in adults with diabetes. Results of a 5-year follow-up study. *Diabetes Care*, *11*, 605–612.

Maunder, R. G., & Esplen, M. J. (2001). Supportive-expressive group psychotherapy for persons with inflammatory bowel disease. *Canadian Journal of Psychiatry*, *46*, 622–626.

Méndez, F. J., & Beléndez, M. (1997). Effects of a behavioral intervention on treatment adherence and stress management in adolescents with IDDM. *Diabetes Care*, *20*, 1370–1375.

Miller, W. R., & Rollnick, S. (2002). *Motivational Interviewing: Preparing People for Change* (2nd edn). New York: Guilford Press.

Miller, W. R., Rollnick, S., & Moyers, T. B. (1998). *Motivational Interviewing* (6-tape series). Albuquerque, NM: University of New Mexico.

Mussell, M., Böcker, U., Nagel, N., Olbrich, R., & Singer, M. V. (2003). Reducing psychological distress in patients with inflammatory bowel disease by cognitive-behavioural treatment: exploratory study effectiveness. *Scandinavian Journal of Gastroenterology*, *38*, 755–762.

Nathan, P. E., & Gorman, J. M. (eds) (1998). *A Guide to Treatments That Work*. New York: Oxford University Press.

Payne, A., & Blanchard, E. D. (1995). A controlled comparison of cognitive therapy and self-help support groups in the treatment of irritable bowel syndrome. *Journal of Consulting and Clinical Psychology*, *63*, 779–786.

Prochaska, J. O., & DiClemente, C. C. (1983). Stages and processes of self-change of smoking: toward an integrative model of change. *Journal of Consulting and Clinical Psychology*, *51*, 390–395.

Redd, W. H., Montgomery, G. H., & DuHamel, K. N. (2001). Behavioral intervention for cancer treatment side effects. *Journal of the National Cancer Institute*, *93*, 810–823.

Rollnick, S., & Miller, W. R. (1995). What is motivational interviewing? *Behavioural and Cognitive Psychotherapy*, *23*, 325–334.

Rubin, R. R., & Peyrot, M. (2002). Was Willis right? Thoughts on the interaction of depression and diabetes. *Diabetes/Metabolism Research and Reviews*, *18*, 173–175.

Rubin, R., Walen, S. R., & Ellis, A. (1990). Living with diabetes. *Journal of Rational-Emotive and Cognitive-Behavior Therapy*, *8*, 21–39.

Sharpe, L., Sensky, T., Timberlake, N., Ryan, B., Brewin, C. R., & Allard, S. (2001). The efficacy of a cognitive-behaviour therapy programme as a treatment for recently diagnosed rheumatoid arthritis: preventing psychological and physical morbidity. *Pain*, *89*, 275–283.

Sharpe, L., Sensky, T., Timberlake, N., Ryan, B., Brewin, C. R., & Allard, S. (2003). Long-term efficacy of a cognitive-behavioural treatment from a randomized controlled trial for patients recently diagnosed with rheumatoid arthritis. *Rheumatology*, *42*, 435–441.

Snoek, F. J., & Skinner, T. C. (2002). Psychological counselling in problematic diabetes: does it help? *Diabetic Medicine*, *19*, 265–273.

Sobel, D. S. (2000). The cost-effectiveness of mind-body medicine interventions. *Progress in Brain Research*, *122*, 393–412.

Talbot, F., & Nouwen, A. (2000). A review of the relationship between depression and diabetes in adults: is there a link? *Diabetes Care*, *23*, 1556–1562.

van der Ven, N. C. W., Lubach, C. H. C., Hogenelst, M. H. E., van Iperen, A.,

Tromp-Wever, A. M. E., Vriend, A., et al. (2005). Cognitive behavioural group training (CBGT) for patients with type 1 diabetes in persistent poor glycaemic control: who do we reach? *Patient Education and Counseling, 56,* 313–322.

Verhaak, P., Heijmans, M., Peters, L., & Rijken, M. (2005). Chronic disease and mental disorder. *Social Science and Medicine, 60,* 789–797.

Chapter 10

Effective socialization in cognitive behaviour therapy: the Collaborative Interviewing in Mathematical Analogy Technique (CLIMATE)

Lefteris Konstadinidis, Panagiota Goga and Gregoris Simos

In the initial session(s) of cognitive behaviour therapy (CBT) clients usually ask questions such as, 'What is my problem?', 'Why doesn't this problem remit?', 'Is there a cure or solution to my problem?', and 'What is CBT?' At the same time, therapists ask themselves, 'Is this client motivated?', 'Is he suitable for CBT?', 'Will he be able to respond favourably to CBT?', 'What are his expectations from the therapist and this therapy?', 'Is he willing to try to take an active role in therapy?', or 'How possible is it that he will drop out of therapy?'

The socialization phase of CBT

Socializing the client into CBT and making clear what CBT is, are an integral part of any CB treatment. Socializing and educating the client about the cognitive model and also the nature of his problem is a very important step of treatment. In the beginning of therapy, it is very important for the client and the therapist to have a common understanding of the model that will be used during treatment (DeRubeis, Tang, & Beck, 2001). Quite often, this process has an additional therapeutic effect; for some clients, it may actually be the first time they have a good chance to understand their problems and see them from a very different and meaningful perspective. At the same time, the therapist instils hope and consequently enhances a given client's necessary motivation and willing collaboration in treatment. Nevertheless, CBT texts do not always give adequate emphasis to the socialization phase, and therefore many therapists mistakenly do not insist enough on this basic phase of CBT, and they also socialize the client very briefly (Kuehlwein, 2002).

Quite often, during this socialization phase of therapy, therapists provide the client with an information handout on his specific problem, as well as with a handout on CBT in general. Therapists also describe the cognitive model and recommend relevant bibliotherapy (DeRubeis et al., 2001; Leahy & Holland, 2000). But are all these approaches enough to socialize most of the clients in the therapeutic model? Although the above approaches are very useful, they sometimes seem very limited in their effect. On the other hand, a given client's psychopathology and personality, as well as his cognitive and intellectual abilities, decrease this effect even further. CBT uses a variety of cognitive techniques; cognitive techniques vary according to phase of treatment, the therapist's overall goals, or the therapist's specific goals from a given session (Leahy, 2003). Motivational techniques are also rarely used in this early phase of treatment (Miller & Rollnick, 2002). Although there are plenty of different cognitive techniques for different major or minor interventions, there is a relevant paucity in techniques corresponding to the early socialization phase in CBT. Collaboration between therapist and client is a *sine qua non* aspect of contemporary CBT. Although therapists routinely emphasize the importance of a collaborative therapeutic relationship, this aspect of therapy remains mainly verbal, at least at the first session. Active client involvement in such collaboration is not always achieved in this early treatment phase (Konstadinidis, Goga, Gouzaris, Lioura, & Simos, 2005).

Correlation between analogies, mathematics, philosophy, and CBT

Nothing happens in isolation in this world; consequently, our environment is full of metaphors of relationships and interactions (Burns, 2001). CB therapists use anecdotes, metaphors, short stories and analogies in their daily practice, when assessing suitability for treatment, challenging unhelpful styles of thinking, and addressing maintaining behaviours. The collaborative development of metaphors, stories and analogies can enhance rapport, help clients gain a new perspective upon their problems, increase personal impact and clarity of meaning, and reinforce clients' motivation to effect therapeutic change (Blenkiron, 2005).

If someone looks carefully, he will see that there is an analogy between CBT and mathematics. Mathematics is the science that is mainly concerned with and focuses on the solution of problems. CBT is problem-oriented, since it also focuses on problems in order to provide a client with alternative solutions to his distressing problems. The field of problem-solving corresponds directly to the science of mathematics, but problem-solving is a process very often incorporated in CBT (D'Zurila & Nezu, 1988). There are common keywords in CBT and mathematics (Konstadinidis, Goga, Simos, Nikolaidis & Gouzaris, 2003), such as 'problem', 'solution', 'problem-solving', 'collaboration', 'education and teaching', 'heuristic', 'homework', 'trying and effort', 'thinking', 'techniques', 'help' and 'learn'.

There is a connection between ancient Greek philosophy and mathematics, since mathematicians used to refer to philosophical methods and principles, while philosophers used to refer to mathematical-geometrical methods and principles. Many ancient Greek philosophers seem to have been inspired by Greek mathematics, and at the same time the science of mathematics was studied at their academies (Konstadinidis et al., 2003).

In Plato's *Meno* dialogue, Socrates, in order to prove that 'All I know is that I know nothing', used a geometrical paradigm with a servant boy. Socrates also proposes to Meno that if they are to investigate whether virtue is teachable or not, they must follow the way of the geometers – geometrical analysis – and he suggests that they somehow adapt this method for their own search (Beaney, 2003). The Socratic questioning and the dialectic methods are basic and sometimes difficult-to-apply principles of CBT (DeRubeis et al., 2001). The Socratic method constitutes a cognitive therapist's basic instrument; through questioning, a therapist helps a client to think. For this reason, the therapist uses memory, translation, interpretation, application, analysis, synthesis and evaluation questions (Bloom, 1956; Gross, 2002; Sanders, 1966).

The Socratic method is a heuristic method. Heuristics, or 'the art of solving problems', is the work of three men, Euclid, Apollonius of Perga, and Aristaeus the Elder, and it teaches the procedures of analysis and synthesis. Heuristics and heuristic problem-solving have been in use for centuries, and can be traced back to at least Socrates (469 BC) and Pappus (AD 300). They were also considered and used by scientists such as Descartes, Liebnitz, Bolzano, Mach, and Newton (Beaney, 2003).

The Greek method of analysis motivated many seventeenth-century mathematicians. Analysis is a method used by the Greek mathematicians to solve problems; analysis is a heuristic method too. The method of analysis and synthesis was made known in Europe by Pappus of Alexandria, a Greek mathematician who flourished at the end of the third century AD. According to the theory of analysis and synthesis, a solver's thought comprises a chain of reasoning or mediations. At the phase of synthesis, this chain proceeds from the hypothesis (or given data or facts) towards the conclusion (or solution); this phase is considered to be the final phase. Nevertheless, what usually comes first is the phase of analysis. During this phase, the solver makes an actually paradoxical hypothesis: what is to be concluded has already been found, and the solver tries to relate the solution to other more profound prerequisites; that is, he tries to relate his solution to possible variables that could have resulted in the conclusion. The final objective for the solver is to find a chain of mediations that arise from the conclusion and proceed towards the given data or facts, a chain that can be and consequently will be reversed in the phase of synthesis. Pappus reports that Plato was the first to develop the method of analysis (Beaney, 2003; Polya, 1945).

Plato is the best known of Socrates' students. If one root of modern conceptions of analysis lies in ancient Greek geometry, the other main root lies in the dialectic method that Socrates used in Plato's dialogues (Beaney, 2003). In his dissertation *Plato's Philosophical Use of Mathematical*

Analysis, Mark Andrew Faller (2000) defends the thesis that Plato employs methods of philosophical analysis that are akin to and based upon mathematical analysis. Plato was the inventor of geometric analysis, and the success of his philosophy is closely tied to a method of conceptual development that had been appropriated from mathematics (Faller, 2000). It is certainly not coincidental that at many of the junctures of explaining philosophical method, Plato makes references to specific problems in mathematics (Beaney, 2003).

Taking into consideration all of the above, we developed a technique that seems to be especially promising. This technique was especially welcome when we presented it in the form of a mini-in-congress workshop at the Congresses of the European Association for Behavioural and Cognitive Therapies in Manchester (Konstadinidis & Simos, 2004) and Thessaloniki (Konstadinidis & Simos, 2005).

We have called this technique 'CLIMATE'; an acronym derived from 'Collaborative Interviewing in Mathematical Analogy Technique'. However, CLIMATE is not simply a metaphor, a story or an analogy, but a procedure based on the theories of Socrates, Plato and Pappus. The technique was developed in order to achieve the following: (a) a successful socialization into CBT; (b) a client's motivation for therapy; and (c) the recruitment of a client's best possible collaboration. It is easy to apply the CLIMATE technique to everyday clinical practice and it takes approximately 19 minutes to complete.

During CLIMATE, the client works in the same way as in mathematics and follows the steps of analysis and synthesis. In the context of the stage of analysis, the client starts from the end – he assumes that there is a solution to his problems. Then, through Socratic questioning, he is guided to discover the steps that are necessary to solve his problems. Finally, in the context of the stage of synthesis, and in collaboration with the therapist, he is able to link the steps that give the solution to his problems with the corresponding CBT the therapist offers.

What is CLIMATE?

CLIMATE is a step-by-step analysis and synthesis of CBT through the Socratic method in the context of a mathematical analogy procedure. In accordance with the model of analysis and synthesis, the CLIMATE process asks the client to start from the solution of a problem, and through Socratic questioning the client is guided backwards in order to discover the basic and necessary steps to this solution. CLIMATE is a highly structured interview. This highly structured technique has the form of an interview between the therapist and the client, during which the therapist asks the client a series of 35 specific questions. Since the range of possible answers is rather restricted, what actually happens is that the therapist gets almost invariably the answer he anticipates. From its development up to its present form, CLIMATE has been revised several times. Unforeseen difficulties and idiosyncratic responses to this technique were appropriate cues for constant revision. CLIMATE or its precursors have been applied to a large variety of clients suffering also from a large variety of DSM mental disorders (more than 300 clients). Its present form seems to be quite applicable to all kinds of clients, regardless of their psychopathology, financial condition, or age. However, we found that clients with rather low intellectual ability have difficulties in following the CLIMATE process. Minor adaptations for these clients are therefore necessary.

The therapist applies CLIMATE after history taking and intake evaluation. First, the therapist gives the client the opportunity to summarize and at the same time clarify a series of important matters, by asking the following three questions:

- What is the client's request and what exactly does he ask from the therapist? What does the client want to achieve, in collaboration with him?
- Does the client believe that his problem can be solved?
- What has the client done until now to solve his problem?

The therapist writes down whatever the client answers, irrespective of his own assumptions about the client's problem. By doing so, the therapist clarifies the client's initial request and defines whether this request or expectation is a concrete or an obscure one. The therapist also clarifies the client's beliefs on the therapy outcome. Does the client believe that his problem can be solved or not? Finally, in this initial stage of CLIMATE, the therapist enquires what the client has done to solve his problem up to now. The above information is very important for the therapy outcome, because we have found that clients who have a concrete request, believe that their problems can be managed, or who exhibit even minor evidence of current adaptive management of their problems, are more eager to collaborate and are also more likely to remain in therapy (Konstadinidis et al., 2007). After this initial three-question stage, the therapist, through Socratic questioning, guides his client to think that there is a solution to his problems and that, in order to be able to find it, he has to become able to think in a realistic way and to take the appropriate steps towards the solution of his problems. Through this dialogue, the client finds that in order for him to solve his problems he has to acknowledge what his problems are, collaborate with his therapist in the context of CBT, and try to do his best on a rather constant basis. All the above are considered to be achieved in the context of CLIMATE and its 15 steps.

CLIMATE: interview

What follows is CLIMATE's structured interview; as mentioned above, it consists of 35 questions asked by the therapist in a specific order. The CLIMATE interview takes place at the end of the first session and constitutes both the beginning of formal cognitive therapy, and the socialization of the client into the therapeutic model that will follow. During the interview, the therapist writes down the client's answers in a specific 12-box form. Figures 10.1 and 10.2 present a blank form and a filled-in form, respectively.

The following interview comes from the initial session with a social phobia patient. The selection of this case report was due to the fact that this client responds to the therapist's questions in a way that matches the most commonly given answers, those answers that are actually anticipated by the therapist. For the reader's convenience, questions are numbered as Q1, Q2 . . . CLIMATE's steps are also given a name that actually specifies the process in hand.

An actual CLIMATE interview

First step: scrutiny

Therapist: (Q1a): Suppose that it's our last session. Please think and tell me, what would you like to have accomplished in therapy?

Client: There are three – four things actually! First of all, I would like not to be so anxious and to be more realistic and not so romantic in my relationships with women. Also, I would like not to be so embarrassed by women. Also, I would like to learn how to be more assertive and not to be submissive with friends and colleagues. Also, I would like to expand my social activities and to escape from daily routine.

Therapist: (Q1b): What exactly do you mean by the word 'escape'?

Client: To go for a drink or dinner with friends, to go fishing or to see a football match and to escape from work, not stay at home all day.

Therapist: (Q2): Do you believe that all these problems of yours can be solved in the context of our collaboration?

Client: Yes! Actually, I believe that they can be solved, but I don't know how this could be done.

Therapist: (Q3a): What have you done until now to solve these specific problems?

Client: I've tried to do some things occasionally, like going out for a drink by myself or with friends, but, as I said, occasionally.

Therapist: (Q3b): What do you usually do?

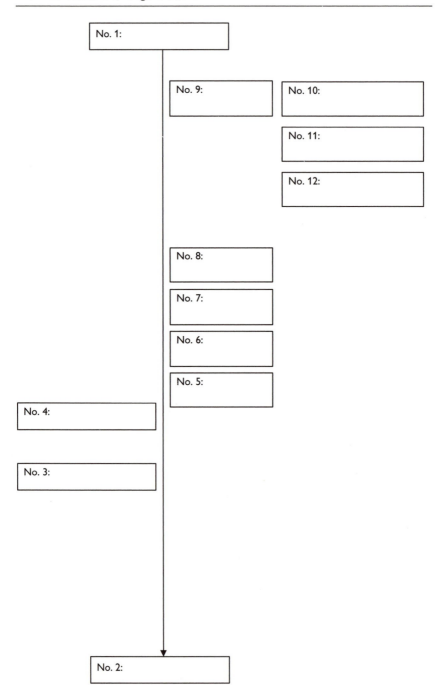

Figure 10.1 The CLIMATE form

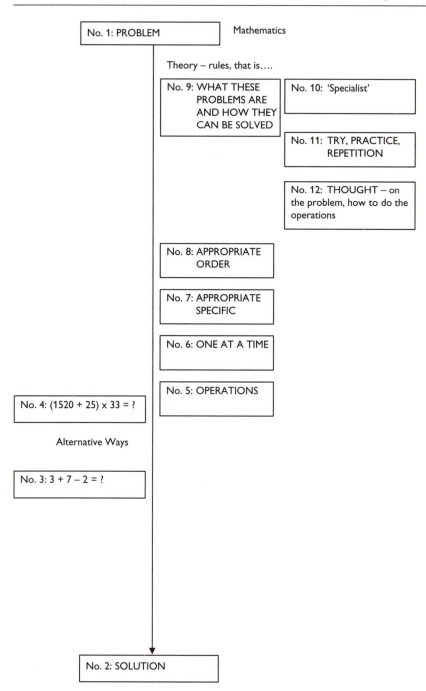

Figure 10.2 A filled-in CLIMATE form

Client: Actually, I don't do many things.
Therapist: (Q3c): What do you prefer to do instead of going out?
Client: Most of the time I prefer to stay at home. I avoid my problem.

Second step: retrospection – analogy principle

Therapist: (Q4): So, to summarize, you came here because of this. [The therapist writes the word 'PROBLEM' in box no. 1 of the CLIMATE form and shows it to the client.] Let's forget these specific problems for a while, and let's go, for a moment, back to the past and specifically to the high school years. I'd like you to think and tell me, what school subject centres upon problems. Please, do not think of a school subject you may have had problems with, but which subject had to do with problems.
Client: Mathematics. [The therapist writes the word 'mathematics' at the right side of box no. 1.]

Third step: there is a solution to the problem

Therapist: (Q5): As regards mathematics, what are we looking for in problems?
Client: The solution. [The therapist writes the word 'SOLUTION' in box no. 2.]

Fourth step: alternatives

Therapist: (Q6): Let us suppose for a moment that we have the exercise '3 + 7 – 2 = ?' [The therapist writes '3 + 7 – 2 = ?' in box no. 3.] What is the solution?
Client: It's eight.
Therapist: (Q7): Very well! What have you done in order to find the solution?
Client: I said, 'Three and seven equals ten, minus two equals eight.'
Therapist: (Q8): Very well! Suppose I say, 'Three minus two equals one, plus seven equals eight.' Is that wrong?
Client: No, it is the same.
Therapist: (Q9): Fine! Suppose I say, 'Seven minus two equals five, plus three equals eight.' Is that wrong?
Client: No, it is the same, too.
Therapist: [summarizes]: So in mathematics there is a solution to a given problem, and we can use alternative ways in order to find the same solution. [The therapist writes the words 'alternative ways' over box no. 3.]

Fifth step: action

Therapist: (Q10): Suppose we are in high school and the teacher in the classroom says, 'I would like you to solve the following exercise.' [The therapist notes in box no. 4 $(1520 + 25) \times 33 = ?$] I don't want you to solve it at once because our goal is not to learn mathematics, but, instead, tell me what you would do to solve it.

Client: I would do the addition in the brackets first and I would multiply the result by 33.

Therapist: (Q11): Very well! What are the additions and the multiplications called in mathematics terminology?

Client: Operations.

Therapist: (Q12): Very well! So you would do the operations. [The therapist notes in box no. 5 the word 'OPERATIONS'.] You said that you would do the addition in the brackets first and then the multiplication. Could you do both the operations at the same time?

Client: No. I would do one first and then the other.

Therapist: (Q13): [The therapist notes in box no. 6 the words, 'ONE AT A TIME'.] So, you will do your operations, but one at a time. Could you say, 'Come on, he asks me to multiply, but this is a difficult operation. I'd better subtract.' Would you get the right solution?

Client: No, I can't do this. The problem asks for multiplication.

Therapist: (Q14): So, you would do appropriate and specific operations to solve it. [The therapist notes in box no. 7 the words 'APPROPRIATE/SPECIFIC'.] Very well! Could you do the multiplication first and then the addition?

Client: No, that can't be done.

Therapist: So you would do the operations in a specific, more appropriate order. [The therapist notes in box no. 8 the words 'APPRO-PRIATE ORDER' and summarizes.] So, as you say, and I completely agree with you, the way to solve this problem is to do the appropriate specific operations, one at a time, and in an appropriate order. [The therapist at the same time shows the corresponding words he has written on the CLIMATE form.]

Sixth step: theory and learning

Therapist: (Q15): To get to the point of learning about such mathematical problems and knowing how to do the specific operations, what has to be learnt and known in general?

Client:	I have to learn the theory (or 'I have to learn the rules', or 'I have to learn how these operations can be done').
Therapist:	(Q16): Very well! So, you need to know the theory, the rules, and how these operations can be done. That means you have to know what these problems are and how they can be solved. [The therapist notes over box no. 9 the phrase, 'Theory – rules, that is . . .'], and inside the same box he writes the phrase, 'WHAT THESE PROBLEMS ARE AND HOW THEY CAN BE SOLVED'.] Where and how do you learn these specific things? Did you know them the moment you were born?

Seventh step: the necessity of a specialist

Client:	No, I didn't know them the moment I was born.
Therapist:	(Q17): How and where did you learn them, then?
Client:	I studied and learned them at school.
Therapist:	(Q18): Did you do it alone?
Client:	No, together with the teacher.
Therapist:	(Q19): Very well! You learned them in collaboration with the teacher. What teacher was it? The literature teacher?
Client:	No, the mathematician.
Therapist:	(Q20): So, there was a special teacher, the mathematician, that you collaborated with in order to learn how to solve such problems. [The therapist writes in box no. 10 the word 'Specialist'.] But was this enough? I mean, did the teacher do all the talking and you just instantly learned? Was there anything else necessary?

Eighth step: effort and repetition

Client:	No, I guess this was not enough. I also had to study and try. I had to practise.
Therapist:	(Q21): So, you say that the teacher's efforts were not enough. You say that it was also necessary for you to really want to do it and try to practise. But whenever you tried, did you try only once?
Client:	No, I did it several times.
Therapist:	[summarizes]: So, apart from the specialist's collaboration, what is also needed is your repeated efforts – you try again and again – so that you learn how to solve such mathematical problems. [The therapist writes in box no. 11 the words, 'TRY, PRACTICE, REPETITION.']

Ninth step: thought

Therapist:	(Q22): Suppose we are in high school. The teacher enters the classroom and asks you to do this specific exercise. [The therapist points to the exercise in box no. 4.] As for you, you have already collaborated with the mathematician, you have already made the relevant and necessary efforts, and you have already learnt how to solve such exercises. But the very moment you do these specific operations, do you also do anything else besides writing? [The therapist touches his forehead with his forefinger pretending he is thinking.]
Client:	Yes, I'm thinking.
Therapist:	(Q23): Are you thinking something like 'What am I going to eat tomorrow?' or 'I'd better not try because I won't solve it?'
Client:	No, I'm thinking about how to solve the problem, how to do the operations.
Therapist:	[summarizes]: Very well! So what is necessary for you to do is to think at the time you do the operations and focus on the problem. [The therapist writes in box no. 12 the words, 'THOUGHT – on the problem, how to do the operations'.]

Tenth step: rejection of the 'easy solution'

[From the tenth step and on, the therapist goes back to the CLIMATE form and shows his client the specific points he is referring to.]

Therapist:	(Q24): I have a query! Isn't there an easier way to solve this problem? Isn't there a way to bypass all this procedure, and nevertheless reach the same conclusion?
Client:	Mm . . . I guess that one can use a calculator . . . One can also ask someone else to solve the problem for them.
Therapist:	(Q25): Good. One can use both ways. But, could they learn how to solve such problems and would they be able to solve them any moment they show up? Could they also feel adequate enough to solve problems?
Client:	No, they wouldn't.
Therapist:	(Q26): How would they feel then?
Client:	Helpless or miserable.
Therapist:	[summarizes]: So, the easy solutions may 'solve' mathematical problems temporarily, but they make people feel helpless, and this isn't the best result.

Eleventh step: review

Therapist: (Q27): So, to summarize. For the mathematical problem in hand, if you don't do the appropriate and specific operations, one at a time, and in appropriate order, will it be solved?

Client: No.

Therapist: (Q28): If you don't think about the problem the moment you do the operations, will you be able to solve it?

Client: No.

Therapist: (Q29): If you have never learnt from a mathematician what these problems are and how they can be solved, if you don't try enough and you don't practise on similar problems, will you be able to solve them?

Client: No.

Therapist: [summarizes]: So, in mathematics, as you have told me, there is a solution to a given problem. In order for us to find such a solution, we may have to follow one of the probably more than one available alternative processes, and we have to do the appropriate operations, one at a time, and in the appropriate order. To accomplish this task, it is necessary to keep a problem-oriented way of thinking. It is also necessary that we have already learned from a teacher what these problems are and how they can be solved, and consequently we have taken the time to practise in the context of a continuous effort.

Twelfth step: analogy between mathematics and CBT

Therapist: (Q30): OK. Let's forget mathematics now and let's go back to your own problems. Real-life problems and psychotherapy are not, of course, mathematics, but, as we will see, there is a clear analogy between mathematics and the way we solve our real-life problems. Going back to your problems, would you say that your actions, your behaviours have helped you solve them?

Client: No, they usually do not help. Sometimes they make my problems worse.

Therapist: (Q31): Whenever you face such a problem, would you say that your way of thinking is helpful?

Client: No, on the contrary. Sometimes it brings the opposite results.

Therapist: (Q32): Has the use of the 'easy solution', and I mean your tendency to depend on others to solve the problem, or to avoid situations, brought the expected result?

Client: Sometimes it helped. Other times, things got worse.

Therapist: (Q33): Have you ever been to a 'specialist'? In case you had, has he made clear to you what your problems are and in what specific ways you can solve them? Having a clear identification and description of your problems is necessary in order for you and your therapist to follow an appropriate plan and also make appropriate and goal-directed efforts.

Client: I can usually imagine what my problems are, but I don't really know what they are.

Thirteenth step: socialization to CBT

Therapist: (Q34): So, there are your presenting, both short- and long-term, problems, and you and I, as a working team, will collaboratively try to identify clearly each problem of yours, and, by applying the principles we have seen to be useful in mathematics, we will try to find appropriate solutions. For this purpose, allow me to be the 'expert – the mathematician'. Both you and I should try to maintain a problem-oriented attitude in the context of what we call 'cognitive behaviour therapy'. The term 'cognitive' comes from the word 'cognition', which actually comes from the Latin word *cognosco* or the ancient Greek word *gignosco*, which means 'to learn and to know'. Cognitive therapy will provide you with all necessary means to allow you to take a more realistic stance toward your problems, that is, a more realistic way of thinking. This way of thinking will be the leverage to enable you to devise appropriate solutions and also implement them in an appropriate and effective way. The term 'behavioural', on the other hand, comes from the word 'behaviour' and involves techniques that will transform and guide your behaviour and actions towards the effective solution of your problems. To summarize, our objective, which is also an educational one, is for you to acquire a thinking and behaving pattern that will allow you to handle by yourself any present and future problems. Like being trained and competent in applying mathematics to solving problems, CBT will train you in accurately conceptualizing everyday life problems and devising and applying appropriate strategies to these problems. The process of CBT has a clear analogy with what we came across in filling in this form. [The therapist shows the CLIMATE form.] Is it clear what CBT is?

Client: Yes.

Fourteenth step: contract

Therapist: (Q35a): As you have already mentioned, and I completely agree with you, every problem has a solution, and quite often there is more than one way of solving it. Therefore, we will work together to discover the best applicable solutions. Nevertheless, there is one last thing: we have to choose among three important options! [The therapist counts slowly with his fingers and at the same time shows box no. 11.] 'We try, try, or try.' You have already mentioned that 'trying' is essential to solve simple mathematical problems, let alone more complex and substantial problems like yours.

Client: [surprise] And why did you mention it three times?

Therapist: (Q35b): Because I want to emphasize the importance of this part of the therapeutic process. So, you may think about it for a while, if you want, and let me know what you choose to do.

Client: [smiling] I'll try.

Fifteenth step: closure

On the therapist's initiative, therapist and client shake hands, giving thus a more official flavour to their collaboration. The therapist makes a final summary and gives the client a copy of the CLIMATE handout (Figure 10.3) and at the same time notes that the identification and reconceptualization of the client's problems could be a provisional item for the agenda of the next session.

The therapist also gives the client all relevant questionnaires as part of this week's homework, stressing that filling them in is a basic part of the overall effort. The therapist also gives an information handout of CBT in general. Bibliotherapy and any information specific to a client's presenting problem are usually given at the second session, after the therapist has educated the client about his problem.

What the therapist has to know and pay attention to

The application of any techniques has its inevitable difficulties and also requires flexible adaptation. In order for the therapist to foresee difficulties or minimize any difficulties during the CLIMATE application, there are certain points that a therapist has to pay attention to and take into consideration, as well as necessary adaptations. These are as follows:

•   What is the client's reaction (positive or negative) at the moment he sees or hears the word 'problem,' since there are times that clients do not like the term 'problem'? The therapist may use terms such as 'difficulties' or 'distress' instead, although for the sake of CLIMATE he has to adhere to 'problem(s)'. The therapist has to take care to be flexible enough towards the client's negative responses during the technique. During the first steps of the technique, some clients will

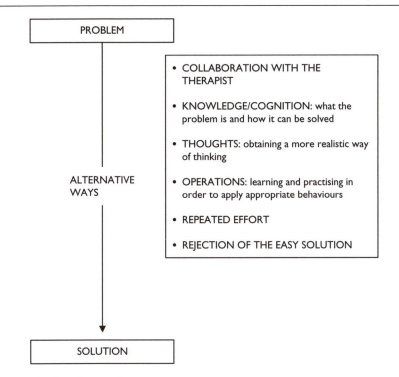

Figure 10.3 The CLIMATE handout

relate the mathematical example to their own problem and make a positive remark (e.g., 'Oh! I can understand now why we are doing this'), a remark that is rather in favour of the CLIMATE outcome.

- When a client cannot find an answer to a given question, the therapist asks the question again, more slowly and more expressively. When a client cannot find an answer to a given question even if the therapist has asked this question more than once, the therapist does not insist and gives the answer himself, not as a definite option, but rather as a possibility ('Might it be . . .?').
- The first steps of CLIMATE usually give the therapist useful hints about a given client's intellectual and educational level. For clients with a lower educational level (below secondary school), the therapist does not use the complex mathematical exercise. In that case, the therapist chooses a less difficult exercise for box no. 4, or he continues working with the first exercise (the one at box no. 3).
- If a client has difficulty in answering the fourth, fifth and sixth questions, the therapist quits the technique.
- It is necessary for the therapist to summarize from time to time. The therapist reviews what the client has said up to that moment in a way

that reinforces the already given answers and also highlights the client's adaptive way of thinking. At the same time, the therapist stresses the fact that the client comes to conclusions by himself and therefore the therapist responds with comments such as 'as you have mentioned and I fully agree with you', 'as you have found out', or 'as you have said'.

- The therapist responds to a client's answers (even if they are not what he expects or they are obviously out of context) in an empathic, non-critical and rapport-maintaining way. The therapist quite often makes a 'very well' or 'very good' response in order to reinforce and encourage the client's adaptive, problem-oriented, and concrete way of thinking. Psychotic clients who experience the rejection of their way of thinking as being illogical on a daily basis find through CLIMATE that their thoughts about the solution to their problem are accepted, something that reinforces further collaboration.

- Collaborative empiricism is an attitude that applies both to the therapist and the client. No matter how collaboratively and empirically oriented a therapist is, therapy will not progress if a client is unwilling to or cannot work in a similar way. The client's responses to CLIMATE provide the therapist with useful hints about a given client's attitude to therapy and the therapist. The client with answers such as 'I know what my problem is and how this can be solved', or 'My way of thinking helps me with my problems', or 'My way of acting helps me with my problems' will not probably stay in therapy, despite the therapist's efforts to introduce the possibilities of alternative beliefs and behaviours.

- In question 24, the therapist asks for 'easier' alternative and probably non-adaptive ways of solving the problem (use a calculator, ask someone else to solve the problem). Clients who are relatively more functional may not be able to answer this question, whereas clients who use 'easy' and 'on the spot' solutions (e.g., depend on others, rely heavily on safety/avoidant behaviours) are better able to provide the therapist with alternative options.

- In question/answer 25, the client agrees that using 'easy' solutions does not help him acquire problem-solving abilities and instead promotes personal inadequacy, something that consequently (question/answer 26) may make him feel 'helpless . . . miserable'. It is quite probable that at this part of the interview what the client really expresses is his own everyday life feelings, rather than the feelings of a person who is trying to solve a mathematical problem. At the same time, the therapist has the chance to see whether the client can express and focus on specific emotions (e.g., 'anxious', 'at a loose end', 'desperate') or expresses himself in more general, non-emotionally tuned terms (e.g., 'bad', 'lousy').

- There are two ways of solving the mathematical exercise [$(1520 + 25) \times 33 = ?$] we have chosen: (a) $1520 + 25 = 1545 \times 33 = 50,985$; (b) $1520 \times$

33 = 50,160, 25 × 33 = 825, 50,160 + 825 = 50,985. Regardless of the client's response, the therapist may choose to intervene and suggest that there is also an alternative procedure. Some clients argue that they could first do the multiplications and next the addition. The therapist agrees that this is another appropriate procedure to the solution of this problem, but it is certainly more complicated, as it requires more operations (two multiplications and an addition). If the client answers that we cannot do the multiplication first and then the addition, the therapist considers the client's answer as a right one, and goes on with the technique. Besides, the therapist's objective when using CLIMATE is not to teach the client mathematics. Sometimes clients devise more complicated, less profound, but still successful ways of solving it, such as {[(520 + 25 = 1545) × 3 = 4635] × 10 = 46,350} + 4635 = 50,985.

- CLIMATE is not appropriate for: (a) elderly and cognitively impaired people, (b) naive or uneducated people, or (c) overly psychotic, disorganized, disoriented or confused clients.
- Although CLIMATE implies that in order for us to learn how to solve problems we need an 'expert', the therapist takes every possible precaution not to behave and respond as '*the*' expert, but rather as an available and willing collaborator.
- Although the vast majority of clients find CLIMATE useful and the concluding remarks are invariably the same for almost any client, there are certain instances where the therapist may choose to adapt his process. Some variations of CLIMATE have been shown above. Nevertheless, there are additional remarks. When a client is psychotic, it is advisable that the therapist skip the 'contract' part of the process, in order for the client not to feel overwhelmed and consequently drop out of treatment. Had the client been moderately to severely depressed, somewhat confused or disorganized, or suffering from a severe personality disorder such as borderline personality disorder, it is better for the therapist to skip the contract part of the interview. Instead, the therapist may choose to emphasize the collaborative nature of CBT.
- Additionally, it is important to know that a very small number of clients say at the end of CLIMATE that their emotions or other problems are not mathematics. Although the therapist has already mentioned in the twelfth step that 'Real-life problems and psychotherapy are not, of course, mathematics', he fully agrees with the client and says that the purpose of the interview is to help the client understand, think and say by himself the way to solve his problems.

CLIMATE: benefits and conclusions

Most of our clients feel more comfortable when they know what to expect from therapy, when they fully understand their, as well as their therapist's, responsibilities and duties, and when they have a concrete request or expectation related to the therapy outcome. One of the therapist's basic aims is to present the treatment process in the most comprehensive and understandable way (Beck, 1995). CLIMATE's aim is to help both the client and the patient in this direction; in other words, we could just briefly say that CLIMATE sets the 'therapeutic climate'. As we have seen, this technique is applied at the very first session, and any client may achieve at this very first session a cognitive orientation towards or conceptualization of the nature of his problem(s) and what must be done in order for him and his therapist to solve it (them). At the same time, the client discovers, directly or indirectly, that the basic solution to his problem is CBT, irrespective of whether he follows it or not later on.

In general and taking into account the above interview, we argue that CLIMATE is useful, because it makes clear to a client the following:

• what the client's problems are and how they can be solved
• what CBT is
• what is the objective and the process of CBT are
• the collaborative role of the therapist
• the collaborative role of the client
• the nature of the therapeutic contract.

CLIMATE also makes clear to the therapist the following:

• the identification of a client's motivation for therapy
• the identification of a client's willingness for collaboration
• the identification of a client's suitability for CBT.

This technique is also useful in the achievement of the therapist's basic goals, which are as follows:

• to develop a general cognitive conceptualization of the client's problem
• to develop a collaborative therapeutic relationship
• to educate the client about his problems in general
• to introduce the CBT model
• to help the client recognize that he, as well as the therapist, is responsible for any personal change
• to help the client develop optimism about CBT
• to help the client begin to understand that his maladaptive thoughts and behaviour do not always help.

In one of our studies (Konstadinidis et al., 2005), we investigated the relationship between the application of CLIMATE and consequent treatment dropout from CBT, and we found that CLIMATE can be useful as a minimizing factor of dropout from CBT. We administered CLIMATE to 142 clients with a variety of DSM-IV diagnoses just after their intake and evaluation interview (CLIMATE group, n = 142). These clients were compared with a control group of 142 age- and gender-matched clients with a variety of DSM-IV diagnoses who were not administered CLIMATE (non-CLIMATE group, n = 142). There were non-significant age differences (CLIMATE: 31.7 years, SD = 11.2; non-CLIMATE: 29.8 years, SD = 9.8, F = 2.32, P = 0.128) or male–female ratio differences (CLIMATE male/female: 63/79; non-CLIMATE male/female: 62/80). What we found was that proportionally more clients from the non-CLIMATE group dropped out of treatment, and this difference was statistically very significant (P < 0.001). Our current CLIMATE research is focused on the following: (a) the identification of significant demographic and clinical variables that may predict responses to specific CLIMATE questions and the implication that these relationships may have on treatment outcome; (b) the CLIMATE–other variables interaction that may lead to consequent dropout; and (c) the impact that CLIMATE may have on the outcome of CBT.

References

Beaney, M. (2003). Analysis. In E. N. Zalta (ed.), *Stanford Encyclopedia of Philosophy*. http://plato.stanford.edu/archives/sum2003/entries/analysis/ (accessed 1 July 2007).

Beck, J. S. (1995). *Cognitive Therapy: Basics and Beyond*. New York: Guilford Press.

Blenkiron, P. (2005). Stories and analogies in cognitive behaviour therapy: a clinical review. *Behavioural and Cognitive Psychotherapy, 33*, 45–49.

Bloom, B. (1956). *Taxonomy of Educational Objectives: The Classification of Educational Goals*. New York: Longmans, Green.

Burns, G. W. (2001). *101 Healing Stories: Using Metaphors in Therapy*. New York: Wiley.

DeRubeis, R. J., Tang, T. Z., & Beck, A. T. (2001). Cognitive therapy. In K. S. Dobson (eds), *Handbook of Cognitive-Behavioural Therapies* (pp. 349–392). New York: Guilford Press.

D'Zurila, T. G., & Nezu, A. M. (1988). Problem solving therapies. In K. S. Dobson (ed.), *Handbook of Cognitive-Behavioural Therapies* (pp. 211–245). New York: Guilford Press.

Faller, M. A. (2000). *Plato's Philosophical Use of Mathematical Analysis*. Athens, GA: University of Georgia Press. http://polar.alaskapacific.edu/mfaller/mfaller phd3.pdf (accessed 1 July 2007).

Gross, R. (2002). *Socrates' Way: Seven Keys to Using Your Mind to the Utmost*. New York: Tarcher/Putnam.

Konstadinidis, L., Goga, P., Gouzaris, A., Lioura, T., & Simos, G. (2005, September). CLIMATE as a factor predicting dropout in CBT. Poster presentation at the 35th Annual Congress of the European Association for Behavioural and Cognitive Therapies, Thessaloniki, Greece.

Konstadinidis, L., Goga, P., Simos, G., Nikolaidis, N., & Gouzaris, A. (2003,

September). 'Mathematical logic': an introductory step-by-step analysis and synthesis of CBT using a mathematical paradigm. Poster presentation at the 33rd Annual Congress of the European Association for Behavioural and Cognitive Therapies, Prague. Book of Abstracts, p. 127.

Konstadinidis, L., Goga, P., Simos, G., Nikolaidis, N., Gouzaris, A., & Lioura, T. (2007, June). Is the client suitable for cognitive behaviour therapy? Poster presentation at the V World Congress of Behavioural and Cognitive Therapies, Barcelona.

Konstadinidis, L., & Simos, G. (2004). Collaborative Interviewing in Mathematical Analogy Technique (CLIMATE): Socializing the patient into CT using step-by-step analysis and synthesis technique. *In-Congress Mini Workshop at the 34th Annual Congress of the European Association for Behavioural and Cognitive Therapies*, Manchester, UK.

Konstadinidis, L., & Simos, G. (2005). Effective socialization in CBT. *In-Congress Mini Workshop at the 35th Annual Congress of the European Association for Behavioural and Cognitive Therapies*, Thessaloniki, Greece.

Kuehlwein, K. T. (2002). The cognitive treatment of depression. In G. Simos (ed.), *Cognitive Behaviour Therapy: A Guide for the Practising Clinician*, vol. 1 (pp. 3–48). Hove, UK: Routledge.

Leahy, R. L. (2003). *Cognitive Therapy Techniques – A Practitioner's Guide*. New York: Guilford Press.

Leahy, R. L., & Holland, S. J. (2000). *Treatment Plans and Interventions for Depression and Anxiety Disorders*. New York: Guilford Press.

Miller, W. R., & Rollnick, S. (2002). *Motivational Interviewing* (2nd edn). New York: Guilford Press.

Polya, G. (1945). *How to Solve It: A New Aspect of Mathematical Method*. Princeton, NJ: Princeton University Press.

Sanders, N. (1966). *Classroom Questions: What Kinds?* New York: Harper & Row.

Chapter 11

Homework assignments in cognitive behavior therapy

Nikolaos Kazantzis and Jeanne Daniel

The notion of 'learning through doing' has been a guiding principle of cognitive therapy since its inception (Beck, Rush, Shaw, & Emery, 1979). The guiding principles of 'outward focus' and 'collaborative empiricism' require that we consider the therapy room analogous to the laboratory, and that the everyday situations and relationships in which the patient's problems exist represent an opportunity to gather data to test beliefs (Blackburn & Twaddle, 1996). In this way, homework extends what was discussed in-session, and provides an opportunity for data collection, skill practice and maintenance, as well as evaluation of situational, cross-situational, and core-level beliefs. Homework is a core and not an optional part of cognitive therapy. The implication is that a therapy that does not include homework cannot be considered cognitive therapy (Thase & Callan, 2006).

Homework often includes providing a list of cognitive distortions and dysfunctional thought records to help patients to record thoughts, physiological sensations, and emotions. With practice, patients proceed with full thought records that provide opportunity to identify negative automatic thoughts, evaluate evidence and generate alternatives to their thoughts, and generate balanced alternatives to alleviate distress. Behavioral experiments are powerful tools to build alternative explanations for beliefs that have a peripheral or central role in the etiology and maintenance of presenting problems. Reduction of compensatory strategies associated with underlying assumptions, rules, and intermediate beliefs are also achieved through behavioral experiments and graded task assignments. Although these types of homework are often represented in cognitive therapy for a range of clinical problems, the selection of tasks is ideally tailored according to the individualized cognitive conceptualization. The range of tasks that can be assigned for homework is vast; the key elements are that they are focused on the patient's goals and targeted on evaluation of unhelpful cognitions. In broad terms, homework can be defined as any out-of-office activity discussed with the therapist and intended to have a therapeutic effect if undertaken during therapy (Kazantzis, 2005).

In this chapter, we briefly outline the theoretical and empirical basis for homework in the practice of cognitive therapy. The main portion of the chapter will discuss clinical case examples to demonstrate the effective design of homework (i.e., task selection based on a generic model and individualized conceptualization), assignment of homework (i.e., collaboration on the pragmatics of completing the task), and review of homework assignments in cognitive therapy. Emphasis will be placed on the therapeutic collaboration and cognitive conceptualization in the integration of homework assignments into therapy. Several recommendations for the supervision of cognitive therapists' practice will also be included. The benefit of using the cognitive conceptualization to examine the therapist's own beliefs, emotions, and behaviors in using homework will be discussed on the basis of our work in clinical supervision. The foundation for this material is primarily Aaron T. Beck's (1976) cognitive theory and system of psychotherapy. Guidelines are also drawn from the recent 'Guiding Model for Practice' by Kazantzis, MacEwan, and Dattilio (2005), designed to make explicit the processes for the effective integration of homework in Beckian cognitive therapy, also called cognitive behavior therapy (CBT) (Beck et al., 1979).

Behavioral and cognitive theory determinants of engagement

The reasons for using homework in CBT and the explanations for patient engagement in those tasks are based on behavioral and cognitive theory (Kazantzis & L'Abate, 2005, 2007). The trigger to apply a technique between sessions is often environmental stimuli, such as difficult interpersonal interactions, exposure to distressing objects and situations, and the patient's personal experience of emotional distress (with or without clearly identified precipitants). At the same time, the benefits of activities, such as engaging in activities associated with mastery and pleasure, interpersonal interaction, and gathering information to evaluate beliefs, provide immediate contingencies for engaging in homework activities. The patient's decision to engage in the task depends not only on recognizing these antecedents and consequences, but also on the capacity to overcome any practical obstacles that may be involved in its completion. Thus, classical and operant conditioning processes provide a foundation for clinicians' understanding of how adaptive behaviors can be practiced and maintained.

The process of using homework directly involves the patient's belief system. According to various social cognition theories, the patient's thoughts about the task when it is first presented in-session represent important clinical markers for determining whether the patient will engage with the task (Bandura, 1977, 1989; Stretcher, Champion, & Rosenstock, 1997). When a patient engages in homework tasks, increases in personal mastery and progress towards goals facilitate the reduction in unhelpful thinking and the production of lasting cognitive change. Therefore, the opportunity to have some in-session practice and experience of the benefits of the assignment is paramount. Similarly, patients' predictions about their readiness, willingness, and confidence to engage in the homework once the specifics have been collaboratively discussed at the end of the session, and their synthesis of the actual experience once attempted between sessions, further determine engagement with tasks (Conoley, Padula, Payton, & Daniels, 1994; Dunn, Morrison, & Bentall, 2006; Miller & Rollnick, 2002).

The centrality of the cognitive conceptualization to CBT filters through all aspects of the therapy, and is essential for the effective integration of homework. The aforementioned beliefs at each stage of using homework can be expected to make sense in the context of the patient's belief system. For example, patients with helplessness schema (i.e., the core beliefs, 'I am powerless', 'I am vulnerable', 'I cannot cope') will benefit from careful design of achievable homework that they have the opportunity to practice repeatedly in-session. Patients with failure schema (i.e., 'I am a failure', 'I am not good enough') will benefit from a gradual progression from home-work tasks that provide an early success experience before moving to more challenging tasks. Patients with social desirability schema and unrelenting standards may also experience activation of their beliefs system in not wanting to displease the therapist or 'fail' the assignment (Beck, 2005; Persons, 1989). Given that the homework may itself trigger the patient's belief system, the therapist should seek patient feedback about their beliefs about the task in designing, assigning, and reviewing homework. The central role of the conceptualization in the effective use of homework is further discussed in the case study below.

Empirical data to support the use of homework

Homework assignments have been the focus of increased empirical investi-gation. The majority of the existing research addresses the causal and correlational effects, with symptom reduction assessed at termination. First, the data demonstrate that homework produces small-sized effects in trials where therapies are contrasted with and without homework. Second, the data show that compliance with homework is positively associated with symptom reduction (see review by Kazantzis, Deane, & Ronan, 2000). These findings have been demonstrated in a variety of populations, including individuals suffering mood disorders (Addis & Jacobson, 2000; Bryant, Simons, & Thase, 1999; Burns & Nolen-Hoeksema, 1991; Burns & Spangler, 2000; Coon & Thompson, 2003; Kazantzis, Ronan, & Deane, 2001; Neimeyer & Feixas, 1990; Persons, Burns, & Perloff, 1988; Startup & Edmonds, 1994) and anxiety disorders (Leung & Heimberg, 1996; Rees, McEvoy, & Nathan, 2005; Schmidt & Woolaway-Bickel, 2000). Studies have also examined couples in treatment (Holtzworth-Munroe, Jacobson, DeKlyen, & Whisman, 1989) and patients with psychotic symptoms (Bailer, Takats, & Schmitt, 2002; Dunn et al., 2006) and cocaine dependence (Carroll, Nich, & Ball, 2005; Gonzalez, Schmitz, & DeLaune, 2006).

The processes by which homework helps to reduce symptom distress, increase functioning, and facilitate cognitive changes have not been carefully studied. In addition, existing conceptual frameworks attempting to explain what leads patients to complete homework assignments (Detweiler & Whisman, 1999; Malouff & Schutte, 2004) have not comprehensively considered the behavioral and cognitive theory determinants of engagement with homework (Kazantzis, Dattilio, & McEwan, 2005). The data to guide practitioners' use of homework have been gathered in isolated studies without a guiding theoretical framework. Nevertheless, there are clear patterns that emerge when the findings are reviewed as a group.

Table 11.1 presents a summary of those process findings and shows that there are meaningful therapist, patient, and in-session factors associated with compliance with homework. A limited number of studies have sought to examine the degree of skill acquisition (i.e., quality of homework completion) as a predictor of outcome. Since patients may regularly complete homework without experiencing benefit or changes in beliefs, we advocate increased focus on skill acquisition and the theoretically meaningful determinants of engagement with homework (Kazantzis, Deane, & Ronan, 2005).

In this first part of the chapter, we have summarized the theoretical and empirical support for homework in CBT. Homework has been evaluated and can be considered an important and necessary feature of CBT. Engagement with homework increases a patient's chances of benefit from therapy. While there has been increasing research attention to this aspect of CBT process, there is reason to believe that greater connection with the theory foundations undergirding this aspect of Beckian cognitive therapy would provide an evidence base to support the process for integrating homework into clinical practice.

A model for using homework in CBT

The process of integrating homework into therapy can be delineated into three steps: (a) designing (or selecting) tasks; (b) discussing the specifics of how the homework will be carried out; and (c) reviewing homework. In this manner, a framework for integrating homework – regardless of the presentation of and interactions between patients' highly individualized arrays of historical and contemporary contextual features, therapy goals and problem lists, under- and overdeveloped behavioral strategies, case conceptualization, and diagnosis – is interwoven throughout each individual session and the more significant time between sessions. The model is presented in

Table 11.1 Summary of process research on homework

Study	n	Sample	Main finding
Therapist behaviors			
Bryant et al. (1999)	26	Depression	Therapist competence in reviewing homework predicted compliance
Cox et al. (1988)	30	Mixed	Making a written note of the homework assignment predicted compliance
DeRubeis & Feeley (1990)	25	Depression	A factor representing use of 'concrete' or symptom-focused interventions was associated with symptom reduction early, but not later in therapy; homework was one of the interventions in this factor
Detweiler-Bedell & Whisman (2005)	24	Depression	Therapist behaviors in designing homework (setting concrete goals and discussing barriers to homework completion) predicted outcomes
Shaw et al. (1999)	53	Depression	Therapist competence on the structuring factor of the CTS (i.e., agenda, homework, pacing) predicted outcomes
Worthington (1986)	61	Mixed	Involving patients in homework assignments early in therapy, some prior history of homework adherence, and therapist's checking patient's attitude predicted adherence
Patient factors			
Edelman & Chambless (1993)	56	Social phobia	Symptom severity associated with homework compliance
Edelman & Chambless (1995)	52	Social phobia	Patient dependency traits as well as high levels of symptomatology predicted homework compliance
Fennell & Teasdale (1987)	34	Depression	Demoralization 'depression about depression' associated with a more rapid response to CBT and homework adherence
Neimeyer & Feixas (1990)	63	Depression	Impact of homework adherence greatest for those with high initial BDI scores
Persons et al. (1988)	70	Depression	Impact of homework adherence greatest for those with high initial BDI scores
In-session factors			
Addis & Jacobson (2000)	150	Depression	Early and midtreatment compliance with homework associated with acceptance of treatment rationale
Burns and Nolen-Hoeksema (1991)	307	Depression	Pretreatment willingness to try a coping strategy predicted symptom reduction; homework compliance added a separate contribution to symptom change

continues overleaf

Table 11.1 Continues

Study	n	Sample	Main finding
Burns & Nolen-Hoeksema (1992)	185	Depression	Global rating of therapist empathy was independently associated with treatment response and did not influence homework adherence
Conoley et al. (1994)	37	Mixed	Patient beliefs regarding the difficulty of the task, match with goals, and designing tasks that used patients' strengths, predicted compliance
Dunn et al. (2006)	29	Schizo-phrenia	Therapeutic alliance predicted homework compliance
Fennell & Teasdale (1987)	34	Depression	Early treatment response correlated with patients' positive responses to initial homework assignments (Coping with Depression booklet) and completion of homework between second and third weeks of therapy
Leung & Heimberg (1996)	104	Social phobia	Homework compliance early in therapy predicted compliance in the final stages of therapy
Woody & Adessky (2002)	53	Social phobia	Decreased compliance with increasing therapeutic alliance as treatment progressed
Skill acquisition			
Bogalo & Moss-Morris (2006)	31	IBS	Quality of homework completed correlated with outcome
Carroll et al. (2005)	60	Cocaine dependence	Quantity and quality of coping skills
Gonzalez et al. (2006)	123	Cocaine dependence	Homework compliance in combination with readiness to change predicted less cocaine use during treatment
Neimeyer & Feixas (1990)	63	Depression	Quality of homework (thought record) positively correlated with outcome
Schmidt & Woolaway-Bickel (2000)	48	Panic disorder	Quality of homework (exposure) positively correlated with employment status (greater with unemployment) and outcome
Woods et al. (2002)	82	Mixed anxiety	Quality of homework (SUDS during exposure) negatively associated with outcome

This table presents a representative summary of the CBT process research related to homework compliance. Readers are directed to Kazantzis et al. (2000) for a summary of the research on the relationship between homework compliance and treatment outcome.
BDI: Beck Depression Inventory; CTS: Cognitive Therapy Scale; IBS: irritable bowel syndrome; SUDS: Subjective Units of Distress Scale.

the following subsections with particular emphasis on the therapist behaviors that increase patients' engagement with homework tasks.

Case outline

Mary, a 62-year-old divorced woman, lived alone and was estranged from her two adult children. She sought therapy because she had been reprimanded at work for frequent absences and was concerned that she would lose her job as a travel agent. Her father had left the family when Mary was 6 years old. Mary's mother had long-standing alcohol use, was diagnosed with liver disease, and died when Mary was 19 years old. Mary was required to provide care for her mother in the time leading up to her death, and she described her mother's parenting style as 'rejecting, cold, and physically abusive'.

In the 8 months prior to therapy, Mary said she had been 'depressed' and described a predominantly sad mood with some anxiety, tearfulness, difficulty with early waking from sleep, reduced appetite, and reduced interest and pleasure from activities, as well as difficulties with focusing on tasks and making decisions. She noted that she was withdrawing from social interaction and her level of alcohol consumption had increased. Specifically, she was drinking at least 6 glasses of wine per night, and would increase this to 10 glasses on weekends. After an evening of heavy drinking, Mary often vomited and felt nauseous the next day. Her absences had been steadily increasing during the past 4 months, and in the month prior to therapy, she had missed 1 day of work per week.

At intake, Mary's completed various psychometric measures: Beck Depression Inventory – Revised (Beck, Steer, & Brown, 1996; score 24 – moderate), Beck Hopelessness Scale (Beck, 1988; score 11 – moderate), State Trait Anxiety Inventory – State (Spielberger, 1983; score 62nd percentile compared to nonclinical female norms in her age group), and Dysfunctional Attitude Scale (DAS) (Weissman & Beck, 1978; score 198 – depressed). Her therapist completed the Hamilton Rating Scale of Depression (HRSD) (Hamilton, 1967; score 30 – severe) and Suitability for Short-Term Cognitive Therapy Scale (SST) (Safran, Segal, Vallis, Shaw, & Samstag, 1993; score 40 – suitable) at intake.

Selecting/designing homework tasks

In the first instance, homework tasks should be drawn from generic cognitive models that are relevant to the patient's presenting problem(s). Mary's therapist presented the activity schedule (Beck et al., 1979) to investigate the link between situations, distressing emotions, and cognitions serving as triggers for her binge drinking. Many therapies for substance abuse, including those targeting relapse prevention (Dimeff & Marlatt,

1995) and coping skills training (Monti, Kadden, Rohsenow, Cooney, & Abrams, 2002), integrate an adapted activity schedule (see also Apodaca & Monti, 2007; Najavits, 2005). The therapist's objective was to obtain more detailed information regarding her activities throughout the day, the fluctuations in her emotions, and the frequency, intensity, and duration of drinking behavior.

By exploring the patient's perceptions of a particular task, unhelpful beliefs about an assignment may be discovered in advance and worked through collaboratively. Such a discussion can result in a variation of the task that fits with the patient's perceived ability to complete it.

Mary's initial response to the activity schedule was that 'it is too complex' and 'I won't be able to complete it.' In this instance, it was useful to ask Mary to use this situational conceptualization diagram to capture her emotional, physiological, and cognitive experience before and after in-session practice of the activity schedule. As illustrated in Figure 11.1, the activity schedule enabled Mary to test her prediction that she would not be able to complete it, while at the same time providing an opportunity to practice the new skill. Using Socratic dialogue, the therapist guided Mary to arrive at the conclusions that 'I have previously worked through therapy forms', 'When things initially seemed quite overwhelming to me, I could break them down into component parts, and ask for assistance.'

As a general rule, discussing with the patient the rationale for a particular assignment provides an opportunity to increase motivation to complete the homework. This includes a discussion of how the task will provide clinical benefit and the extent to which the benefits outweigh the costs (e.g., financial cost, time commitment, exposure to unpleasant emotions and physiology, re-engaging with activities and social interaction). Homework tasks should also be aligned with the patient's specific treatment goals. Mary's long-term objective was to maintain her employment, and her specific therapy goal was to relieve tension in her relationships with work colleagues, which she considered strained by emotional fluctuations associated with the 'hangover' effects of heavy drinking. Thus, the rationale for the activity schedule was further expanded by noting that it would provide insight on patterns to her drinking, and guide the application of interventions to address drinking.

Therapists should ensure there is sufficient time in the therapy session agenda to enable in-session practice of the homework. The initial practice provides the opportunity for the patient to ask questions about the task, and clarify what is required and how it will assist them. The experience of the task's benefits contributes to motivation and consolidates the rationale. If in-session practice is not feasible or appropriate, the therapist can guide the patient to complete the task by using imagery for a hypothetical scenario, or, in the case of interpersonal interactions, engaging in a role-play with the therapist.

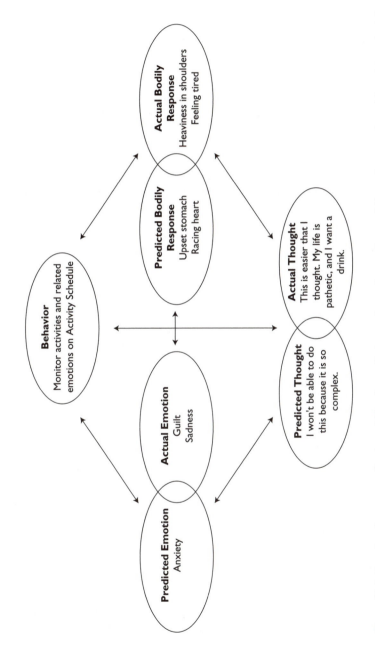

Figure 11.1 Situational conceptualization of Mary's prediction and actual experience of in-session practice with activity schedule

Mary's therapist began by helping her fill in the activity schedule for the current day through the session time. Mary initially found the recordings for activities, emotion, and urges to drink difficult and cumbersome, so further practice to capture Mary's experience on the previous day enabled Mary to experience a degree of mastery in completing the task. Mary was then guided, through imagery, to rehearse how she would continue to add information to the form later that evening.

Negotiating the specifics (assigning) homework tasks

In setting the agenda for the session, a portion of time should be allocated to the end to discuss the specifics of how the homework task(s) will be carried out. This provides an opportunity for patients to discuss concerns about abilities or difficulties related to the task, and express their beliefs about performing the task. As there may be several homework tasks assigned in any given session, it is useful to allocate 10 or 15 minutes at the end of the session to collaborate on specifics. The patient and therapist can consider any ongoing tasks (e.g., ongoing thought records and positive data logs) in the context of 'new' homework tasks linked to the present therapy session. This discussion should be collaborative, and include explicit discussion regarding when, where, and how often the task will be performed and how long it will take. The patients are the expert on their own daily/ weekly schedule, so this process requires a large amount of facilitation from the therapist, but the patient can ultimately be required to judge what will be reasonable and practically possible in the context of their existing commitments. In addition, brainstorming a list of practical obstacles that may interfere with completion, and problem-solving how these might be averted or resolved will help ensure that the patient is prepared to undertake the task.

Reviewing homework tasks

Review of homework should occur early on the agenda of each therapy session. Not only does this display respect for the time and energy the patient has spent engaging in a task, but it also conveys that homework is an important part of therapy. It is necessary to review the amount of homework carried out and to understand the patient's difficulties or decision not to complete the entire assignment, but also to review the *quality* of homework completion (or degree of learning). The patient's actual completion of a homework assignment, both in terms of quantity and quality, can be facilitated by using a process of successive approximation so that small, achievable portions of the skills can be shaped to a more complex skill. The intrinsic benefits gained through these smaller achievements and the ultimate acquisition of the overall task will determine the extent to which the behavior or skill is maintained.

The patient should be praised for any aspect of the homework that has been completed. Of course, patients will synthesize their experience of the homework prior to the session, and will have their own intrinsic sense of pleasure, mastery, and sense of progress toward their therapeutic goals. Thus, the therapist can quickly move to asking the patient about their synthesis from the learning task, and genuinely focus on the fact that the patient was responsible for the gains achieved. This review should include Socratic questioning to reveal the conclusions the patient may have gained regarding beliefs or behaviors that maintain his or her problems, the extent to which a particular assignment contributed to the patient's hypothesis-testing skills, and how – or if – the patient perceives that an assignment has provided movement toward his or her individualized treatment goals.

With the use of a situational conceptualization, such as that shown in Figure 11.1, the therapist can assist the patient in clarifying the cues or triggers for completion as well as the patient's beliefs about the homework. In conjunction with the case conceptualization diagram, as shown in Figure 11.2, the therapist can make sense of noncompletion and the beliefs that underlie recurrent unhelpful behaviors. Conceptualizing homework behaviors protects against falling into an interpretive therapeutic stance, where partial or whole homework noncompletion might be viewed as 'resistance' or 'transference' to the therapist (see discussion in Rudd & Joiner, 1997). Maintaining a collaborative therapeutic relationship that aims to take account of the patient's worldview is crucial when reviewing homework. Sometimes obstacles to homework are simply obstacles.

A review of homework early in the session also provides an opportunity to assess difficulties and to synthesize the patient's learning before proceeding to other agenda items. In many instances, the agenda for the session refines or extends the work for homework. In other instances, the work done between sessions alters the priorities for the session agenda.

When working with Mary, the therapist utilized all of the above strategies when reviewing homework. Mary and her therapist spent sessions 1 and 2 on the skills to identify and distinguish her emotions on a visual analogue scale. Mary had considerable difficulty in finding words to describe her emotional experience, and had difficulty in rating emotional intensity. Mary arrived at session 3 having completed the assigned homework, which in the first instance involved rating several situations for the degree of 'sad', 'guilty', and 'angry' feeling, but still had difficulty in appreciating the gradation in her emotions. Thus, the initial speed of therapy was slower than initially anticipated as a function of Mary's existing coping strategy to avoid emotions and distract herself by drinking and engaging in various other unhelpful behaviors. Without such careful attention and adjusting the pace of therapy according to the patient's skill level, the activity schedule

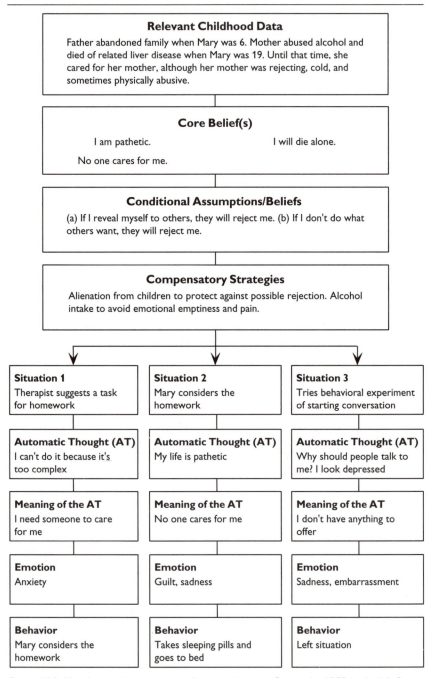

Figure 11.2 Mary's cognitive conceptualization diagram. Copyright 1993 by Judith S. Beck, Ph.D. Adapted with permission from *Cognitive Therapy: Basics and Beyond* by Judith S. Beck, 1995, Guilford Press

may have been introduced too soon, and the necessary foundations for thought records may not have been sufficiently well laid.

In this second part of the chapter, we discussed specific therapist behaviors for enhancing engagement with homework assignments in therapy. We emphasized the role of the individualized cognitive conceptualization in each stage of selecting (designing), planning (discussing specifics), and reviewing homework. We recommended that basic CBT conceptualization be combined with Socratic questioning and guided imagery. To facilitate therapist skill and mastery in integrating homework into therapy by making the process more explicit, we summarized the specific behaviors in the 'therapist quick reference' (Figure 11.3).

Therapist beliefs about homework

Homework assignments represent a feature of all CBT sessions, and as outlined above, require that the therapist 'adhere' to recommended guidelines. Consequently, the same behavioral and cognitive theory determinants of adherence that help us understand patients' adherence to between-session homework tasks can assist our understanding of the therapist in using homework. There are at least two broad classes of therapist beliefs that require attention in this context, namely, therapist beliefs about the process of using homework in therapy, and therapist beliefs about the patient's level of engagement with homework.

Some data suggest that therapist beliefs about the process of using homework in therapy are related to their use of homework. Data gathered in a survey of German psychologists ($n = 140$; Fehm & Kazantzis, 2004) and in a random sample of North American psychologists ($n = 827$; Kazantzis, Lampropoulos, & Deane, 2005) show a clear link between therapists' self-reported beliefs and practices. Specifically, CBT therapists were more likely to use homework assignments if they considered homework a process that facilitates the acquisition of adaptive skills and increases patient awareness, and if they considered homework helpful in promoting sustained long-term benefit, and in enhancing a patient's sense of mastery, self-control, or self-efficacy. Not surprisingly, those less likely to use homework considered the process to overemphasize a directive therapist style, place unrealistic expectations on patients, not benefit therapeutic outcomes, and undermine the natural learning process.

The process of integrating homework into therapy is often rushed, poorly executed, or forgotten. Some novice therapists engage patients in a cursory discussion at the end of the session, 'prescribing' or 'assigning' the patient homework without the opportunity for discussion, in-session practice, or adequate planning. If such an approach is typical of a therapist's practices, it suggests that there are therapist beliefs relevant to homework requiring attention. For some therapists, this behavior is explained by a belief that

Quick Reference Summary of Model for Practice*

1. HOMEWORK REVIEW	2. HOMEWORK DESIGN	3. HOMEWORK ASSIGNED
• Discuss Non-Completion and Quantity and Quality of Completion	• Guided Discovery to Identify Coping Strategies and Beliefs	• Ask Client to Summarize Rationale in Relation to Therapy Goals
• Provide Verbal Reinforcement for any Portion Carried-Out	• Use Disorder Specific Cognitive Model and Individualized Conceptualization	• Collaborate to Specify How the Task Will be Practically Possible (i.e., when, where, how often, and how long it will take)
• Situational Conceptualization to Identify Beliefs about the Consequences to Homework (i.e., synthesis of learning)	• Collaboratively Select Tasks	• Consider Potential Difficulties (i.e., link to obstacles identified during review)
• Use Individualized Conceptualization to Make Sense of Non-Completion	• Present a Rationale and Aligns with the Client's Treatment Goals	• Emphasize Learning 'Experiment' Focus
• Problem-Solve Obstacles	• Ask about Client's Ability and Perceived Task Difficulty	• Ask Client to Summarize Task and Obtain Rating of Readiness, Importance, and Confidence (renegotiate if < 70%)
• Record Homework Completion in Session Notes	• In-Session Practice of Task	• Make a Written Note of the Homework for the client (or use Homework Form)
	• Guided Imagery to Begin Experiential Learning	
	• Situational Conceptualization to Identify Beliefs and Situational Triggers	

Figure 11.3 Therapists' quick reference. Copyright 2005 by Nikolaos Kazantzis, Frank Deane, and Kevin Ronan. Adapted from *Using Homework Assignments in Cognitive Behavior Therapy* edited by Nikolaos Kazantzis, Frank Deane, Kevin Ronan, and Luciano L'Abate, 2005, Routledge

'the session is the therapy' or 'the work in-session is where the main adaptive changes occur'. We encourage these therapists to view homework *as therapy*, and test their assumptions by placing greater emphasis on homework.

Other therapists experience difficulties in selecting homework assignments. They typically miss opportunities to link the new task with the patient's goals or the patient's existing coping strategies. Patients often have completed various activities in the past that either carry the concept of learning through between-session practice (e.g., noticing that children learn new skills; learning an art or craft; reading about home renovation, gardening, or car repair work; studying at college or university; business coaching; or sports training), or those that carry similar aims and intentions to techniques of CBT (e.g., keeping a diary of thoughts and emotions, writing pros and cons, setting goals, problem-solving, trying new behaviors). We encourage therapists to assign only homework that is relevant to the patient's therapy goals and framed so that it aligns with existing coping strategies.

The most common difficulties that therapists experience in using homework assignments relate to their own beliefs and emotions when patients either partially, or wholly do not complete their homework. Some therapists experience activation of their own core beliefs about their abilities as a therapist, their patients, or the effectiveness of the therapy when therapy does not proceed as planned (Bennett-Levy et al., 2001; Leahy, 2001). When working with Mary, the therapist encountered a number of negative automatic thoughts at session 10 after the first thought record had been assigned.

Mary had just sold her house, and was currently in the process of relocating to be closer to her two adult children. She presented for the therapy session having read a self-help chapter on cognitive restructuring, but left the thought record until the day prior to the session, and had only attempted one thought record. On the thought record, Mary identified the thoughts, 'I'm not able to do this', 'What is the use of this form?', and 'Why is life so unfair?', said she was 'irritated with the therapist', and explained, 'I don't see the point of doing this!' Her therapist experienced frustration with Mary's level of engagement with the homework, and reverted to completing a situational conceptualization to capture patient thoughts, emotions, physiology, and behaviors in specific problematic situations. As a high degree of frustration was experienced, Mary's therapist brought this situation to therapy, and in discussion with the supervisor identified the following:

Thoughts: 'She does know what the point is of doing this – I explained the rationale TWICE last session!'
'Mary has had so much trouble identifying and rating moods – she is NEVER going to grasp the thought record!'

'Her unrelenting standards are being activated here – she is avoiding the thought record because of the performance concerns identified on the DAS.'

Emotions:	Frustration – 60 percent
	Irritation – 40 percent
Physiology:	Increased autonomic arousal, face flushed
Behavior:	Reverted to previous therapy skill

When Mary's therapist wrote down the thoughts she experienced in this therapy interaction, she was surprised, and could see the merit in using a thought record to evaluate the evidence supporting her predictions about therapy outcome. This supervision activity was helpful in identifying the therapist's assumptions that 'patients should complete their homework' and 'if patients don't complete their homework, it means that therapy is not going well/the patient is not motivated/the patient is not suitable for CBT'. Following this session, the therapist wrote down several beliefs advocated in the guiding model for practice, namely that 'homework non-completion is common', 'is often part of the learning process', and 'represents an opportunity to use the cognitive case conceptualization to make sense of the patient's behavior' (Kazantzis, MacEwan, & Dattilio, 2005, p. 367). We encourage therapists and supervisors to use the Therapeutic Belief System (TBS) (Rudd & Joiner, 1997) as a conceptual model for understanding the particular types of beliefs, assumptions and behaviors commonly experienced by therapists and patients associated with homework (see also Haarhoff & Kazantzis, 2007).

These two broad classes of therapist beliefs about the process of using homework and the patient's level of engagement with homework often overlap. Table 11.2 presents a series of common therapist beliefs that reflect the interplay between patient and therapist schemas. A series of associated unhelpful therapist behaviors is also presented. The therapist beliefs outlined are examples from our experiences in clinical supervision and are intended as an illustration. There are also instances where some of the listed therapist behaviors may be indicated (e.g., vague discussion of homework specifics with a highly autonomous patient who consistently completes the homework and prefers to make his own plan for integrating the task into his life). Nevertheless, this table can be used as a reference for therapists and supervisors and as a guide for overcoming persistent difficulties with patient nonengagement with homework.

This final section of the chapter emphasized that therapists' own beliefs, from time to time, may lead to behaviors that may inadvertently contribute to patient nonengagement with homework tasks. Identifying and working with therapist beliefs in supervision enables CBT therapists to experience the importance of the effect of their beliefs on the therapeutic relationship in using homework. We have offered some practical suggestions for

Table 11.2 Unhelpful therapist beliefs and behaviors

Beliefs about patient's homework	Therapist in-session behavior
'I am responsible for the positive changes in the patient's life – the session *is* the therapy'	No homework assigned
'He obviously has not done the homework – this patient is never going to improve'	Homework not reviewed
'Talking about the homework will only make the patient worse off'	Avoiding homework when distressed
'Patients should do what I tell them – I know what is best – I'm the expert here'	Directive style with homework
'This patient is simply not motivated – he has too many activated personality beliefs'	Frustrated/irritated with noncompletion
'They know what to do – I can't be bothered getting into specifics'	Vague discussion of specifics of task
'I feel bad asking them to do homework that is challenging – gosh, they have done well!'	Excessive praise in review

The therapist beliefs outlined in this table are examples from our experiences in clinical supervision and are intended as examples only. There are also instances where some of the above-listed therapist behaviors may be indicated (e.g., vague discussion of homework specifics with highly autonomous patient who consistently completes the homework and prefers to make his own plan for integrating the task into his life).

addressing therapists' beliefs about homework and patient engagement with homework in a manner consistent with the cognitive model.

Summary

The aim of this chapter was to provide guidance on the effective use of homework assignments in CBT. This chapter integrated knowledge from CBT outcome and process research, behavior and cognitive theories, and traditional CBT methods. It discussed the role of the therapist in facilitating a collaborative therapeutic relationship and using the cognitive conceptualization diagram to guide the use of homework, and make sense of homework noncompletion using a case study. This chapter presented an overview of a three-step model for the integration of homework into therapy. In particular, the processes in selecting (designing), planning (assigning), and reviewing homework assignments with the case study were discussed. Addressing unhelpful therapists beliefs and behaviors in supervision represented the focus of the final section.

Homework assignments are a standard feature of CBT sessions. Thus, the guidelines outlined in this chapter can benefit a broad range of patient populations, especially those that present with persistent interpersonal difficulties and complex presentations. In addition, the model can help therapist understanding of patient nonadherence and serve as a useful tool in clinical training and supervision.

References

Addis, M. E., & Jacobson, N. S. (2000). A closer look at the treatment rationale and homework compliance in cognitive behavioral therapy for depression. *Cognitive Therapy and Research, 24*, 313–326.

Apodaca, T. R., & Monti, P. M. (2007). Substance abuse. In N. Kazantzis & L. L'Abate (eds), *Handbook of Homework Assignments in Psychotherapy: Research, Practice, and Prevention* (pp. 369–388). New York: Springer.

Bailer, J., Takats, I., & Schmitt, A. (2002). Individualized cognitive-behavioral therapy for schizophrenic patients with negative symptoms and social disabilities. II. Responder analysis and predictors of treatment response. *Verhaltenstherapie, 12*, 192–203.

Bandura, A. (1977). Self-efficacy: toward a unifying theory of behavioral change. *Psychological Review, 84*, 191–215.

Bandura, A. (1989). Human agency in social cognitive theory. *American Psychologist, 44*, 1175–1184.

Beck, A. T. (1976). *Cognitive Therapy and the Emotional Disorders*. New York: International Universities Press.

Beck, A. T. (1988). *Beck Hopelessness Scale*. San Antonio, TX: Psychological Corporation.

Beck, A. T., Rush, A. J., Shaw, B. F., & Emery, G. (1979). *Cognitive Therapy of Depression*. New York: Guilford Press.

Beck, A. T., Steer, R. A., & Brown, G. K. (1996). *Manual for the Beck Depression Inventory-II*. San Antonio, TX: Psychological Corporation.

Beck, J. S. (1995). *Cognitive Therapy: Basics and Beyond*. New York: Guilford Press.

Beck, J. S. (2005). Cognitive therapy for challenging problems: what to do when the basics don't work. New York: Guilford Press.

Bennett-Levy, J., Turner, F., Beaty, T., Smith, M., Paterson, B., & Farmer, S. (2001). The value of self-practice of cognitive therapy techniques and self-reflection in the training of cognitive therapists. *Behavioural and Cognitive Psychotherapy*, *29*, 203–220.

Blackburn, I., & Twaddle, V. (1996). *Cognitive Therapy in Action*. London: Souvenir Press.

Bogalo, L., & Moss-Morris, R. (2006). The effectiveness of homework tasks in an irritable bowel syndrome cognitive behavioural self-management programme. *New Zealand Journal of Psychology*, *35*, 120–125.

Bryant, M. J., Simons, A. D., & Thase, M. E. (1999). Therapist skill and patient variables in homework compliance: controlling an uncontrolled variable in cognitive therapy outcome research. *Cognitive Therapy and Research*, *23*, 381–399.

Burns, D. D., & Nolen-Hoeksema, S. (1991). Coping styles, homework compliance, and the effectiveness of cognitive behavioral therapy. *Journal of Consulting and Clinical Psychology*, *59*, 305–311.

Burns, D. D., & Nolen-Hoeksema, S. (1992). Therapist empathy and recovery from depression in cognitive behavioral therapy: a structural equation model. *Journal of Consulting and Clinical Psychology*, *60*, 441–449.

Burns, D. D., & Spangler, D. L. (2000). Does psychotherapy homework lead to improvements in depression in cognitive-behavioral therapy or does improvement lead to increased homework compliance? *Journal of Consulting and Clinical Psychology*, *68*, 46–56.

Carroll, K. M., Nich, C., & Ball, S. A. (2005). Practice makes progress? Homework assignments and outcome in treatment of cocaine dependence. *Journal of Consulting and Clinical Psychology*, *73*, 749–755.

Conoley, C. W., Padula, M. A., Payton, D. S., & Daniels, J. A. (1994). Predictors of client implementation of counselor recommendations: match with problem, difficulty level, and building on client strengths. *Journal of Counseling Psychology*, *41*, 3–7.

Coon, D. W., & Thompson, L. W. (2003). Association between homework compliance and treatment outcome among older adult outpatients with depression. *American Journal of Geriatric Psychiatry*, *11*, 53–61.

Cox, D. J., Tisdelle, D. A., & Culbert, J. P. (1988). Increasing adherence to behavioral homework assignments. *Journal of Behavioral Medicine*, *11*, 519–522.

DeRubeis, R. J., & Feeley, M. (1990). Determinants of change in cognitive therapy for depression. *Cognitive Therapy and Research*, *14*, 469–482.

Detweiler-Bedell, J. B., & Whisman, M. A. (2005). A lesson in assigning homework: therapist, client, and task characteristics in cognitive therapy for depression. *Professional Psychology: Research and Practice*, *56*, 219–223.

Detweiler, J. B., & Whisman, M. A. (1999). The role of homework assignments in cognitive therapy for depression: potential methods for enhancing adherence. *Clinical Psychology and Psychotherapy*, *6*, 267–282.

Dimeff, L. A., & Marlatt, G. A. (1995). Relapse prevention. In R. K. Hester & W. R. Miller (eds), *Handbook of Alcoholism Treatment Approaches: Effective Alternatives* (2nd edn, pp. 188–212). Boston: Allyn and Bacon.

Dunn, H., Morrison, A. P., & Bentall, R. P. (2006). The relationship between patient suitability, therapeutic alliance, homework compliance and outcome in cognitive therapy for psychosis. *Clinical Psychology and Psychotherapy*, *13*, 145–152.

Edelman, R. E., & Chambless, D. L. (1993). Compliance during sessions and homework in exposure-based treatment of agoraphobia. *Behaviour Research and Therapy*, *31*, 767–773.

Edelman, R. E., & Chambless, D. L. (1995). Adherence during sessions and homework in cognitive-behavioral group treatment of social phobia. *Behaviour Research and Therapy*, *33*, 573–577.

Fehm, L., & Kazantzis, N. (2004). Attitudes and use of homework assignments in therapy: a survey of German psychotherapists. *Clinical Psychology and Psychotherapy*, *11*, 332–343.

Fennell, M. J., & Teadale, J. D. (1987). Cognitive therapy for depression: individual differences and the process of change. *Cognitive Therapy and Research*, *11*, 253–271.

Gonzalez, V. M., Schmitz, J. M., & DeLaune, K. A. (2006). The role of homework in cognitive-behavioral therapy for cocaine dependence. *Journal of Consulting and Clinical Psychology*, *74*, 633–637.

Haarhoff, B. A., & Kazantzis, N. (2007). How to supervise the use of homework in cognitive behavior therapy: The role of trainee therapist beliefs. *Cognitive and Behavioral Practice*, *14*, 325–332.

Hamilton, M. (1967). Development of a rating scale for primary depressive illness. *British Journal of Social and Clinical Psychology*, *6*, 278–296.

Holtzworth-Munroe, A., Jacobson, N. S., DeKlyen, M., & Whisman, M. A. (1989). Relationship between behavioral marital therapy outcome and process variables. *Journal of Consulting and Clinical Psychology*, *68*, 166–170.

Kazantzis, N. (2005). Introduction and overview. In N. Kazantzis, F. P. Deane, K. R. Ronan, & L. L'Abate (eds), *Using Homework Assignments in Cognitive Behavior Therapy* (pp. 3–8). New York: Routledge.

Kazantzis, N., Dattilio, F. M., & MacEwan, J. (2005). In pursuit of homework adherence in behavior and cognitive behavior therapy: comment on Malouff and Schutte (2004). *Behavior Therapist*, *28*, 179–183.

Kazantzis, N., Deane, F. P., & Ronan, K. R. (2000). Homework assignments in cognitive and behavioral therapy: a meta-analysis. *Clinical Psychology: Science and Practice*, *7*, 189–202.

Kazantzis, N., Deane, F. P., & Ronan, K. R. (2005). Assessment of homework completion. In N. Kazantzis, F. P. Deane, K. R. Ronan, & L. L'Abate (eds), *Using Homework Assignments in Cognitive Behavior Therapy* (pp. 61–72). New York: Routledge.

Kazantzis, N., & L'Abate, L. (2005). Theoretical foundations. In N. Kazantzis, F. P. Deane, K. R. Ronan, & L. L'Abate (eds), *Using Homework Assignments in Cognitive Behavior Therapy*. New York: Routledge.

Kazantzis, N., & L'Abate, L. (2007). *Handbook of Homework Assignments in Psychotherapy: Research, Practice, and Prevention.* New York: Springer.

Kazantzis, N., Lampropoulos, G. L., & Deane, F. P. (2005). A national survey of practicing psychologists' use and attitudes towards homework in psychotherapy. *Journal of Consulting and Clinical Psychology, 73,* 742–748.

Kazantzis, N., MacEwan, J., & Dattilio, F. M. (2005). A guiding model for practice. In N. Kazantzis, F. P. Deane, K. R. Ronan, & L. L'Abate (eds), *Using Homework Assignments in Cognitive Behavior Therapy* (pp. 357–404). New York: Routledge.

Kazantzis, N., Ronan, K. R., & Deane, F. P. (2001). Concluding causation from correlation: comment on Burns and Spangler (2000). *Journal of Consulting and Clinical Psychology, 69,* 1079–1083.

Leahy, R. L. (2001). *Overcoming Resistance in Cognitive Therapy.* New York: Guilford Press.

Leung, A. W., & Heimberg, R. G. (1996). Homework compliance, perceptions of control, and outcome of cognitive-behavioral treatment of social phobia. *Behaviour Research and Therapy, 34,* 423–432.

Malouff, J. M., & Schutte, N. S. (2004). Strategies for increasing client completion of treatment assignments. *Behavior Therapist, 27,* 118–121.

Miller, W. R., & Rollnick, S. (2002). *Motivational Interviewing: Preparing People for Change* (2nd edn). New York: Guilford Press.

Monti, P. M., Kadden, R. M., Rohsenow, D. J., Cooney, N. L., & Abrams, D. B. (2002). *Treating Alcohol Dependence: A Coping Skills Training Guide* (2nd edn). New York: Guilford Press.

Najavits, L. M. (2005). Substance abuse. In N. Kazantzis, F. P. Deane, K. R. Ronan, & L. L'Abate (eds), *Using Homework Assignments in Cognitive Behavior Therapy* (pp. 263–282). New York: Routledge.

Neimeyer, R. A., & Feixas, G. (1990). The role of homework and skill acquisition in the outcome of group cognitive therapy for depression. *Behavior Therapy, 21,* 281–292.

Persons, J. B. (1989). *Cognitive Therapy in Practice: A Case Formulation Approach.* New York: Norton.

Persons, J. B., Burns, D. D., & Perloff, J. M. (1988). Predictors of dropout and outcome in cognitive therapy for depression in a private practice setting. *Cognitive Therapy and Research, 12,* 557–575.

Rees, C. S., McEvoy, P., & Nathan, P. R. (2005). Relationship between homework completion and outcome in cognitive behaviour therapy. *Cognitive Behaviour Therapy, 34,* 242–247.

Rudd, M. D., & Joiner, T. (1997). Countertransference and the therapeutic relationship: a cognitive perspective. *Journal of Cognitive Psychotherapy, 11,* 231–250.

Safran, J. D., Segal, Z. V., Vallis, T. M., Shaw, B. F., & Samstag, L. W. (1993). Assessing patient suitability for short-term cognitive therapy with an interpersonal focus. *Cognitive Therapy and Research, 17,* 23–38.

Schmidt, N. B., & Woolaway-Bickel, K. (2000). The effects of treatment compliance on outcome in cognitive-behavioral therapy for panic disorder: quality versus quantity. *Journal of Consulting and Clinical Psychology, 68,* 13–18.

Shaw, B. F., Elkin, I., Yamaguchi, J., Olmsted, M., & Vallis, T. M. (1999).

Therapist competence ratings in relation to clinical outcome in cognitive therapy of depression. *Journal of Consulting and Clinical Psychology, 67,* 837–846.

Spielberger, C. D. (1983). *Manual for the State-Trait Anxiety Inventory (STAI).* Palo Alto, CA: Consulting Psychologists Press.

Startup, M., & Edmonds, J. (1994). Compliance with homework assignments in cognitive-behavioral psychotherapy for depression: relation to outcome and methods of enhancement. *Cognitive Therapy and Research, 186,* 567–579.

Stretcher, V. J., Champion, V. L., & Rosenstock, I. W. (1997). In D. S. Gochman (ed.), *Handbook of Health Behavior Research. I. Personal and Social Determinants* (pp. 71–91). New York: Plenum Press.

Thase, M. E., & Callan, J. A. (2006). The role of homework in cognitive behavior therapy of depression. *Journal of Psychotherapy Integration, 16,* 162–177.

Weissman, A. N., & Beck, A. T. (1978). Development and validation of the Dysfunctional Attitudes Scale: a preliminary investigation. Paper presented at the meeting of the American Educational Research Association, Toronto, Canada.

Woods, C. M., Chambless, D. L., & Steketee, G. (2002). Homework compliance and behavior therapy outcome for panic with agoraphobia and obsessive compulsive disorder. *Cognitive Behaviour Therapy, 31,* 88–95.

Woody, S. R., & Adessky, R. S. (2002). Therapeutic alliance, group cohesion, and homework compliance during cognitive-behavioral group treatment of social phobia. *Behavior Therapy, 33,* 5–27.

Worthington, E. L. (1986). Client compliance with homework directives during counseling. *Journal of Counseling Psychology, 33,* 124–130.

Chapter 12

Resistance: an emotional schema therapy (EST) approach

Robert L. Leahy

Cognitive therapy has often been criticized for not adequately addressing the role of emotions in therapy and the importance of the therapeutic relationship. Indeed, many novices in cognitive-behavioral therapy (CBT) rely heavily on 'empirically supported treatments', manualized approaches, agenda-setting, or targeted behaviors and cognitions, but fail to recognize appropriately the role of the therapeutic relationship and the opportunities provided in addressing resistance and non-compliance. Empirically supported treatments 'work' (as the title implies), but only if the patient enters therapy, maintains a therapeutic relationship, and actually engages in homework and exposure exercises. Many patients drop out prematurely. If the patient is not in treatment, then no help is found.

A number of clinicians within the CBT tradition have addressed the issues of resistance, therapeutic alliance and non-compliance. For example, Safran, Muran and colleagues have identified the opportunities for deepening therapy by focusing on ruptures in the therapeutic relationship (Safran & Muran, 1995, 2000; Stevens, Muran, & Safran, 2003). Motivational interviewing has been used to improve compliance in substance abuse treatment (Marlatt & Gordon, 1985) and in the treatment of anxiety disorders (Westra, 2004). Traditional cognitive therapy techniques have been utilized to improve homework compliance (Kazantzis & L'Abate, 2007) and to help patients and therapists overcome impasses in treatment (Beck, 2005). Dialectical behavior therapy (DBT) has focused on therapy-interfering behaviors and how emotional regulation strategies can be employed to avert these problems (Linehan, 1993a). Gilbert has employed 'compassionate mind therapy' to help self-loathing patients overcome their sense of contempt, shame, and self-hatred (Gilbert, 2007). All of these approaches provide helpful directions in addressing resistance in treatment. The current chapter will develop a more comprehensive model of resistance, outlining a number of dimensions of resistance in treatment and developing a model of emotional schema therapy (EST) that directly addresses the problems with emotional regulation and both patient and therapist schemas about the nature of emotional experience.

Emotional schemas and resistance to change

Even though I do cognitive therapy, I have never had a patient come to therapy because of a 'thought'. No one pursues therapy because they think they are 'not using the evidence' or that they are 'irrational'. No one has come to see me because of some mistake in a truth table. People pursue therapy because they are emotionally distraught, life has lost meaning, their relationships are falling apart, and they are not getting their needs met. Their emotional brain is telling them 'something is wrong'. Although CBT refers to 'cognitive' and 'behavioral', it is really the 'emotional' component that needs to be addressed. If you change cognition and modify behavior – but the emotional part is not addressed – there is nothing really gained. People want to 'feel better' or 'find meaning' – they are not concerned about their thinking or their behavior.

I think we can expand cognitive therapy to include a recognition that 'how you deal with your emotions' is a key element in depression, anxiety, personality disorders, and interpersonal relations, and, to this end, I have advanced the EST to address this issue. All of us experience feelings of sadness, anxiety, fear, and even hopelessness. But the key element is, 'What do you do, think, or feel *after* you have that emotion?' For example, Bill's partner has left him. He now feels sad ('I miss her'), anxious ('Will I ever find someone to love?'), fearful ('It's going to be hard being alone'), and even hopeless ('I could be alone forever'). Bill's problem is not the experience of the breakup, but that he handles his emotions in the most problematic way. He believes that his feelings don't make sense ('Why should I be so upset after only a few months of a relationship?'); he thinks that these emotions are going to last forever and that they will overwhelm him ('My God, how will I be able to work when I'm so anxious and depressed?'); and he thinks that a 'real man' shouldn't be so upset. He feels ashamed of his feelings, so he won't share them with Roger, his best friend, and he won't get any validation because he's all alone with his feelings. Like many times in his life when he has had to face problems, Bill turns to drinking as a way to cope.

The emotional schema model is depicted in Figure 12.1, reflecting normalizing and pathological styles of coping with emotion. Bill could have normalized his feelings and recognized that painful emotions often follow a breakup, that emotions are temporary and, in some cases, can point to your higher values ('valuing a loving relationship'). Rather than using avoidance and rumination as strategies, one can use acceptance, behavioral activation and developing more meaningful supportive relationships to cope with emotions.

EST is a form of CBT that stresses the following:

- Painful and difficult emotions are universal.
- These emotions were evolved to warn us of danger and tell us about our needs.

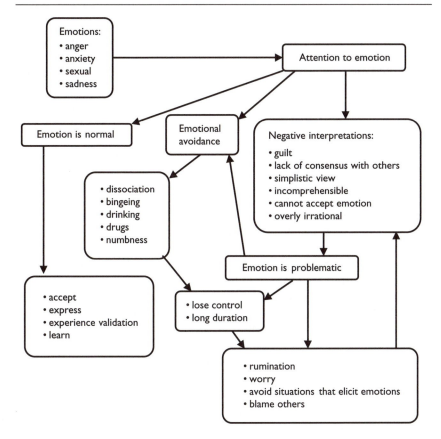

Figure 12.1 A model of emotional schemas

- Underlying beliefs and strategies (schemas) about emotions determine the impact that an emotion has on the escalation or maintenance of an emotion.
- Problematic schemas include catastrophizing an emotion, thinking that one's emotions do not make sense, and viewing an emotion as permanent and out of control, shameful, unique to the self, and needing to be kept to the self.
- Emotional control strategies, such as attempts to suppress, ignore, neutralize or eliminate through substance abuse and binge eating, help confirm negative beliefs of emotions as intolerable experiences.
- Expression and validation are helpful insofar as they normalize, universalize, improve understanding, differentiate various emotions, reduce guilt and shame, and help increase beliefs in the tolerability of emotional experience.
- EST assists the patient in the following:

- identifying a variety of emotions and helping to label them
- normalizing emotional experience, including painful and difficult emotions
- linking emotions to personal needs and to interpersonal communication
- identifing problematic beliefs and strategies (schemas) that the patient has for interpreting, judging, controlling, and acting on an emotion
- collecting information, using experiential techniques, and setting up behavioral, interpersonal and emotional 'experiments' to develop more helpful responses to emotions.

This form of therapy is consistent with a more traditional cognitive model, such as Beck's model, but it does provide the following advantages:

1   The patient's interpretations and strategies about emotional experience and regulation are directly addressed.
2   The inevitable and helpful functions of emotion are enhanced.
3   The nature of the emotional experience, including earlier transference and relational experiences and messages about emotion, is a focus of treatment.
4   The therapist's emotional schemas and their impact on the therapeutic relationship are addressed.

Therapist beliefs that interfere with emotional expression

Invalidation beliefs

As therapists, we bring to the therapeutic relationship our own 'philosophies' about emotional expression and experience. Some therapists, perhaps overly committed to the 'rationality' and 'problem-solving' nature of CBT, may recognize their own automatic thoughts that occur when a patient experiences and expresses intense emotion: 'Strong emotions interfere with effective treatment', 'I need to stick with my agenda', 'I need to get the patient to feel better', 'The patient may lose control of her/his emotion', and 'The patient needs to learn how to solve problems or to think rationally'. Similarly, the therapist may have negative beliefs about the patient's crying: 'I feel uncomfortable when the patient is crying', 'Crying gets in the way of getting the job done', 'I feel that I identify too much with the patient's painful feeling', and 'I feel I may lose control of my own feelings when the patient is upset'.

These negative beliefs about emotional expression and intensity may contribute to reinforcing the patient's negative emotional schemas. For example, the belief that strong emotions interfere with therapy may confirm the patient's beliefs that 'My feelings don't matter to other people', 'No one wants to hear about my problems', and 'My feelings are a burden to others'. These may be similar to the messages that the patient heard from parents: 'Stop crying and pull yourself together', 'You're just not thinking right', and 'You think you are the only person with problems'. Negative beliefs about crying may result in the therapist jumping in too soon to calm the patient: 'Things will work out, so there's no reason to feel bad'. This confirms the patient's beliefs that painful emotions cannot be tolerated – one must suppress them or, better still, avoid experiences that give rise to these emotions.

Emotion connection beliefs

Some therapists recognize that intense emotional expression and experience can be opportunities for deepening therapy – by accessing the 'hot cognitions', the core beliefs, and the imagery and memories associated with significant life events. These therapists would likely endorse the following beliefs:

- Painful feelings are a chance to form a closer relationship.
- I can matter more when the patient is feeling this way.
- Painful feelings are part of life.
- I can also imagine myself in this situation.
- Painful feelings are not permanent.
- I should respect the patient's suffering and pain.

If I believe that the patient's feelings can lead to a closer and more meaningful relationship, I may allow more time and 'space' for the patient to reflect, open up, cry, and feel intense emotion. I can also serve the patient in a more fulfilling way if the patient is able to trust me by sharing and experiencing emotion in the session. This does not mean that I would not use standard cognitive therapy techniques to address automatic thoughts or use behavioral techniques to increase a sense of mastery or pleasure. However, by allowing the patient to access the negative and painful memory, the techniques that I employ later will have more impact. Consider the following interaction with a patient who escaped injury on 9–11 at the World Trade Center:

Patient: I was running away from the building and there was debris falling all around me.
Dr Leahy: What were you thinking and feeling at that moment?
Patient: I thought that I wouldn't get away. I thought I was going to die [visibly shaken].

Dr Leahy: That must have been terribly difficult to feel like you were going to die. What did things look like?

Patient: [Becoming more anxious] There were people running everywhere and dust all over us. I felt trapped. I felt no one could save me [begins to cry].

Dr Leahy: [Pauses] Feeling all alone and afraid is terribly frightening to you. [Pauses] I can see how painful that memory is right now, to feel no one can save you. How do you feel sharing that with me at this moment?

Patient: [Still crying] I don't know if anyone can really protect me.

Dr Leahy: It feels like you don't know if you can trust anyone. I notice now that you are crying and sharing that with me. How does that feel to you right now?

Patient: I'm not sure. I don't really know you. But I guess I feel safe right now.

Dr Leahy: Do you feel that other people wouldn't know how bad it must have been for you – and how bad it is now for you?

Patient: Yes. I don't want to burden anyone with my problems. I should be over it by now. It's been 10 months. But whenever I see a plane in the sky, I think, 'It's happening again'.

Dr Leahy: So, your feelings don't make sense to you and you feel embarrassed about the way you feel and that no one can really understand this. And so you feel all alone with those feelings, very much like you felt when you were running away from the building when it was collapsing – 'All alone and no one that I can talk to. No one can help me.'

Patient: That's how I feel. Yes, right. That's it. All alone. And that there's something really wrong with me.

Dr Leahy: And that you feel now – as you did then – no one could help you?

Patient: Yes, you understand. You understand.

Getting stuck in a feeling

We often sense that our feelings 'happen to us', as if the feeling is a wave that comes over us and envelops us. This sense of being a victim of his own feelings can make the patient fearful of allowing a feeling to exist and may lead him to struggle against an emotion that he thinks he needs to get rid of. For example, John had been cheated out of money by his boss. Even though he had moved to another company, he was enraged with the loss and he ruminated about getting back at the boss and the unfairness of the entire experience. He complained about lack of sleep, tension, anxiety, helplessness, and anger. John had become stuck in a legitimate, but dead-end, feeling of rage and I decided to help him construct an alternative.

Patient:	I can't get over the idea that he cheated me out of this money.
Dr Leahy:	Yeah, it just keeps going around in your head and driving you crazy. It sounds like you are ruminating about this and don't know what to do.
Patient:	I wish I could get back at him, but there's very little that I can do.
Dr Leahy:	And it's unfair to be in that position, because he really shouldn't have treated you this badly. It really is unfair.
Patient:	That's why I can't get it out of my head.
Dr Leahy:	Let's recognize for now that you will have those feelings of anxiety, rage, regret, and helplessness *about this*. But I'd like to try a different exercise today – let's aim for a different set of feelings about other things in your life – things that have nothing to do with this event.
Patient:	I don't understand.
Dr Leahy:	Let's imagine that everything has been taken away – your senses, your body, your family, your job, money, house, everything is gone. You are now nothing. Now, here is the exercise. You can have everything back – one at a time – but only if you make a case that you really appreciate it. You have to show that this one thing that you will get back *really matters to you*.
Patient:	I'd like my family back.
Dr Leahy:	You have three girls. Which one do you want back?
Patient:	Do I have to choose?
Dr Leahy:	Good answer. OK. Let's start with your oldest child. Make a case that you appreciate her. [The patient goes through her qualities – some of which have been problematic – and indicates how important she is. He describes her face, her hair, her learning difficulties, the moments they spend together. The therapist then asks him to describe the other two daughters, what he appreciates, and then his wife.]
Dr Leahy:	OK. You have your family back. What else would you want back?
Patient:	My eyesight.
Dr Leahy:	Close your eyes. You have learned that you will be blind for the rest of your life. But now I tell you that you can have your eyesight back if you make a case for it. If you could open your eyes, what would you really want to see?
Patient:	My family.
Dr Leahy:	You can see them every day. Your homework assignment is to spend 15 minutes each day focusing on something quite simple, quite mundane, that you need to appreciate more. Do you

think that this money – if you could have gotten it – would
have been on your list?

Patient: No.

Dr Leahy: Then you can recognize when you have these rageful feelings
that your feelings make sense. But there may be other feelings
that can be your goal and they can be feelings of appreciation
and gratitude.

The patient used this exercise. Because of scheduling, he did not come back
for 3 weeks, but when he returned he said that this appreciation exercise
helped him set aside a lot of his rage and rumination.

In addition to the appreciation exercise described above, it is also helpful
to consider emotions as *goals*. This is very different from thinking of an
emotion as 'the only feeling I can have right now' or 'something *that
happens to me* over which I have no control'. Just as we can make choices as
to the food we eat at a buffet, we can also make choices as to the emotions
we are going to aim for today. As in the DBT technique of improving the
moment (Linehan, 1993a, 1993b), with EST we can also decide which
emotions to 'go for'. The following may be helpful to the patient:

1 *Recognition of choice*: 'You can decide if you want to experience and
   focus on the current emotion or see if there is a way to have another
   emotion'. 'What would be the advantages of having a different emotion
   – about something entirely different in your life – rather than the
   current emotion?'
2 *Setting an emotion as a goal*: 'Which emotion would you like to create
   for yourself? Happiness, curiosity, appreciation, fear, confusion,
   challenge, gratitude?'
3 *Activating memories and images*: 'Let's take the emotion of "pride".
   Close your eyes and try to recall a moment in your life when you felt
   proud of doing something.' [Therapist uses imagery induction to guide
   the patient through memories, images, thoughts, sensations and
   feeling.] Another alternative is to use family 'scrapbooks' of photo-
   graphs that bring back other memories.
4 *Using activity to make the emotion real*: 'Let's imagine that over the
   next week you were going to try to catch yourself or other people
   feeling proud. What would be some examples of this? What are some
   things that you could do – even very small things that you might do –
   to catch some examples for yourself of your feeling proud?'

In addition, traditional activity scheduling can assist the patient in recognizing that other emotions occur according to the activities engaged in.

Positive psychology exercises can often be helpful in EST by directing the
patient toward alternative emotions and empowering the patient to 'do

something' other than feel bad. These exercises help address patients' negative beliefs that their emotions are out of control, permanent, dangerous, and shameful. With these emotion-induction techniques, the patient can learn that he is not a victim of emotions, but the one who can generate emotions.

Constructive therapist strategies

The therapist can address the emotional schemas that the patient may be stuck in by directly raising the dilemmas within the therapeutic experience – that is, the dilemma of activating painful feelings in order to process them, the inevitability of disappointment and even suffering in a life that has fuller meaning, and the difficulty in trusting a therapist who is really a stranger that has not yet merited trust with the most private, perhaps shameful, feelings that the patient has. The following can be helpful in deepening the trust, increasing validation, and enhancing the meaning of the therapeutic experience.

- *Indicate that emotions are the key in therapy.* Here the therapist can directly say, 'Even though we are doing cognitive therapy, we should always keep in mind that your feelings, your emotions, are the most important thing. Your sadness, happiness, anxiety, fears, hopefulness, confusion and anger are what we should be aware of and respectful of. Your feelings matter. That's why we are here.'
- *Acknowledge that cognitive therapy can seem invalidating.* Cognitive therapy can appear to invalidate the suffering that the patient experiences. If the patient is stuck in validation or victim resistance, attempts to challenge or modify thinking may seem invalidating. It is helpful to directly address this dilemma: 'Sometimes we will talk about different ways of thinking or acting, and that might appear to you that I am saying that what happened to you is fair, or OK. This is a dilemma in therapy, since we want to see if you can feel better, but we also recognize that your hurt feelings count.'
- *Ask about a range and variety of feelings.* Too often we can focus on one feeling without exploring the range and complexity of feelings. For example, Greenberg (2002) distinguishes between primary and secondary emotions. By increasing the differentiation of the feelings that the patient may have, we help the patient recognize that there are alternative feelings that one can have – one is not stuck with one response – and we also allow for discovery of whether one emotion ('anger') is really a cover for another more disturbing emotion ('anxiety' or 'humiliation').
- *Link painful emotion to higher values.* It is not possible to have meaningful relationships without experiencing painful emotions. Sometimes,

painful emotions are the natural consequence of deeper, more important values. For example, Martha Nussbaum, in *Upheavals of Thought* (2001), describes her sense of overwhelming sadness at the death of her mother, and she asks the reader, convincingly, 'How could I say I loved my mother if I did not feel sad?' A man who recently separated from his wife told me he felt sad – and apologized because he thought this was 'irrational'. I asked him why he felt sad, and he said, 'Because I miss my daughter'. I replied, 'Do you want to be the kind of man who does not feel sad when he misses his daughter?' It became clear to him that feeling sad was the price of a higher value – to love your children. Consequently, he did not feel bad about feeling sad. Similarly, the therapist can say, 'Loneliness means that you care about intimacy and love – because you are a loving person.'

- *Make emotions universal.* It is very hard to think that you are the only one who suffers. Many patients feel defective because they are depressed and lonesome and they feel ashamed of their problem. Perhaps an attraction of drama, romance, and ballads is that they help us recognize that we are not alone in our suffering. The therapist can assist the patient in this recognition by normalizing pain: 'This is how many of us feel when we are lonely.'

- *Acknowledge that sometimes life feels 'awful'.* Despite rationalizations that 'nothing is awful', there are many things in life that are awful – that is, that inspire us with awe, feelings of being overwhelmed, and feelings that we cannot bear it. A woman contemplating couples therapy was soothed when the therapist acknowledged, 'Things can feel really bad – really awful.' A man whose son died suddenly from a brain hemorrhage was bewildered by the loss. The therapist said, 'This sounds so awful to me. It is hard to imagine how bad this feels for you. I cannot imagine that you could ever be consoled.' By sharing the 'awfulness' of the loss, the patient felt, at least, the therapist understood that life can be awful – and was for him at the present time.

- *Recognize that an emotion 'feels like forever' but can also pass with time.* Strong emotions may appear to us to be permanent: 'I will always be depressed'. The feeling appears to be a fact, and rational disputation may only appear to invalidate the 'reality' for the patient. No one feels better after a breakup when someone says, 'You will get over it' or 'Time heals everything'. Platitudes are not effective therapy. Yet the therapist can reflect for the patient that these feelings do feel like forever – 'You feel right now that you will never get over this, that your sadness will always be part of your life. And, so, when people say, "Feelings are not permanent", it seems that they are invalidating how bad it feels and how real the permanence appears to you.' In this case, the therapist is not 'telling' the patient that feelings will change. The observation is tentative. In fact, it acknowledges that the foregoing statement may not be helpful right now. Because it is tentative – and recognizes its own possible futility – it will be more believable for the patient.

Schematic mismatch

Just as patients have personal schemas (about abandonment, helplessness, control, or special status), therapists also come to the therapeutic relationship with their own schemas. For example, some therapists have demanding standards ('I should cure all my patients'), others are concerned about abandonment ('What if my patients leave therapy?'), and others are excessively self-sacrificing ('If I take a vacation, my patients will be angry with me'). Of particular interest is the case in which the patient's and therapist's personal schemas are in conflict or serve to confirm the patient's underlying fears. Let's consider an example of a dependent patient with concerns about abandonment and a therapist with a similar schema about abandonment.

Dependent patient	*Therapist with abandonment schema*
Does not have an agenda of problems to solve. Frequently complains about 'feelings'.	If my patient is bothered with therapy, she might leave.
Calls frequently between sessions.	It's upsetting when patients terminate.
Wants to prolong sessions.	I might end up with no patients.
Does not think he can do the homework, or believes that homework will not work.	
Upset when therapist takes vacations.	

The therapist who fears losing a patient may use compensatory strategies, including constantly reassuring the patient, prolonging sessions, and apologizing for absences. Or the therapist may avoid confronting the patient's fears of abandonment and helplessness by not bringing up difficult topics, avoid discussing the patient's dependent behavior, not set limits on the patient, and avoid using exposure techniques. The patient may interpret the compensatory behaviors (e.g., reassuring the patient) as evidence of the following: 'I need to rely on others to solve my problems', 'I must be incompetent', 'I can't get better on my own', or 'The only way to get better is to find someone to take care of me and protect me'. Similarly, the patient may interpret the therapist's avoidance as evidence that he really cannot face difficult emotions and problems: 'My emotions must be overwhelming to other people', 'Doing new things will be risky and terrifying', 'My therapist must think I am incapable of doing things on my own', 'I should avoid independent behavior'. Thus, the patient and therapist – with similar schemas about abandonment – inadvertently confirm the patient's underlying emotional schemas of being incapable of dealing with his emotions on his own.

Addressing the therapist's counter-transference

Recognizing one's own personal schemas can be helpful in addressing both the patient's underlying emotional and personal schemas and using counter-transference to help the patient. For example, if the therapist has fears of abandonment (losing patients), he can use cognitive therapy techniques to address these fears. Consider the rational responses in Table 12.1 for typical counter-transference fears.

Other rational responses that can be helpful in addressing one's counter-transference are shown in Table 12.2. The advantage of a cognitive therapy and EST approach is that many of the issues that psychodynamic therapists talk about (and which can be important) can, with the current approach, be addressed actively and directly.

Addressing the patient's emotional schemas in the transference

The advantage of the EST approach is that we can directly identify the problematic emotional schemas in the transference and begin to use the therapeutic relationship as a venue for modifying these schemas. Let's consider patients who are dependent and have fears of abandonment. How do we respond to their problematic strategies?

What would it mean if you did not get reassurance?

Some people believe that reassurance will give them a sense of security, comfort, or certainty. But reassurance is only an attempt to soothe – it does not tell us anything about the future. Anxiety is often based on intolerance of uncertainty when uncertainty is equated with a negative outcome, lack of responsibility and helplessness (Dugas, Buhr, & Ladouceur, 2004). Rather than seeking reassurance, the patient can be asked to examine the advantages of accepting some uncertainty, consider problem-solving strategies, and confront situations that he is avoiding.

What is the advantage of not having an agenda?

Agenda-setting is a key feature in CBT. It is really an existential issue, since setting an agenda requires that you think about *your goals*, you exercise a sense of proactive responsibility in setting the goals, and you believe there is

Table 12.1 Counter-transference beliefs for therapist fearing abandonment

Negative beliefs	Rational responses
If I say something that upsets the patient, she will leave therapy.	Patients may leave therapy because the therapy is not useful. If you do not make the therapy emotionally significant, the patient will not address important issues. What is the evidence that talking about certain things is so upsetting that the patient leaves? Haven't you had patients get upset in therapy and come back? Don't people assume that their emotions will be aroused in therapy?
It's terrible when people are anxious.	It may be uncomfortable, but people are anxious and that is why they come to therapy. In order to do exposure techniques, the anxiety has to be activated. You have to go through it to get past it. What is the terrible thing that will happen if the patient is anxious?
If this patient quits therapy, I could end up with no patients.	Patients quit therapy all the time. Ask someone who has had a practice for a long time. It is normal for patients to quit therapy. The goal is to help patients – and to do this you have to get the patient to tolerate uncomfortable feelings.

something that you can do to achieve them. Not having an agenda may reflect more general problems in the patient's life, such as going through life reacting to events, feeling aimless and helpless, deferring to others, not setting goals and not feeling competent. Many dependent patients follow the agendas of other people, especially rescuers who they think will solve their problems. It may be useful to focus on agenda setting as a way of life – an approach to getting your needs met – and to explore the patient's rationale for not having an agenda. Some dependent patients will say, 'I never think that way', 'I don't know how to set goals', or 'I don't think that I can achieve anything'. The therapist can explore this issue by asking, 'Is the lack of an agenda similar to your lack of goals and plans in life?', 'Do you let other people set the agenda for you?' or 'Do you believe that you cannot handle your feelings on your own?'

Explore emotional schemas

The dependent patient often feels overwhelmed with emotions, either relying on others to soothe, give reassurance, or meet needs or to rely on avoidance as a way to deal with difficult challenges in life. The therapist can address these emotional schema beliefs and strategies directly:

- 'What do you typically do when you have unpleasant feelings? Do you get other people to take care of them?' Patterns of dependency – both in

Table 12.2 Counter-transference cognitive distortions

Distortion	Example	Rational response
Personalizing	'The patient isn't getting better because I'm not that good a therapist.'	Patients do not get better for a lot of reasons. The patient had this problem before therapy began. You have helped a lot of other patients.
Catastrophizing	'It's awful that the patient is thinking of suicide.'	Thinking about suicide is very common with depressed patients. You are here to help people think through their problems. There is no advantage in your getting catastrophic. Nothing terrible has happened yet. There are a lot of things that you can do to help: you can counsel the patient on alternatives, examine short-term and long-term goals, help the patient challenge his negative and hopeless thinking, modify the medication, get assurance with a suicide contract, and arrange for hospitalization during this time of crisis.
Labeling (of patient)	'This patient is just a pain to deal with.'	The patient is a human being who is suffering. He doesn't want to suffer, and the difficulty and resistance that the patient expresses is probably causing him more discomfort than it is causing you. Try to see life through his eyes and develop a shared curiosity with the patient about the current problems.
Labeling (of self)	'I must be a lousy therapist.'	There are some people you work well with and others that you don't. Even the 'famous' therapists make mistakes. Consider the range of patients that you have worked with – aren't there some who have been helped? No therapist is perfect.
Mind-reading	'The patient thinks I'm incompetent.'	That's unlikely if the patient keeps coming for help. Even if the patient did think you were incompetent, it doesn't follow that you are. You probably don't know what the patient is really thinking. If the patient thinks you are incompetent, it may be that this is the way that the patient responds to support in his life.
Fortune-telling	'This patient will never get better.'	You don't know that this is true. In reality, many people improve a little bit and have good times and bad times. Look back at the mood fluctuations of this patient over time and you will discover some better times. There are a variety of techniques and interventions that you have yet to try.

Table 12.2 Continued

Distortion	Example	Rational response
All-or-nothing	'Nothing seems to work.'	Again, there may be some fluctuation in functioning for this patient. Have the patient keep a mood log and you will find that his mood varies with time of day, activities and thoughts.
Emotional reasoning	'I feel lousy seeing this patient, so the therapy must be going poorly.'	Your feelings are no guide as to whether the patient is getting anything out of treatment. However, you might examine whether the way you are feeling may be similar to the way other people feel in trying to help this person.
Discounting the positives	'Anyone could have helped that patient.'	You don't know whether that's true, but even if it were, you helped someone. That's what counts.
Over-generalizing	'I didn't help this patient. I can't help any patients.'	You don't really know that you did not help this patient. But, even if you did not help him, you still have helped others, and you still can help new patients.

From R. L. Leahy (2001). *Overcoming Resistance in Cognitive Therapy*. New York: Guilford Press.

and out of therapy – can be examined. For example, the patient may turn to her partner to give her reassurance that 'everything will be OK', but this may reconfirm her belief that she cannot get her needs met on her own and that she cannot tolerate uncertainty and anxiety. Emotion-regulation techniques, such as improving the moment, mindfulness, acceptance, distraction, and goal setting, can be used to self-soothe and adapt to difficult moments. It is important to realize that both the patient and the 'caregiver' get some reinforcement from the reassurance-seeking/soothing relationship – the patient gets immediate gratification and the caregiver gets to feel powerful and needed. Addressing these problematic interactions as self-confirming of negative emotional schemas is essential: 'What negative beliefs about your emotions and needs are being confirmed by this reassurance-seeking?'

• *Do your feelings make sense to you? Do other people have these feelings? Will your painful feelings go away on their own?* The therapist can help patients see their feelings as following from the negative automatic thoughts, assumptions and schemas that are the source of these feelings. For example, the patient can learn that the feelings of loneliness, helplessness and despair follow from the beliefs, 'I can't make myself happy', 'I am helpless', 'I need to wait for someone to rescue me', and 'You can't be happy on your own'. Behavioral experiments of independent activity, problem-solving strategies, goal setting, self-reward and affect tolerance can help address feelings of helplessness in regard to one's emotions. Additionally, normalizing feelings of loneliness, sadness, and anger can help the patient feel less alone with the feeling of loneliness. Tracking feelings of sadness through activity scheduling, graded task assignments, self-reward, and mindfulness exercises can help the patient realize that not only are emotions temporary, but also that they change depending on what you are doing. Finally, the therapist can help the patient 'inoculate' himself to feeling 'alone' with feelings by asking the patient to develop a 'self-help plan' for painful feelings: 'If you were not able to get in touch with me, could you use some techniques to handle your thoughts and feelings?'

Conclusions

Despite the significant gains in CBT there are still many patients who drop out prematurely, do not comply with homework assignments, resist exposure and response prevention, and do not gain the benefits of treatment. Moreover, some cognitive therapists, enamored with the methods and techniques, often miss the bigger picture – the difficulties in processing emotion and dealing with inevitable problems of life that our patients, and we ourselves, will experience. EST helps us understand both the patient's and therapist's problematic approaches to emotion, helps identify family of origin issues in emotional schemas, provides a model of more adaptive emotional strategies, and helps reconcile schematic conflicts in the therapeutic relationship.

The cognitive model – after gaining ascendency for years and replacing the psychodynamic model as the 'treatment of choice' – is now undergoing its own crisis of identity. Confronted with 'third wave' challenges that suggest that experiential avoidance, willingness, flexibility and values are important (Hayes, Luoma, Bond, Masuda, & Lillis, 2006), the EST approach may provide the many advantages of the cognitive model and the ecological validity of the third wave models. The implication is that thinking and emotional experience cannot be separated from one another. The charioteer in Plato's metaphor needs the power of the horses to drive him forward.

References

Beck, J. S. (2005). *Cognitive Therapy for Challenging Problems: What to Do When the Basics Don't Work*. New York: Guilford Press.
Dugas, M. J., Buhr, K., & Ladouceur, R. (2004). The role of intolerance of uncertainty in the etiology and maintenance of generalized anxiety disorder. In R. G.

Heimberg, C. L. Turk, & D. S. Mennin (eds), *Generalized Anxiety Disorder: Advances in Research and Practice* (pp. 143–163). New York: Guilford Press.

Gilbert, P. (2007). Evolved minds and compassion in the therapeutic relationship. In P. Gilbert & R. L. Leahy (eds), *The Therapeutic Relationship in the Cognitive Behavioural Psychotherapies* (pp. 106–142). London: Brunner-Routledge.

Greenberg, L. S. (2002). *Emotion-Focused Therapy: Coaching Clients to Work Through Their Feelings.* Washington, DC: American Psychological Association.

Hayes, S. C., Luoma, J. B., Bond, F. W., Masuda, A., & Lillis, J. (2006). Acceptance and commitment therapy: model, processes and outcomes. *Behaviour Research and Therapy, 44,* 1–25.

Hayes, S. C., Strosahl, K. D., & Wilson, K. G. (2003). *Acceptance and Commitment Therapy: An Experiential Approach to Behavior Change.* New York: Guilford Press.

Johnson, S. L., & Roberts, J. E. (1995). Life events and bipolar disorder: implications from biological theories. *Psychological Bulletin, 117,* 434–449.

Johnson, S. L., Turner, R., & Iwata, N. (2003). BIS/BAS levels and psychiatric disorder: an epidemiological study. *Journal of Psychopathology and Behavioral Assessment, 25,* 25–36.

Kazantzis, N., & L'Abate, L. (eds) (2007). *Handbook of Homework Assignments in Psychotherapy: Research, Practice, and Prevention.* New York: Springer.

Kennedy-Moore, E., & Watson, J. C. (1999). *Expressing Emotions: Myths, Realities and Therapeutic Strategies.* New York: Guilford Press.

Leahy, R. L. (1997). An investment model of depressive resistance. *Journal of Cognitive Psychotherapy, 11,* 3–19.

Leahy, R. L. (1999). Decision-making and mania. *Journal of Cognitive Psychotherapy, 13,* 1–23.

Leahy, R. L. (2001). *Overcoming Resistance in Cognitive Therapy.* New York: Guilford Press.

Leahy, R. L. (2002). Improving homework compliance in the treatment of generalized anxiety disorder. *Journal of Clinical Psychology, 58,* 499–511.

Leahy, R. L. (2004). Decision making and psychopathology. In R. L. Leahy (ed.), *Contemporary Cognitive Therapy: Theory, Research, and Practice* (pp. 116–138). New York: Guilford Press.

Leahy, R. L. (2005). Clinical implications in the treatment of mania: reducing risk behavior in manic patients. *Cognitive and Behavioral Practice, 12,* 89–98.

Leahy, R. L., Beck, A. T., & Beck, J. S. (2005). Cognitive therapy for the personality disorders. In S. Strack (ed.), *Handbook of Personology and Psychopathology* (pp. 442–461). New York: Wiley.

Linehan, M. M. (1993a). *Cognitive-Behavioral Treatment of Borderline Personality Disorder.* New York: Guilford Press.

Linehan, M. M. (1993b). *Skills Training Manual for Treating Borderline Personality Disorder.* New York: Guilford Press.

Marlatt, G. A., & Gordon, J. R. (eds) (1985). *Relapse Prevention: Maintenance Strategies in the Treatment of Addictive Behaviors.* New York: Guilford Press.

Nussbaum, M. C. (2001). *Upheavals of Thought: The Intelligence of Emotions.* Cambridge: Cambridge University Press.

Safran, J. D., & Muran, J. (1995). Resolving therapeutic alliance ruptures: diversity and integration. *In Session: Psychotherapy in Practice, 1,* 81–92.

Safran, J. D., & Muran, J. C. (2000). *Negotiating the Therapeutic Alliance: A Relational Treatment Guide*. New York: Guilford Press.

Stevens, C. L., Muran, J. C., & Safran, J. D. (2003). Obstacles or opportunities? A relational approach to negotiating alliance ruptures. In R. L. Leahy (ed.), *Roadblocks in Cognitive-Behavioral Therapy: Transforming Challenges into Opportunities for Change* (pp. 274–294). New York: Guilford Press.

Westra, H. A. (2004). Managing resistance in cognitive behavioural therapy: the application of motivational interviewing in mixed anxiety and depression. *Cognitive Behaviour Therapy, 33*, 161–175.

Chapter 13

Developing a compassion-focused approach in cognitive behavioural therapy

Paul Gilbert

Compassion-focused therapy (CFT) grew out of efforts to understand and help people with major difficulties in self-experiences (Gilbert, 2000, 2005; Gilbert & Irons, 2005; Gilbert & Procter, 2006). These are individuals with high shame and self-critical problems (Gilbert, 1998, 2003; Zuroff, Santor, & Mongrain, 2005). They are likely to have come from harsh, neglectful or abusive backgrounds, which have orientated their sense of 'self' to be very threat focused (Bifulco & Moran, 1998). Indeed, they can be quick to perceive the threat of rejection, exclusion, put-down and shame coming from the outside world and to activate internal, self-critical attacks on themselves. Under these conditions, they are caught in a pincer movement of attacks from the outside and the inside; there is nowhere 'safe'. Even if one helps such people to tone down the sensitivity to these threats and be less self-critical, they can still find it difficult to feel much better. They also commonly experience another problem many clinicians will be familiar with; they may say, 'I can see the logic of the CBT approach but it does not change how I feel about myself; I know, logically, that I am not a bad or unlovable person, but I still feel it', or 'I know I was not to blame for the abuse, but I still feel there must be something wrong with me' (Lee, 2005). Stott (2007) has given a fascinating overview of such difficulties, referring to them as rational-emotional dissociation. His ideas are based on the increasing awareness that we process information through multiple channels, which include fast-affect routes (on how something feels) and other cognitive routes derived from explicit knowledge of situations (see also Baldwin, 2005; Hiadt, 2001). Brewin (2006) has explored such phenomena in terms of accessibility of emotional memories.

A compassion-focused approach to these difficulties has been via a consideration of neuroscience that suggests there are in fact different affect-processing systems that provide information on threat and safeness (Gilbert, 1989, 1993, 2005). It is possible, therefore, that people can experience affective arousal in threat systems (based on fast threat processing) but lack accessibility to affect systems that process information in term of safeness and help regulate threat. So, for example, people who feel they are unlovable may not respond to objective evidence that they are lovable because they have few emotional memories, or access to an affect system that gives rise to the feelings of being loved; in effect, they do not actually know what 'being loved' feels like; such feelings may seem alien or even frightening. In addition, feeling unlovable also operates as a basic strategic orientation to threat; that is, if one expects others to treat one as unwanted and unlovable, then one will have to orientate oneself to a range of possible threats. To dismantle or override well-entrenched strategic (or phenotypic) threat orientations to social life can itself be rather frightening because it implies a range of new strategies that involve, for example, reducing vigilance to social threat, increasing trust, coping with interpersonal conflicts in new ways, reducing submissive and appeasement behaviours, and changes in a self-identity and sense of self (Gilbert, 2007a).

If this view has value, it suggests that only focusing on threat processing, and reducing threat sensitivities and safety behaviour, may not be enough to help some people develop more positive affects and mood states of safeness, well-being and contentment. We may need to work specifically on helping people develop access to feelings of safeness and safeness processing. However, while threat-processing systems have been subject to much research attention (e.g., Le Doux, 1998) and focus in CBT (Beck, Emery, & Greenberg, 1985; Stott, 2007), safeness systems have been less well researched or integrated into CBT. Since compassion-focused therapy is based on the need to increase activation and accessibility to safeness systems, a short exploration of them is necessary here.

The role of attachment and soothing systems for the sense of well-being

Mammals evolved reproductive strategies to have few offspring but provide care, protection and safeness for them. Research has shown that from the first days of life the most important source of affect regulation is not the self but the mother or primary caregiver (Gerhardt, 2004; Schore, 1994). The infant or young child is unable to meet any of its own needs and requires protection, feeding, warmth and soothing from the parent. In regard to the regulation of distress, therefore, it is the access to a soothing, caring other that is crucial (Bowlby, 1969, 1973). This means that mammalian infants, who require various aspects of caring to survive, must have internal mechanisms that can detect and respond to caring and soothing cues from another. Over many years, Bowlby's theory has generated a large number of studies on both animal and human attachment processes (Cassidy & Shaver, 1999). There is not the space to review the findings of these studies except to say that there is now good evidence that the quality of early attachment experiences, especially in regard to how soothing, loving and caring children experience their parent to be, has major effects on brain maturation (Gerhardt, 2004; Schore, 1994) and various schema and working models of self and others (Leahy, 2005; Mikulincer & Shaver, 2004; Wallin, 2007). We can, however, address one key aspect of recent research relating to threat regulation and safeness systems.

The study of attachment and affiliation has led to important findings about positive affect-regulation systems and their relationship to threat/ stress systems. In a major review of neurophysiological studies, Depue and Morrone-Strupinsky (2005) point out that there are at least *two types* of positive affect-regulation systems. One gives us a sense of drive and vitality – to seek out rewards and positive things, while another system operates when we have consumed or achieved and no longer need to seek things, and are not under threat (i.e., it turns off seeking and drive) – we are content. Both systems have been 'borrowed' and used by evolution to regulate behaviour in social relationships. For example, the possibility of new positive relationships 'activates' us, and we seek them out – we get a buzz when starting a new love relationship, or are chosen to be on the team. However, the contentment system has also evolved into a system that registers care, love and affection signals, acceptance and social safeness (Carter, 1998; Depue & Morrone-Strupinsky, 2005; Wang, 2005). When social signals of affiliation and 'being cared for and about' trigger this system, we feel calmed, and soothed by the support, kindness and care of others (Gerhardt, 2004; Schore, 1994). These feelings are strongly linked to feelings of contentment, safeness and well-being, and they regulate both the drive-seeking and threat systems. Although the neuroscience is complex, and these systems are in constant states of co-regulation, a simplified model of these three affect systems is given in Figure 13.1.

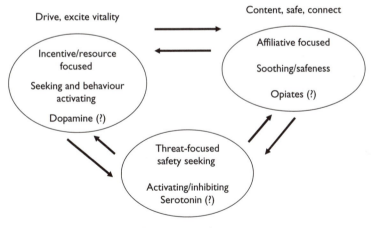

Figure 13.1 Types of affect regulation systems

Social signals of affiliation and care have the qualities of soothing and involve neurohormones such as oxytocin and opiates (Carter, 1998; Depue & Morrone-Strupinsky, 2005; Panksepp, 1998; Uväns-Morberg, 1998). Signals and stimuli such as stroking, holding, voice tone, facial expressions, concerned interest/attentiveness and social support are *natural* stimuli that activate this system (Field, 2000; Uväns-Morberg, 1998; Wang, 2005). Depue and Morrone-Strupinsky (2005) distinguish affiliation from agency and sociability. Agency and sociability are linked to control and achievement seeking, social dominance and the (threat-focused) avoidance of rejection and isolation. In contrast, affiliation and affiliative interactions have a more calming effect on participants, alter pain thresholds and the immune and digestive systems, and operate via an oxytocin-opiate system. Heinrichs, Baumgartner, Kirschbaum, and Ehlert (2003) found that oxytocin is linked to social support and buffers stress, those with lower oxytocin having higher stress responsiveness. So evidence points to the possibility that this oxytocin-opiate system is particularly linked to soothing and calming and regulates the production of the stress hormones such as cortisol (Carter, 1998; Depue & Morrone-Strupinsky, 2005; Field, 2000; Wang, 2005). It can therefore be regarded as part of a safeness system (Gilbert, 1989, 2005, 2007a).

Soothing systems are off-line

Armed with these insights, we can return to the problems of people who struggle to feel safe and soothed in the world. As noted, these individuals often come from abusive and neglectful backgrounds. They may have few emotional memories of feeling loved or wanted. Indeed, those individuals who should have provided these inputs for them (and thus stimulate their soothing systems) were just as likely to be unavailable, or to be threatening and over-stimulate their threat-processing systems (Perry et al., 1995). There are a number of consequences of these early experiences. First, in order for the soothing system to lay down neural connections with other parts of the brain, and act as a regulator of threat, it has to be stimulated by appropriate inputs (Schore, 1994). Lack of such input can thus compromise the soothing systems, leaving the infant and child having to find alternative ways to self-regulate distress and threat. Second, threatening parents can produce serious approach–avoidance conflicts. While there will be innate motives to seek out soothing agents, there will also be learnt fears and reasons to avoid them (Liotti, 2000). Like all major approach–avoidance conflicts, these can disorganize response systems, leading to various forms of disturbance (Gray, 1979), elevated stress, and problems in thinking and reflecting on experiences (Fonagy & Target, 2006; Wallin, 2007). Third, Ferster (1973) pointed out that internal emotions can act as stimuli for other emotions. For example, if a child's expression of anger or affection-seeking is constantly punished, this will generate anxiety and fear of punishment. Thus, the inner stimuli/feelings of anger or affection-seeking will be associated with fear. Eventually, the arousal of anger or affection-seeking automatically elicits a conditioned fear/anxiety response. In this context, the child may gradually become unaware of feelings of anger or affection-seeking feelings in the context where these could (normally) be useful. Instead, they are only aware of the secondary conditioned anxiety to stimuli, and not anger feelings or affection-seeking motives and feelings. This can have serious consequences for the child's abilities to recognize certain emotions and mature them in helpful ways.

So safeness is not just the absence of threat, but there are specialized systems in the brain linked to social cues. Thus, soothing systems are regulated via different pathways from those of threat. Moreover, there are a number of different dimensions that relate to how we feel safe with others, and reassured by them. In the first stage of life (and subsequently), there are cues of physical affection (facial, holding, touch comforting) – which are highly sensory based. Second, needs can be met and soothed, and we can experience contentedness. Third, the way others relate to us (e.g., showing pleasure in our actions) helps us learn how we live in the minds of others (that we can create positive affects in the minds of other about the self). Fourth, via empathic connections and reflections from others to our emotions, we also learn about our own mind. For example, this emotion is tolerable; this emotion is bad. Fifth, we engage in social referencing (via information provided by others, and also by observing their behaviours and emotions in certain contexts). Thus, we learn what is safe or threatening from others and can come to trust their judgements. From these sources of physical care, expression of positive affect from others, and being provided with reliable information, we create internal memories of others as soothing, supportive, kind and forgiving, and the self as lovable. All these play different roles in threat regulation and feeling safe/content.

These experiences lay down various emotional memories and coalesce around basic interpersonal schema of self and others (Baldwin, 2005). Neglect or abuse can compromise any of the routes into developing the safeness-processing system. The consequence is that for some people the ability to access the soothing system, which is a source of feeling safe, reassured, and content and having a sense of well-being, is compromised.

Formulation

In this model, people's difficulties of shame and self-criticism are formulated as forms of threat-focused safety behaviours. There is considerable overlap with the Beck et al. (2004) approach to personality disorders. They suggest that with more complex cases, and those sometimes labelled as personality disordered, the formulation focuses on a number of central domains. These are as follows:

1   views of self and others (I am . . . they are . . .)
2   core and conditional beliefs about the self, the world and others (e.g., I am helpless; the world is a dangerous place; I need others to help me)
3   rules for living (I must succeed to make others notice and care about me)
4   key fears and threats (rejection, abandonment and shame)
5   basic life strategies (avoidance of conflicts, submissive behaviours or constantly trying to impress others)
6   domain of emotions (anxiety, dysphoria, anger).

The formulation in CFT is somewhat similar. It goes though a series of stages.

Background and historical influences

Here the therapist explores the basic early attachment styles and life events that illuminate issues of feeling cared for or about. These experiences will have patterned various neurophysiological systems and the coordination of the various affect systems noted in Figure 13.1. The therapist searches for key emotional memories that act a focus for self-experience and can be triggered by life events (Brewin, 2006). Some people, however, may have poor recall of negative events, or be averse to revealing themselves and 'going onto the history'. Careful history taking, however, can be important, even if it emerges over time, because it is not just 'fact finding' but also offers key opportunities to compassionately empathize and validate people's experiences (Leahy, 2005), and enables people to develop a coherent story and narrative out of their difficulties. Therapy may be the first time people have experienced another person's mind orientated towards them in this interested, non-judgemental, containing, empathic and caring way (Wallin, 2007).

The life history also offers ways that people can see the sources of their 'felt sense of self and others' that can also be conceptualized in schema terms (Beck et al., 2004). In regard to a sense of shame and 'feeling alone', these can often be linked to specific emotional memories. For example, Sally could easily recall in imagery the contempt on her mother's face when she told Sally that she was 'a stupid and ugly child'. 'It is the same horrible "wanting to disappear" feelings that go through me when people criticize me,' she said. When Jon felt distressed he would feel overwhelmed with feelings of 'total aloneness'. His mother admitted to him that when he was young she was depressed and that he often cried in the night but she felt unable to go to him. Jon came to connect these early memories with the feeling of being totally alone when distressed.

Key threat and fears

Early background experiences can enable us to feel safe and secure or easily threatened (Mikulincer & Shaver, 2004). As Gilbert (1989) and Beck et al. (2004) note, key fears are often around archetypal and innate themes of abandonment, rejection, shame and abuse/harm. In CFT, we distinguish between external threats and internal threats. External threats pertain to what the world or others might do, whereas internal threats are related to what emerges, or is recreated inside oneself. For example, a person might be frightened of losing control or becoming overwhelmed by anxiety, anger or depression. Indeed, it can be the fear of becoming depressed (again) that can set in motion rumination, avoidance, dread of the future and even suicide (Gilbert, 2007a).

Safety strategies

People will obviously develop a range of strategies to try to get safe and self-protect. These safety strategies will vary as to whether they are aimed at external threats or internal ones. Avoidance of conflicts and submissive behaviours may be aimed to ward off external threats, whereas (say) distraction, dissociation and use of alcohol can be used to cope with internal threats.

Unintended consequences

Key domains of threat and their safety strategies often lead to unintended consequences. For example, to ward off being criticized or rejected individuals may fail to develop healthy assertiveness and instead focus on submissive and appeasement behaviour, or forms of perfectionism. In consequence, they may lose (or fail to develop) the competencies to articulate and actualize their own values and life goals, are constantly wary of others, and become self-critical when safety strategies fail to protect them (Gilbert, 2007a). Although shame and self–criticism have many sources, the therapist helps the patient to recognize and be compassionate to the consequences of understandable safety strategies.

Therapeutic interventions

The focus of the therapeutic intervention is on generating experiences of reassurance and safeness that can counter shame and self-criticism. In particular, the focus is on developing the self-compassion and kindness that recruit the soothing system (Gilbert, 2000, 2007a; Neff, 2003). Research suggests that teaching self-compassion can help with coping with difficult life events (Leary, Tate, Adams, Allen, and Hancock, 2007). In behavioural terms it is like working with anxiety while one teaches relaxation; one cannot be anxious and relaxed at the same time. Similarly, one cannot be engaged in self-soothing and self-attacking at the same time. The therapy unfolds in a series of steps following formulation. First, the therapist introduces the model of the three circles (see Figure 13.1) and discusses with patients whether elevated threat processing and problems with feeling safe, connected and reassured reflects their difficulties. We then explore whether it would be useful to begin to generate experiences of soothing and safeness. One way of exploring the value of this is to discuss with the client how our images and thoughts can stimulate physiological systems in our brains. One can draw an outline of a brain and then work through some examples (Gilbert, 2007a). When we are hungry, both seeing a meal and just imagining one can stimulate an area of our brain that will send messages to the body so that our mouth will start to water and our stomach acids get going. Seeing something sexy on TV or just imagining something sexy can stimulate the pituitary and sexual arousal system.

This part of the 'set-up' is to help people gain clear insight into the fact that thoughts and images activate systems in our brains. We give time for discussion because this is a key idea to get across and enables the therapist to move onto the next crucial aspects. We then move to self-criticism. If someone is bullying us and telling us we are no good and there is no point in trying anything, this will affect our stress systems, and make us anxious, angry and unhappy because those emotion systems have been triggered. If the criticism is harsh and constant, it can 'harass' us into feeling depressed. However, as suggested, our own thoughts and images can do the same. So, if we constantly put ourselves down, this can also activate our stress systems and lead to 'self-harassment' and feeling anxious or angry, and tone down positive feelings.

We spend some time on this aspect, linking it to emotion memories and the formulation, and conducting function analysis of self-criticism. This helps people understand that self-criticism can be linked to safety strategies; For example, by being self-critical, we may force or bully ourselves to improve in order to avoid making mistakes and thus avoid being criticized or rejected. Self-criticism might also be used to avoid blaming others and expressing anger, thus again preventing criticism or rejection from others (Gilbert et al., 2004).

We can then move to the issue and benefits of developing self-compassion. We might note that when things are stressful, if there is someone who cares about us, understands how hard it is, and encourages us with warmth and genuine care, this can be soothing. In fact, there are areas of our brain that respond in a certain way to kindness from others and help to soothe and reassure us. Similarly, if we learn how to focus on these feelings within and for ourselves, they can counter the hostility and contempt of self-criticism. Thus, it is the self-soothing areas of the brain we would like to work with.

Although some people are wary of kindness and even frightened of it (e.g., due to beliefs that they do not deserve it or it is weak, or because of conditioned emotional responses to warmth), usually kindness is helpful if we can accept it. Shame-prone people can be very practised at being unkind, harsh and critical of themselves but rather less practised at being kind and supportive. Although some people believe that if they bully themselves and push themselves they will achieve more and then be liked and accepted, we consider with them what part of their brain they are stimulating when they do this. So, using exactly the same idea of imagining how a meal can stimulate feelings in us, we can think about how our own thoughts and images might be able to stimulate the kindness and soothing system. If we can learn to be kind and supportive – to send ourselves helpful messages when things are hard for us – we are more likely to stimulate those parts of our brain that evolved to respond to kindness. This will help us cope with stress and setbacks. This shared overview is the basis for developing collaboration on the value of putting effort into developing self-compassion.

Using the model to develop self-compassion

I was alerted to the problem of being unable to access warmth when treating a number of depressed patients with shame problems. They were able to generate various alternative thoughts to negative self-beliefs; however, the emotional tone of these alternatives was cold, or even at times hostile. Subsequently, I began to focus on the emotional tone that people 'created' in their minds when they thought about alternatives, and it quickly became clear that the ability to generate a warm, supportive and encouraging tone was very difficult for them. When we were able to spend time 'feeling' alternative thoughts with warmth, understanding and gentleness, many patients felt this soothed them and made the thoughts themselves more believable. Others, however, experienced grief or alarm at feelings of warmth.

Since those early days, I have increasingly focused on the emotion of warmth in generating alternatives and in engaging in alternative behaviours and behavioural experiments. This involves clarifying the importance of generating warmth. Further developments of this have been in work with imagery (Holmes & Hackmann, 2004). There are various ways in which this can be used. For example, one can try to generate the experience of warmth, understanding and compassion by helping patients bring to mind a time when they felt someone was very kind to them and to focus on the sensory, bodily feelings and emotions aroused by that memory. Another use for imagery is to engage in guided fantasy. In this work, one helps people create their ideal of a compassionate other and focus on the various sensory qualities of compassion. Sometimes the image is of a person, but at other times it could be that of an animal, a tree or a bright light. The patient is taught to practise these images daily, focusing on key qualities of wisdom, strength, warmth and non-judgement. In other words, one has to imagine that one's compassionate image understands one's human struggle, one's personal experiences, and is compassionate to that struggle. In times of distress, the patient can practise taking a few breaths and then engaging the soothing image (Gilbert, 2000, 2007a, in press; Gilbert & Irons, 2005). Lee (2005) has focused on the nurturing aspects of the image and has called it 'the perfect nurturer'. In addition, she notes the value of anchoring the image with various senses, such as touch or smell. Again attention is directed to the sensory, bodily feelings and emotions aroused by imagery work. There is in fact a range of imagery exercises that can be used for imagining one is in contact with an inner guide, supportive friend, wise sage and so forth (Frederick & McNeal, 1999). The idea is to help patients shift their focus to their soothing affect system as they work at generating alternative and more balanced viewpoints on their difficulties.

A third approach is to work with self-generated compassionate feelings. This involves enabling the person to imagine caring for another person, child or animal in distress, and focusing on their bodies, on how that feels when they create that frame of mind. Generally, most people are able to do this to some degree. One then invites the person to begin to direct those feelings to themselves. This is done by their imagining themselves in the compassionate frame of mind and then looking at their difficulties. It is the transfer of having compassionate feelings for others and then directing them towards self that can be most difficult.

A fourth approach is to use something that is sometimes used in acting where actors have to 'get into role' by imagining themselves to be a particular type of person in order to convince an audience of the role; that is, they have to create certain states of mind within themselves to 'feel' themselves into the role. This is a form of imagination that is about creating states of mind within oneself. The guidance here is,

> Try for a moment, to imagine a wise, kind and compassionate person. Think of the ideal qualities you would like that compassionate person to have. Imagine becoming that person. It does not matter if you are actually like this, because this is about feeling yourself into a role and way of being. Breathe gently and feel yourself slowing down and inner calmness coming over you. Think about your age and appearance, and your facial expressions and postures. Create a slight smile of warmth on your face. Imagine having inner emotions of, say, gentleness, with a

kind voice tone in how you speak. Spend a moment noting how focusing this way feels in your body – now like an actor about to take on a part, feel yourself into this role – become this person.

As people learn to create this state of mind within themselves, they can use this either to revisit their alternative thoughts and how they feel when they are textured by warmth, or imagine generating alternative thoughts from this perspective – called the compassionate reframe (Lee, 2005).

On the nature of compassion

These 'techniques' for trying to access the caregiving system and make it available for self-processing are contextualized within an overall framework of compassion processing. There is no one definition of compassion and different theorists have different views of it (Gilbert & Irons, 2005; Gilbert & Procter, 2006). The evolutionary approach to compassion suggests that its components are related to, and evolved from, caregiving and attachment (Gilbert, 1989, 2005). They form an interlocking set of competencies, and loss of any one of them can throw compassion out of balance. The 'compassion circle' is given in Figure 13.2.

Using this circle, the therapist is encouraged to enact this with his/her patient (Gilbert, 2007b). This is the focus for the therapeutic relationships and is a key process by which a patient may first begin to experience compassion. The therapist thus conveys a genuine sense of care for the well-being and development of the patient. Second, the therapist develops

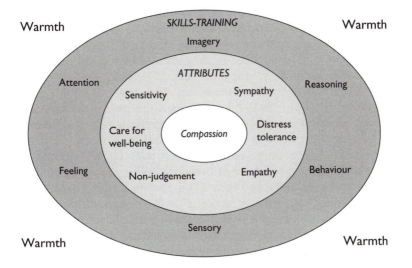

Figure 13.2 Multimodal compassionate mind training

mindful distress sensitivity. What this means is that the therapist can detect subtle cues of distress or affect change, as, for example, with the patient who goes quiet or changes the subject (Wallin, 2007). There may be a shame or an anger issue that is distressing the patient. Sympathy is the ability to be emotionally moved by others' distress. It is an automatic response. Therapists who are emotionally cold may not be able emotionally to tune in, and convey that they are in-tune with the patient's distress and inner world. Distress tolerance requires therapists to be able to tolerate, at times, quite high levels of distress. For example, working with panic, one might have to cope with high levels of anxiety in the patient and possibly in the therapist. For people who have problems with intense rage, being able to tolerate the patient's being silently enraged can be very important, and what some therapists call containment.

Empathy is the more cognitive-focused ability to understand patients on their own terms. This requires effort and imagination, and we now know more about the basic brain processes involved in empathy (Decety & Jackson, 2004). It also bears centrally on what are called reflective functions (Fonagy & Target, 2006; Wallin, 2007). Finally, there is the issue of non-judgement. This does not mean non-preference and that everything is acceptable. For example, even the Dalai Lama would have a strong preference for the world to be free of suffering. Non-judgement is about non-condemning, yet also taking appropriate responsibility.

Hence, the therapeutic relationship becomes a key medium by which patients can experience the 'mind' of their therapist in the care-providing mentality (Wallin, 2007). This does not, however, mean a rushing to the rescue or smothering or over-controlling attitude, but seeks to encourage patients to enter into a cooperative relationship where they are able to take responsibility for their difficulties and for change (Liotti, 2007).

CFT also suggests that one teaches patients how to develop the same elements within themselves. That is, they learn to be focused on their well-being, become sensitive to their distress, and have the ability to be emotionally moved by their distress but also tolerant of it (including distress from the past). In addition, through the process of formulation, therapeutic dialogue and relationship, patients come to understand the nature of their difficulties in an empathic and non-judging way. This is partly because they begin to recognize how their safety behaviours and threat systems have emerged around them to try to protect them but also have unintentionally entrapped them. This enables them to work on those safety behaviours through a process of re-evaluation or exposure, and graded tasks, in a compassionate, supportive and encouraging way. In addition, CFT spends much time focusing on helping people recognize and experience that automatic reactions and safety behaviours are 'not one's fault', while are the same time highlighting that when we give up self-blaming, self-condemning and self-contempt, it is easier to recognize openly our mistakes and unkindnesses and take responsibility for them. In other words, we can clarify distinctions between shame and guilt (Gilbert, 2003).

In both group and individual therapies, patients brain-storm what compassion is, the various components of it, and how they could begin to develop these components within their own lives. They are also provided with handouts and reading materials when helpful (Gilbert & Procter, 2006). At all times, the therapist and patient agree on compassion development as a shared goal based on the three-circles model and that in many ways one is trying to retrain one's brain and develop and access new states of mind with the use of various exercises (Begley, 2007). Various CBT elements, including rationality, balanced thinking, behavioural experiments and mindfulness, are used in the service of developing self and other compassion and are conducted with a warm and compassionate focus.

Conclusion

CBTs have focused on a range of interventions that include Socratic dialogue, guided discovery, behaviour experiments, graded exposures, learning how to monitor and re-evaluate automatic thoughts, and, more recently, mindfulness and attention training. There is a lot of evidence now that these approaches can be very beneficial. However, all therapists recognize the importance of a caring and therapeutic relationship and the ability of a therapist to convey caring and empathy. Recent neuroscience has offered some insights into why this is so important for some patients, especially those with disturbances of self-evaluation.

CFT has suggested that, in addition, patients can learn how to stimulate their self-soothing systems in a variety of ways. These include using imagery and also working on specific components of compassion. Part of the reason for doing this is the view that the soothing systems that normally develop with loving attachments may not be easily accessible for some people from neglectful or abusive backgrounds. To date, research on compassion-focused work is scant, but early indications are that it can be a powerful addition to other focused therapies (Gilbert & Procter, 2006; Leary et al., 2007).

References

Baldwin, M. W. (ed.) (2005). *Interpersonal Cognition*. New York: Guilford Press.

Beck, A. T., Emery, G., & Greenberg, R. L. (1985). *Anxiety Disorders and Phobias: A Cognitive Approach*. New York: Basic Books.

Beck, A. T., Freeman, A., Davis, D. D., & associates (2004). *Cognitive Therapy of Personality Disorders* (2nd edn). New York: Guilford Press.

Begley, S. (2007). *Train Your Mind. Change Your Brain*. New York: Ballantine Books.

Bifulco, A., & Moran, P. (1998). *Wednesday's Child: Research into Women's Experiences of Neglect and Abuse in Childhood, and Adult Depression*. London: Routledge.

Bowlby, J. (1969). *Attachment: Attachment and Loss*, vol. 1. London: Hogarth Press.

Bowlby, J. (1973). *Separation, Anxiety and Anger: Attachment and Loss*, vol. 2. London: Hogarth Press.

Brewin, C. R. (2006). Understanding cognitive behaviour therapy: a retrieval competition account. *Behaviour Research and Therapy*, *44*, 765–784.

Carter, C. S. (1998). Neuroendocrine perspectives on social attachment and love. *Psychoneuroendocrinlogy*, *23*, 779–818.

Cassidy, J., & Shaver, P. R. (eds) (1999). *Handbook of Attachment: Theory, Research and Clinical Applications*. New York: Guilford Press.

Decety, J., & Jackson, P. L. (2004). The functional architecture of human empathy. *Behavioral and Cognitive Neuroscience Reviews*, *3*, 71–100.

Depue, R. A., & Morrone-Strupinsky, J. V. (2005). A neurobehavioral model of affiliative bonding. *Behavioral and Brain Sciences*, *28*, 313–395.

Ferster, C. B. (1973). A functional analysis of depression. *American Psychologist*, *28*, 857–870.

Field, T. (2000). *Touch Therapy*. New York: Churchill Livingstone.

Fonagy, P., & Target, M. (2006). The mentalization-focused approach to self-pathology. *Journal of Personality Disorders*, *20*, 544–576.

Frederick, C., & McNeal, S. (1999). *Inner Strengths: Contemporary Psychotherapy and Hypnosis for Ego Strengthening*. Mahwah, NJ: Lawrence Erlbaum Associates.

Gerhardt, S. (2004). *Why Love Matters. How Affection Shapes a Baby's Brain*. London: Routledge.

Gilbert, P. (1989). *Human Nature and Suffering*. London: Lawrence Erlbaum Associates.

Gilbert, P. (1993). Defence and safety: their function in social behaviour and psychopathology. *British Journal of Clinical Psychology*, *32*, 131–154.

Gilbert, P. (1998). What is shame? Some core issues and controversies. In P. Gilbert & B. Andrews (eds), *Shame: Interpersonal Behavior, Psychopathology and Culture* (pp. 3–38). New York: Oxford University Press.

Gilbert, P. (2000). Social mentalities: internal 'social' conflicts and the role of inner warmth and compassion in cognitive therapy. In P. Gilbert & K. G. Bailey (eds), *Genes on the Couch: Explorations in Evolutionary Psychotherapy* (pp. 118–150). Hove: Psychology Press.

Gilbert, P. (2003). Evolution, social roles, and differences in shame and guilt. *Social Research: An International Quarterly of the Social Sciences*, *70*, 1205–1230.

Gilbert, P. (2005). *Compassion: Conceptualisations, Research and Use in Psychotherapy*. London: Routledge.

Gilbert, P. (2007a). *Psychotherapy and Counselling for Depression* (3rd edn). London: Sage.

Gilbert, P. (2007b). Evolved minds and compassion in the therapeutic relationship. In P. Gilbert & R. Leahy (eds), *The Therapeutic Relationship in the Cognitive Behavioural Psychotherapies* (pp. 106–142). London: Routledge.

Gilbert, P. (in press). Evolved minds and compassion focused imagery in depression. In L. Stropa (ed.), *Imagery and the Threatened Self: Perspectives on Mental Imagery in Cognitive Therapy*. London: Routledge.

Gilbert, P., Clarke, M., Kempel, S., Miles, J. N. V., & Irons, C. (2004). Criticizing and reassuring oneself: an exploration of forms of style and reasons in female students. *British Journal of Clinical Psychology*, *43*, 31–50.

Gilbert, P., & Irons, C. (2005). Focused therapies and compassionate mind training for shame and self attacking. In P. Gilbert (ed.), *Compassion: Conceptualisations, Research and Use in Psychotherapy* (pp. 263–325). London: Routledge.

Gilbert, P., & Procter, S. (2006). Compassionate mind training for people with high shame and self-criticism: a pilot study of a group therapy approach. *Clinical Psychology and Psychotherapy*, *13*, 353–379.

Gray, J. A. (1979). *Pavlov*. London: Fontana.

Haidt, J. (2001). The emotional dog and its rational tail: a social intuitionist approach to moral judgment. *Psychological Review*, *108*, 814–834.

Heinrichs, M., Baumgartner, T., Kirschbaum, C., & Ehlert, U. (2003). Social support and oxytocin interact to suppress cortisol and subjective response to psychosocial stress. *Biological Psychiatry*, *54*, 1389–1398.

Holmes, E. A., & Hackmann, A. (eds) (2004). *Mental Imagery and Memory in Psychopathology* (Special Edition, Memory, Vol. 12, No. 4). Hove: Psychology Press.

Leahy, R. L. (2005). A social-cognitive model of validation. In P. Gilbert (ed.), *Compassion: Conceptualisations, Research and Use in Psychotherapy* (pp. 195–217). London: Brunner-Routledge.

Leary, M. R., Tate, E. B., Adams, C. E., Allen, A. B., & Hancock, J. (2007). Self-compassion and reactions to unpleasant self-relevant events: the implications of treating oneself kindly. *Journal of Personality and Social Psychology*, *92*, 887–904.

LeDoux, J. (1998). *The Emotional Brain*. London: Weidenfeld and Nicolson.

Lee, D. A. (2005). The perfect nurturer: a model to develop a compassionate mind within the context of cognitive therapy. In P. Gilbert (ed.), *Compassion: Conceptualisations, Research and Use in Psychotherapy* (pp. 326–351). London: Brunner-Routledge.

Liotti, G. (2000). Disorganized attachment: models of borderline states and evolutionary psychotherapy. In P. Gilbert & K. Bailey (eds), *Genes on the Couch: Explorations in Evolutionary Psychotherapy* (pp. 232–256). Hove: Psychology Press.

Liotti, G. (2007). Internal working models of attachment in the therapeutic relationship. In P. Gilbert & R. Leahy (eds), *The Therapeutic Relationship in the Cognitive Behavioural Psychotherapies* (pp. 143–161). London: Routledge.

Mikulincer, M., & Shaver, P. R. (2004). Security-based self-representations in adulthood: contents and processes. In N. S. Rholes & J. A. Simpson (eds), *Adult Attachment: Theory, Research, and Clinical Implications* (pp. 159–195). New York: Guilford Press.

Neff, K. D. (2003). Self-compassion: An alternative conceptualization of a healthy attitude toward oneself. *Self and Identity*, *2*, 85–102.

Panskepp, J. (1998). *Affective Neuroscience*. New York: Oxford University Press.

Perry, B. D., Pollard, R. A., Blakley, T. L., Baker, W. L., & Vigilante, D. (1995). Childhood trauma, the neurobiology of adaptation and 'use-dependent' development of the brain: how 'states' become 'traits'. *Infant Mental Health Journal*, *16*, 271–291.

Schore, A. N. (1994). *Affect Regulation and the Origin of the Self: The Neurobiology of Emotional Development*. Hillsdale, NJ: Lawrence Erlbaum.

Stott, R. (2007). When head and heart do not agree: a theoretical and clinical analysis of rational-emotional dissociation (RED) in cognitive therapy. *Journal of Cognitive Psychotherapy: An International Quarterly*, *21*, 37–50.

Uväns-Morberg, K. (1998). Oxytocin may mediate the benefits of positive social interaction and emotions. *Psychoneuroendocrinology*, *23*, 819–835.

Wallin, D. J. (2007). *Attachment in Psychotherapy*. New York: Guilford Press.

Wang, S. (2005). A conceptual framework for integrating research related to the physiology of compassion and the wisdom of Buddhist teachings. In P. Gilbert (ed.), *Compassion: Conceptualisations, Research and Use in Psychotherapy* (pp. 75–120). London: Brunner-Routledge.

Zuroff, D. C., Santor, D., & Mongrain, M. (2005). Dependency, self-criticism, and maladjustment. In J. S. Auerbach, K. N. Levy, & C. E. Schaffer (eds), *Relatedness, Self-Definition and Mental Representation: Essays in Honour of Sidney J. Blatt* (pp. 75–90). Hove, UK: Routledge.

Index

The abbreviation CBT is used for Cognitive Behaviour Therapy.
Page references in *italic* indicate Figures and Tables.